1960

This book may be kept

FOURTEEN DAYS

A fine will be charged for each day the book is kept overtime.

JY 6			
MY 19 '64			
DE 10 '64			
JA 20 14 85			
MR 1 '67 67			
MY 13 '67			
GAYLORD 142			PRINTED IN U.S.A.

THE ARTS AT MID-CENTURY

The Arts at Mid-Century

EDITED BY ROBERT RICHMAN

HORIZON PRESS   NEW YORK   1954

Contents

THE ARTS IN ITALY

THE ARTS IN GERMANY

THE ARTS IN ENGLAND

THE ARTS IN THE UNITED STATES

Preface

Let us admit at once that these forty-one essays, as would any collection of essays discussing the contemporary arts in any age, run the gauntlet between two hazardous conditions. The first is that there are far too many works of art made in any one decade to treat them with any thoroughness or definition. It is sobering to recall that each new generation has had to make its own definitive judgment of Homer.

The second hazard is that when one looks at his contemporaries to explain, to evaluate and to judge, one is tempting both Fate and History, both of whom stand by eager to dash any critic's decisions to havoc. Perhaps Virginia Woolf knew best: she confessed that she did not care to read her contemporaries and the reason could have been, as she had earlier said, that in judging a literary work in English, one must ultimately compare it to Shakespeare.

Even in the face of this, to accept silence at the risk of making an error is foreign to the critical mind, in a manner not unlike that in which the creative spirit would never flinch at the risk of error. No other single attitude marks the true spirit of the twentieth century arts than that very wish to risk, to invent, and to ignore the pastness of traditions and customs in all art. Thus a good critic would be reluctant to seek this easy unemployment, especially when the first half of this century was such an abundant age of art. The fifties and the sixties, it is tempting to predict, will witness an even greater growth of even better criticism; and this does not, in the least, mean that creation in the arts will stop while criticism grows. In a great age of art, creation and scrutiny are more often twins than cousins.

Of the twenty-six contributors to this volume, more than twenty have distinguished themselves with their own art. And as each was willing to look into the past and present decades of this century, so too each would admit at once the long reach and the narrow grasp. Surely none claims to be definitive in his manner nor comprehensive in his survey. The most obvious of gaps are showing: architecture has not been treated in any of the countries under view, nor have the everyday arts allied to it. Nor has the dance. The Hispanic arts (in Europe and in the Latin Americas) and the Scandinavian arts have been neglected. And the contemporary arts on the continents of Asia and of Africa are for the most part unknown on this side of the Atlantic; though the paintings of Munakata and of Okada and the pottery of Hamada—all of Japan, and the work of the dancers and the craftsmen of India, and the best of the fiction and the poetry of the Union of South Africa, as well as of Canada, New Zealand and Australia, indicate enticingly that another symposium on *The Arts at Mid-Century,* and still another, should be held.

These countries and these continents promise much in the arts; but on the remaining geography of the earth, life itself and the arts are in danger of extermination, for not only have the two World Wars but, between them, Fascism and Communism have put the mind and spirit of a third of the world into solitary dungeons and into chains. There, the arts are stillborn, or unborn, or unknown. It is astounding that this the worst century of

wars should have been companion to this the best century of art.

The turn of the half century seemed to call for at least
a partial summing-up: the smell of autumn and maturity
in the arts was in the air; adolescence was gratefully
though wistfully passed by. In the main the arts of the
twentieth century were being accepted in the home, in
the museums, and in the universities. At last, what was
shocking and modern in the arts at 1913 was respectable
and curricular at the mid-century.

With many more exceptions than one would like to
mention or to admit, the most obvious and direct impact
of the literature, music, painting and sculpture, theatre
and films of most of Europe upon America and of America upon Europe, since 1900, has been that of the arts in
France, Italy, pre-Hitler Germany, England and the
United States. Thus in August of 1953, the editors of
the *New Republic,* having arbitrarily delimited the field
to these countries, commissioned these critics and these
specialists—either native or "naturalized"—to discuss
many of the arts in these countries and to consider, at
greater length, some of the general issues in the arts at
this exciting stage of civilization.

The rest is for the reader to enjoy. And there remains
for my part the occasion to give my warmest thanks to all
the contributors; to Michael Straight, the editor of the
New Republic, and Gilbert Harrison, its publisher; and
to Robert Evett, whose guidance and assistance have actually been those of co-editor.

ROBERT RICHMAN

Washington, 1954

SOME GENERAL ESSAYS

Stephen Spender

THE NEW ORTHODOXIES

Shortly before she died, Gertrude Stein is supposed to have asked: "What is the answer?" After this she lay silent for some minutes. Then suddenly, raising herself up in bed, she asked: "What is the question?" Then she died. If this story be true, Miss Stein, on her death-bed, epitomized in these two questions the literary and aesthetic movement which began in the 1850s when Baudelaire noted in his journal that modern civilization created nothing to justify the continuation of life. Baudelaire, in his attempt to achieve a Christian existence by entering the universe of the Divine Comedy through the gateway of his own damnation, sought an answer to nineteenth century materialism. But if we judge his life and work as answer, today we find Baudelaire's satanism absurd and the flowers of evil faded.

Even his insistence on being the poet pursued by furies, the albatross mocked by the hearties, is meretricious. Yet these histrionics do not challenge his position of a supremely great primal modern poet. Why? The reason lies not in the answer but in the question: "how can modern man, with his fallen nature, his classic past, and his role in eternity, live a significant spiritual life within the materialism of modern civilization?"

The reason why we can respect the satanism, the albatross and the yearning for damnation, is because they all serve to re-state the problem—to pose the question. They remind us over and over again, like a hundred variations on one theme, that man has to interpret the life of his soul into the language of the modern city.

The greatness of the modern movement lies perhaps in the fact that after the answer there comes the question. Today there is a reaction from the great individualist visionaries and a trend toward the new orthodoxies partly because, considered as answers, their systems seem inadequate. Rilke's angels, for example, are unsatisfactory spiritual machines invented to cope with material machines. We can't quite believe that above the human landscape of modern life where the genitals of money breed more money and all values are sold at a fare, there stand these objectified projections of the Rilkean poetic task, converting the currency of external things into the symbols of the inner imagination. Shelley thought the poets were the unacknowledged legislators of mankind; Rilke thought that poetry was a kind of Bourse or Exchange in which material values were converted into spiritual ones.

He had fallen into a variety of the Shelleyan fallacy exploded by T. S. Eliot. Yet some form of this fallacy seems inevitable if the poet thinks of himself as isolated communicator of values in a time when they are decaying within the substance of civilization, one who has by himself to relate spiritual existence to modern circumstances, when the institutions and symbols of religion have proved incapable of such convertibility. Although poetry cannot be a substitute for religion the poetic function tends to become a substitute for defective spiritual institutions.

Yet the task of creating substitute spiritual institutions out of the poems of individual poets, the novels of a few extraordinary novelists who exposed their sensibilities to the whole condition of man in their time, produces inevitably a crisis of communication. Religious symbols are familiar to us and in a community brought up on the Bible there is no tremendous difficulty in interpreting them, though meanings may well be clouded or dense or hard. But for a writer to assume the kind of task that Mallarmé or Joyce or Rilke assumed, of re-experiencing everything as though it had never been experienced before, and then expressing it not in terms with which traditions and education have made us familiar but in new ones minted out of his separate sensibility, puts a tremendous burden on both writer and reader. Values have to be created by the total submission of poetic sensibilities to contemporary reality or by the pursuit within subjective life of images and ideas which can be lived and defended against that reality. In the end, though, as the task of individual re-experiencing and re-creating grows, it becomes progressively more difficult for the reader to understand the significance of the writer's symbols and language, without his having experienced the whole process of the writer's experiencing and inventing of his terms.

With Joyce a time came when, to all intents and purposes, he invented a new language. And the difficulty is that in making new words from their derivations in a dozen different languages, and in using myths taken from the cultures of as many nations, he inevitably chose those sources according to the arbitrary principle of what struck his fancy when, in the course of his journeyings, he came up against them. He was a fanatical traditionalist working within no tradition and having to invent one of his own. The understanding of Joyce really implies a special understanding of all the mythology which accumulated in his mind above his private plan of an exile's map of Dublin and its environs. He is in himself a culture and a country with myths and dialects derived from his memories.

So the tremendous attempt of the visionary writers to create works which were substitute spiritual institutions, was justified not by these novels and poems providing answers to the gap in modern spiritual life but in their stating the questions which were not being answered, measuring as it were, the dimensions of the gap, drawing attention to the absence of values. Poetry could not become a substitute for religion but it could draw or create a picture of the absence of religion and describe the modern human situations to which the religions no longer seemed to apply. It could create what Mallarmé called an "absence," and the symbols of the symbolists which seemed to symbolize nothing, could indicate holes in the structure of society where tremendous symbols which once existed within the ritual of living had disappeared.

Nor did the modern movement attack the world in which we live only in the work of the isolated individualists, the great lonely geniuses who stand above the landscape, utterly devoted to receiving impressions and translating them into their own terms. It was in a real sense a movement. That is to say there was an idea, that the human imagination could, through art, digest and transform every manifestation of modern life, even (and perhaps especially) the ugliest, the aesthetically least appetizing. It was a *tour de force* of the spirit to humanize what was most mechanical, to desire what was most hateful; just as Parisians loved the Eiffel Tower because, being a purely scientific demonstration of the utmost that could be achieved in steel construction, their hearts transformed it into a specially cherished toy. Guillaume Apollinaire turned even the Western Front into his private Eiffel Tower.

Thus besides the achievements of the great giants of literature, there was room within modernism for an attack on our industrialized civilization by lesser writers who simply had the sense of belonging to such a general movement. Apollinaire is essentially a cavalier who does not pretend to be a general, a twentieth century Don

Quixote armed with a machine gun who charges into the terrible No Man's Land of the Western Front as though the enemy defenses were windmills, and who with his gaiety, imagination and his love of women, suddenly makes us realize (as indeed Lawrence was to do sometimes) that if we had the courage of our mere humanity, chivalry can be thought of in terms of a modern gaiety of mind and body.

If the greatest modernists improvised substitute spiritual institutions in their immensely complex works, the lesser ones explored the possibilities of an empirical day-to-day humanism, measuring their spirits, minds and bodies, against all that is anti-spiritual, anti-intelligent and anti-sensual in the modern world, and conquering stupidity with a light-hearted avarice for life. In the world of individualist vision there are direct links between the most responsible activities and the least responsible, between the greatest seriousness and the utmost silliness, between, let's say, James Joyce's experiments and those of Gertrude Stein. For what modernism really does is assert the independence and strength of humanity; and at times it does this by gigantic efforts of absorbing a modern experience and improving an almost arbitrarily invented intellectual system to enclose and penetrate at every point this material; at other times by cocking a snook or making a rude noise.

There is no use lamenting over the end of this movement. The reasons for the decline, partly political and social, also lie partly within literature itself. As we have seen, the deeper the writers of the individual vision penetrated into contemporary reality, the greater the difficulty of communication with the reader. Several works have been written during the first half of this century which should terminate not with FINIS or THE END but with the warning DEAD END.

The deeper reasons, though, for the collapse lie within society. For ultimately the single uniting clause of faith of the whole movement lay in the hope that the individual could create his own values and so find his personal solution for his confrontation with the modern world. Paris or London was looked on as a bundle of images striking into his mind through his sensibility. What he must do was develop this sensibility, order these impressions and create his own harmonious inner world. The greatest writer would be he who received and transformed the greatest number of impressions and ordered them within the special inner world of his special vision.

Such a concept of the task of literature is—with modifications and variations—common to all the visionary writers, the modern seers. It breaks down at three points. Firstly, as I have said, the symbols become too complex, the reader cannot follow them. Secondly, the ordering of the impressions requires a religion or philosophy. If the writer invents his own system—as most of these writers have done—or, if, like Baudelaire he interprets in his own way the religion he was born into— there inevitably comes a time when he has to meet the criticism of already existing systems. He may have rejected current beliefs for seemingly good reasons, but all the same, the beliefs he improvises for himself may be less satisfactory than the traditional ones even though he be justified in attacking contemporary institutions.

Thirdly, society today forces us to take sides in certain social conflicts. In the latter part of the nineteenth century and at the beginning of this, people of aesthetic sensibility could regard themselves as the only civilized beings in a world whose values were becoming totally materialist. To the extent that they cared for values of their art which they created they opposed the society in which they lived. Some of them became ecstatic saints of the cult of their art, caring so little for the contemporary world that they expected nothing whatever from it— neither remuneration nor recognition.

Today, to be against the society in which we live is to be for another kind of society. "He who is not with us is against us," is the motto of all societies in the 1950s. Rightly so, because weakness and opposition make them need complete support. It follows then that the opponent of his society is not just for himself and his own vision: he is forced into the position of being a subversive, a social or political opponent. Hence we intelligently read politics into all attitudes: which means that individualist vision has become a delusion.

Roughly speaking, today there are three orthodoxies which influence writing and to some extent all the arts: Unstated Criterion; Communist Doctrine; Christian Theology. The first of the new orthodoxies is so vague that perhaps it is hardly correct to call it an orthodoxy at all. However it is an unstated criterion to which many people attempt to conform in the democracies—especially in England—and it is powerful. By orthodoxy here I simply mean conformity with the pervading presence of authority which demands the "responsibility" of the artist. In England this authority is some governmental body like the BBC or the British Council or the Arts Council which patronizes writers and artists. On the whole these authorities are rather enlightened. They do not consciously attempt to dictate to those who receive their benefits what they should think or write; they do not lay down rules.

All the same the authorities are themselves responsible to a public—they are liable to be bothered by questions in Parliament, for example—and they expect those who benefit to show a proper sense of this. Also these public authorities do have a certain taste. It might be defined best, I think, as Committee taste; and, to go into the matter a little further, Committee taste is a nice compromise between what is conservative and what is advanced. What is advanced might further be defined as that which was most advanced at the moment when the committee first met and which will remain advanced so long as it goes on meeting, though this may be tempered a little by the opinion of independent critics occasionally penetrating into the consultations of the committee. Thus it happens that a certain modern style in the arts in England has suddenly acquired the qualities of that which is academic. Here I am thinking, it is true, not so much of writing as of painting and music. Publishing remains independent, whereas the patrons of the painters and the musicians are, more and more, simply government agencies. But it is also to some degree true of writers, since writers are only in exceptional cases supported by publishers. Whereas the Arts Council or the BBC buys a painting or commissions a work of music, they employ writers who cannot live by writing their books.

In America, the parallel development which has led to this first kind of orthodoxy is the employment of poets by universities. The universities—no more than the corresponding agencies in England—are not of course to be blamed: they are to be congratulated. They have—like the English organizations—saved the writers at the time of the collapse of private patronage and of a general crisis in publishing. Their action is only the last stage in a process which begins with politics and economics.

Nevertheless the result of the entry of the poets into the universities has been a tendency of the modern movement to become academic in American poetry just as modern art has become academic in England. It may seem at present difficult to reconcile academicism with modernism. In a few years time, I fear it will be only too easy to do so. In any case, as I have pointed out, the fact that the spirit of modern art was anti-academic, does not make it, once it has been accepted, any the less a highly suitable (because highly complex) subject for academic study.

In America, though, it is in criticism, much more than in poetry, that one can point to this tendency: and the

fact that a good deal of this criticism is written by poets
is also revealing. There are one or two points I want to
make about a tendency of criticism to develop a kind of
orthodoxy. The first thing to note is that it assumes that
the writing of poetry is a highly intellectual process of
tying up a bundle of experiences and ideas into a poem
which can then be untied again by a highly intellectual
process. It analyzes and elucidates and it shows very little
interest in the relation of literature to life: indeed it is
probably rather vulgar to mention that there could be
such a relationship. It establishes certain works as sacred
texts and then proceeds to examine, analyze and generally probe them, looking always for myths, symbols,
influences, Freudian explanations, and so on.

If you judge a novel primarily by its rootedness in a
great many other literary works, the myth or myths it
refers to or contains, the presence within it of material
capable of Freudian or Jungian dissection, you may over-
look the simplest yet most difficult of all questions about
it, whether it creates an experience of life. When certain
modern critics elucidate works they presuppose the presence of such a complexity of elements to be the necessary
condition of art, that the criticism tends to overburden
the work of art itself. Students might be puzzled to
answer the question why it is that frequently a sophisticated critic, with his grasp of the complexities that
naturally condition poetry, is not able to write poems
better than those of the comparatively simple-minded
poets. The answer may be that the shock of art is lost
when it is absorbed into a complicated machinery of
exigesis.

Twenty years ago T. S. Eliot was being denounced
by dons for a drunken Bolshevik. Today he is accepted,
partly perhaps because we have become familiar with
his kind of sensibility (and this is a distinct gain) but
partly because no one who can be the object of so many
university theses could possibly be regarded as a drunken

Bolshevik. Yet although the words "drunken Bolshevik" were and are inexact, sometimes I wonder whether a hundred volumes explaining the mythology of *The Waste Land* haven't done more to weaken the impact of that poem than calling Eliot rude names has done. Name-calling is a reaction which at least has a certain immediacy, whereas to go into poetry equipped with a contemporary critic's weapons of analysis is like going into a Shelleyan garden of sensitive plants in an armored car.

I do not mean that criticism should be less lax and attentive. But I think that it should be concerned with other things than intellectual analysis, things which perhaps require more attention, as certainly they require more judgment. It should be concerned with deciding what is a poet's relationship to life; for example, Dylan Thomas wrote lines, some good and some bad. He was also a rhetorical writer: but what is his rhetoric about? The analysis of the quality of the poet's feeling for life is more significant than that of the influences that enter into his poetry, and it is also less harmful.

There is a tendency for criticism today to become interlocked in a kind of vicious mental circle with creativity. The critic labels those which are the intellectual elements supposed to enter into the poem. I think it difficult to deny that poets—especially young ones— are influenced by the conscious wish to put these guaranteed substances into their poems. Thus we get a process of qualities being extracted from poems which have been written and fitted into those which are being written. A kind of synthetic poetry is produced which is difficult to distinguish from real poetry, and this further complicates the role of modern criticism as a pervading authority.

Over a large part of the world the dominating orthodoxy is Marxist, which regards the writer as one who has to interpret into the terms of his particular medium the supposedly beneficial and absolutely necessary decrees of a Communist society. In effect the writer is simply asked to be a propagandist. But if he is a Communist he does not think of himself as such, because he believes that the party theoreticians have superior insight into the historic forces which have to be controlled in order to fulfill the Communist destiny, and does not believe that he has any truth of his own that should conflict with it. He asks to be "disciplined" by a "truth" which the Party directors know better than himself.

The very presence in the world of such an orthodoxy tends to produce its opposite, a counter-orthodoxy. For one effect of totalitarianism is to make us distrust individualism, not only because the individual feels weak in the face of such a machine of organized mass activity but because dictatorship itself rests on the will of one supreme individual, and therefore reveals to us the fallacy of putting trust in the authority of an unchallenged human being. Civilized men could almost accept the idea of Rimbaud as demi-god, but when it was changed to Hitler or Stalin, they remembered that men cannot be divine.

Modern life, at the beginning of the second half of the twentieth century, offers us a picture which seems almost to surpass the darkest prophecies of Baudelaire. Half the world has fallen under the control of these tyrants the secret of whose strength is that they are able to convince those whom they rule that their lives are the objects of an inevitable development of history, and that the only right and wrong is that which serves or opposes the purpose of that history imposed by their terrible wills.

All contemporary attitudes actually are related to a choice. Either you choose these historians who have converted sedentary philosophy into the science of their will, or you are against them. But even if you are against them, you may be serving their purposes by making it easier for them to conquer wider and wider areas of mental life.

In Europe today—and perhaps everywhere—it is no longer possible to create a world of individual values which has the power of such a position a hundred years ago, surrounded as it was then by a kind of vacuum within which it floated and which was contained by an outer wall of the individualist passion of bourgeois society. Such was the world of poetic vision miraculously contained within, and yet marvellously isolated from, the materialism of the nineteenth century which began with the Romantics, and whose richness and variety flowered in such different talents as Keats, Rimbaud, Rilke, and E. M. Forster in his early novels. Given the outer wall of a materialist society whose values these writers criticized or rejected, the individualist geniuses could plant towers to last the whole of their spiritual life in the minds of perceptive readers.

But the outer wall could not last. When the fabric of bourgeois society began to collapse then the individualist visionaries who had been hostile to it could only participate in that collapse; could become nihilistic, or rejoice like Yeats in the destruction; or perhaps, like the poets of the 1930s could rally to the hope of a better society.

Today though, to rejoice like Yeats in the destruction which has largely been achieved, or to prophesy *The Waste Land*—which has been largely fulfilled—becomes a pallid mockery. In his book *The Captive Mind* (in which he analyzes the effects of the total organization of thought into the central ideology of Moscow, in contemporary Eastern Europe), the Polish poet Czeslaw Milosz comments on the unreality of *The Waste Land*, after he had experienced the destruction of Warsaw. Poets may prophesy the apocalypse, but their poems seem but imitations when it occurs.

One may feel that to speak too indulgently of death in these days, and to denigrate the values of living, is an occupation where one may find oneself in strange company. Do not the Marxist intellectuals of Eastern Europe also point out that life—as it is lived today—is a thing of little value? Everyone has to die, so if a few million die prematurely in order that the purpose of history may be accomplished, does it matter?

Despair seems better than the kinds of dogmatic orthodoxy which offer us deep truths about life and death, but take our minds off the real problems. The despair of *1984*, even if it offers us no way out, at least keeps our minds open to the fact that what happens in the world of those who are living matters immensely, and shows us that when we forget this, our forgetfulness may be moral complicity in gas chambers and the destruction of freedoms. It reminds us too that while there is any avenue of spiritual or physical self-expression in life— even when it is reduced to the lowest social terms or to depravity—there is hope that man will revolt.

Since the modern world is enormously complex, to accept ethical and social responsibilities is difficult. For example, to improve social conditions implies a great measure of centralization, which in turn may lead us to discover another truth which Herbert Read draws attention to:

All attempts by authoritarian regimes to find a place for the artist in the modern industrial system have only turned the artist into a kind of clown, a jester whose role is to amuse the industrial worker in his off time (decorate the canteen) or keep his mind off disturbing problems. All attempts of the State to find a place for the artist . . . have merely created a type of lifeless academicism which has no relevance to the desires and aspirations of the people at large.

The writers who now live under Communism look for *something* to the West. For what? They do not quite know themselves. Milosz says that among the things they do not seek is to "relinquish the feeling of responsibility for what the public gets from editors and producers. . . . The intellectual . . . makes distinctions between what is worthy of his respect in the West" and what is not.

For what, then? They look surely to the West for writers who understand that situation already existing within the West which tempted the Eastern writers into accepting Communism, in the hope that the Western writers will use their freedom to discover a statement of the problem which is not Communist. Most of what they see in the West, however, is negative. Even that which appears to us to be written to oppose the dictatorship by historical philosophers, from over there may seem merely a confirmation of their worst fears—that we do not understand, that we are potential victims, that we are decadent. Or perhaps we appear to be occupied in setting up shrines—inside the belly of the whale.

The third new orthodoxy is religious, and Christian, for the most part either Catholic or Anglican. This third development is far the most striking in literature today. It is so, for several reasons. One is that against the background of totalitarianism, many writers have turned again to Christian truths which are more profound and more accessible than those which the individualist visionaries tried to work out for themselves. Christianity criticizes both the personal authority of extreme individualism which produced the personal disasters of so many poets and artists, and the public authority of dictators supposedly superhuman. It warns us that the individual who listens to his inner voice is listening only to himself and that this self is a fallen self; and of the evil of absolute power. Both these warnings are reinforced by a whole series of modern disasters.

There are other reasons for the return to some form

of Christian orthodoxy. One reason is that what was best in the individualist vision of the great French writers at the turn of the century was already Catholic, even if these writers had forsaken the Church, so that those who follow after are likely to turn back to what was the starting point of Baudelaire, Verlaine and Rimbaud. Another, and most important, reason is that the individual needs the spiritual authority of the Church to strengthen him against the increasing secular authority of the State.

Nevertheless these reasons are largely negative. They are the results of the failures of the individualist visionaries to stand alone. And they do not answer the questions of Baudelaire, made a hundred years ago, with which I opened this inquiry:

What, under Heaven, has this world henceforth to do? Even supposing that it continued materially to exist, would this existence be worthy of the name of the Historical Dictionary? As a new example, as fresh victims of the inexorable moral laws, we shall perish by that which we have believed to be our means of existence. . . . I appeal to every thinking man to show me what remains of Life. As for religion I believe it useless to speak of it or to search for its relics. . . .

The question which comes after the answer that any new orthodoxy can give is whether this religion when expressed in literature answers or indeed even asks the first question: "What has this world to do?" An answer which treats this question as irrelevant is also treating the most significant development of literature during the past hundred years as irrelevant. And, indeed, that is perhaps what, in spite of its having been turned into objects of academic study, has happened, or is happening among us. Baudelaire and other writers felt that the greatness of the past—the Bible and classical antiquity let us say—had ceased to be applicable to the present. One could only look back on the past, one could not integrate it into the life of the present. And, indeed, to live in the present was, as the nineteenth century ended, more and more to recognize the necessity of sacrificing the past altogether, cutting oneself off from its roots, immersing oneself in the present or even—as in Futurism —the idea of the future.

But the aim of certain writers—James Joyce, Henry James, Rilke and T. S. Eliot—might be stated as that of opening up the past so that it flows over the present, by stating the present in terms of the past. To explain Joyce's attitude to the past we can only describe him as a revolutionary traditionalist. He seeks not just to extend a weakening tradition of past conventions and forms into the present, but to reach back into a remote past, understand and concretize its values and interpret them into a present situation, even if the present is made to appear incredibly sordid and lost as the result of such a comparison. He throws the past into the present like a bomb. His novel *Ulysses* is a military operation of this kind in which we feel that there has been a confrontation of a whole imagined past with a whole imagined present, and the effect is explosive. Much the same confrontation takes place in the opening of the Fire Sermon in Eliot's *The Waste Land*. The theme of D. H. Lawrence is also confrontation, only of a different and more primitive past: the past, continuing into the present, of nature, instinct and primitive society, not the intensely imagined past of the literary mind.

What is noticeable in all these is the very dynamic relation of the past to the present when the writer's sense of modern values is brought into relation with his sense of past ones. The rejection of orthodox Christianity in modern literature was due to the fact that these writers felt that no such confrontation of the most living past and the most materialist present took place within contemporary Christianity of the Churches. For this reason, when writers return to the Church, we have to ask whether their orthodoxy realizes such a confrontation, or whether it is a partial retreat from the present into the past, better, wiser, profounder perhaps than much that has gone before, but perhaps also an abandonment of the problem faced by literature a hundred years ago.

Eliot's orthodoxy seems not to have given him a view of life which includes history. He separates life sharply into tradition and existence, death and life, with the rider added that the dead, because they belong to or are gathered into the past are more living than the living, who are pretty well dead. Edward and Lavinia in *The Cocktail Party* might be described as life partially resurrected compared with the death-in-life view of *The Hollow Men* but still with the mould and mildew of the grave hanging to their wedding garments.

In the *Four Quartets*, by envisioning the religious pattern within our lives, Eliot has immensely strengthened our faith in the reality of spiritual life. Yet even here, his concept of tradition is of an already completed pattern, outside life although existing within our consciousness and behavior. Life seems to consist of the living— who are little more than ghosts—and the spirit and achievements of the dead. In relation to the dead, the living are slightly unreal, at a disadvantage on the existential plane. One asks oneself whether to him "life" was ever real, or rather whether anything happened within time to create the pattern of existence which is now outside our time. Or did history happen outside history?

He is, of course, right in thinking that our true greatness lies in our traditions. But our traditions are living, not by being outside life, but according to our capacity to create them in terms of our contemporary existence. That this may be achieved requires surely that life should not be at such a spiritual disadvantage compared with the past and the dead. Life should be capable of meeting death on equal terms, otherwise we fall into death-worship. In the Renaissance men worshipped antiquity, but they also translated it into their architecture and their statues.

Moreover, life goes on, with all its manifestations which we cannot escape from. If we allow our spiritual lives to be captured by past manifestations, to the exclusion of present ones, then the unredeemed, ugly, and uncultivated modern world will gradually cover us over. The life of the spirit may be outside time, but change nevertheless takes place, and unless we can capture the changing appearances of things with our imaginations, then we will be ghosts living outside the world. We should imagine the past as intensely as we do the present, and we should transform the past into the material of the present.

After all, the writer in English who came nearest to understanding this was D. H. Lawrence. Lawrence saw that the view of tradition which turns us into shadows pursuing the stronger and clearer contours of another shadow-kingdom—the achievements of the dead—can only withdraw us from life into a world of interior cerebration. He realized the significance of the dead having once been alive and of the fact that they created their values out of their lives, out of living, not from a rejection of life. He saw also that what is most traditional in us is not death but precisely life.

Life does, after all, offer us the possibility of choosing to live; and within our own lives even more than within works of art, is the past: the lives of our parents and forefathers, physically and consciously and instinctively existing within our blood. The past as it exists in our physical and spiritual selves is not a separate entity, a pattern outside us, a shrine, a museum. It is ourselves. Tradition is nature as well as myth, religion and art. It is also the universe outside ourselves, still almost untouched by the traces of our history and civilization. And it is nature in ourselves which, with the best or the worst

will, we can do little to alter, but we may fulfill. The
relationships between individual values potential in the
existence of all human beings, and capable of imposing
their pattern on the forms of a new society, remain un-
developed though in the writers of this new orthodoxy.

The most important division of our time is between
what Milosz, in *The Captive Mind,* calls the New Faith
of Communism which is based on an idea of *"historical*
merit and guilt," and the remnants of a Christianity
"based on a concept of *individual* merit and guilt."
Communism analyzes the conflicts in modern society
which produce poverty, crises of overproduction and
war, and whose symptoms are found in every aspect of
human thought and behavior. It offers a solution for
these conflicts which consists in adapting all human
activities to the social goal of Communism. Control of
history by the Communist philosophy becomes the sole
purpose of government and of being governed. Everything is judged by this, what serves these ends is right,
and all that does not serve them, wrong. Communism
rests on an initial, buried decision on the side of justice
by those who then cease to be just, much as some Christian orthodoxy rests on the idea of Original Sin.

The Christian concept of *"individual* merit and guilt"
is, by its implications, the only one that has the power to
withstand the idea of *"historical* merit and guilt," to involve the individual in responsibility for what happens
to his neighbor, and to be the clear concept around
which the idea of a just society, answering the Communist thesis of history, might emerge. Such a concept of
Christianity holds the conscience of each accountable
for the suffering inflicted by society—which happens to
his neighbor. At the same time it analyzes and exposes
the actions of any Christian apologists for Communist
methods, like Hewlett Johnson, the Dean of Canterbury,
who slowly transforms their God into History. Finally,
through drawing attention to the responsibility of the

individual who can incur merit or guilt it puts Christian action back into history.

This, though, is exactly what the new Christian orthodox writers neglect to do. They are concerned with proving theology to themselves, experiencing timelessness, demonstrating the greatness of the past tradition and comparing it with the wretchedness of the present, denigrating the values of living. They evoke the idea of guilt not to prove to modern man his responsibility towards the martyrs (many of whom are Liberals and Jews whom the orthodox do not always approve of) but to draw his attention to the fact that he is fallen, and to make him increasingly preoccupied with his sins. None of this is finally inconsistent with the concept of the responsibility of every man to his neighbor, but in fact it serves to produce a mood of metaphysical introspection where each person examines his experience to prove that he has faith, is sinful, or has a sense of timelessness. The emphasis is on the inner world of isolated experience, now no longer visionary or nihilistic, but Christian, and yet still isolated from society. It is the orthodoxy of the convert preoccupied with his conversion.

Yet for people in the West who still live in comparative freedom, and where writers can receive honor for writing what they believe, to use their freedom in order to describe death as preferable to life seems a dubious use of their position. In the first place it perhaps shows too little awareness of the fate of the millions who have experienced a horrible death, and in the second place it fits in too well with the plans of tyrants who are only too glad to give the bourgeois the death he prefers to life. Of course where there are the conditions which prevail today in so much of the world life cannot seem very attractive. All the same, if the Western writer has any responsibility it is surely to attach value to the idea of life within a pattern of society where men respect the existence of their neighbors.

Probably I shall be accused of writing that Christianity should become political. What I am trying to suggest is the reverse: that politics should be Christian. This, though, can only happen if the Christian accepts his responsibility within time and history. Such a responsibility would tell him that Marxism has been more successful than most philosophies in stating the problem of social justice within an industrial society, but that it has fallen into a fatal error where it disregards the rights of the individual—every separate individual—in ruthlessly supporting a supposedly just—because "scientific" —process of history. The answer to Marxism is to accept the challenge of the necessity of world-wide social change, but at the same time to regard the individual with Christian charity and justice.

John Crowe Ransom

AN AGE OF CRITICISM

The advent of literary genius is unaccountable. The creators appear unheralded, like men coming from the sea. Thereupon, and at once, appear the critics, who are tame creatures of the land, to escort them and mediate for them with their public. There is little mystery about the critics, and the public scarcely expects to see forming for them in turn an escort composed of critics of the critics. The critic springs up like the member of any other profession, because he is needed in the economy of things, to cope with the novel utterances of the creators, and assimilate them into the permanent sense which the race has of its literature. A good deal is done by the critic if he does this. Though he has no existence independently of the creative artist, yet ideally he is formidable, he is possessed of quick sensibility and capable of powerful conviction. By this standard today we have critics of unusual quality. There is also an extraordinary quantity of them, but that is not an accident. Perhaps a fine artist will give employment to half a dozen critics, depending on his felt human importance, and the public difficulty in receiving his innovation. But in the half-century just finished we have witnessed a furious burst of creative activity, and many artists so far ahead of their public, yet causing such a passion of teased interest, that they employed critics for a whole generation before the public could have comfortable possession.

By and large, the critics have made slow work, not quick work, of such artists as Proust and Mann and Kafka, Conrad and Ford, Joyce, Robinson and Frost, Yeats and Eliot, Lawrence and Forster, Dreiser and Anderson, Hemingway and Faulkner, Auden and Dylan Thomas, Shaw and O'Neill and Christopher Fry. (I call names casually, not as trying for a best list.) Evidently the period is not quite finished, nor are the critics finished with the period. But the great surge from the deep seems about to have spent itself at the moment when it is survived by its best and most numerous company of critics, who are left lingering on the strand. Shall we say that they were called into professional existence in force exceeding the occasion? Are they the casualties of an occupation which is only "seasonable"? Or is it their cue now to turn and attack each other to see who is strong enough to take the lean livelihood which is left?

But of course not; these are absurd ideas. For what is it that actually happens? The literature produced in our desperate half-century was both ingenuous and sophisticated, but either way it was almost discontinuous with the literature to which we were accustomed. Only by hard work did the collective critical intelligence master and define it; by straining the existing sense of literature to accommodate it. And unquestionably there were strains which most critics thought they could not make in the name of literature, works which they refused to canonize. But now a reverse operation is proceeding. The illumination cast by the new is turned backward upon the old, and some of the old literature alters appreciably in that light. Our age has to use literature in terms of its own urgencies. Succeeding ages are certain to reject many of our prepossessions, yet some of them may prove to be final; our literature has appealed to human

interests unusually immediate, radical and vital. However that may be the older literary works are under
busy reconsideration by the critics, and some of them
prove sturdier than we knew while others lose substance. In our American literature the modern critics
confer new life upon Dickinson, Hawthorne, Melville,
and James, and find desiccation in other writers once
fully as reputable. Among the giants of British literature
the critics make displacements too; in the fictions, of
course, and in the anthology of lyric poetry. So our
critics still find a great deal of work to occupy them. If
it is not with current production, it is in administering
the ancient literary estate which has been inherited;
that is, in taking the fresh look at it, to keep it liquid
and usable.

But many critics grow in the range of their intellectual interest, and some are brilliantly equipped. They
do not stop with applying their modern perceptions to
the re-study of the older literature. They plunge into
literary theory. They generalize, for example, about the
structural techniques of fiction, or the diction and tropol-
ogy of poetry. This is a study which the philosophers
would bring under logic. Yet that is no stopping-place.
From there they are led into the metaphysics of literature, and discuss its curious manifestations in terms of
a reality-principle. In literature we are in a world of
fantasy and imagination. What is the human purpose
which drives us there, and what is the reality of these
constructions? These questions occupied Coleridge, who
perhaps is first in the line of modern critics. It was out
of entire familiarity with these questions that Matthew
Arnold declared that poetry dealt in the same fluid
existences as did religion, but escaped the dangerous
commitments of religion. But Arnold did not engage in
formal philosophy, nor did he have the modern philosophy of the unconscious. Discussion of this sort is
probably the intellectual limit of our criticism, or of

any criticism. In this area the moderns are in the act of writing their versions of literary aesthetics. It is too soon to tell what it will be worth, but not to say that at a certain point in the growth of a critic it becomes imperative.

So here is criticism, on its modern scale, with its spirited personnel, in its variety and in the unevenness of its intellectual levels. It is tempting to draw a long bow and say that it is a new event which the whole course of literature has been preparing. Professional criticism as we have it could hardly have come into existence till the art of writing had developed, and then the art of printing, and then the technique of mass-producing the books, with its corollary of universal education; and not even then till a spectacular creative outburst could start it off. In our talk about the advent of the creative artist there is usually a pretty figuration, and something of an anachronism. What are we going to do in actual practice with the utterance that "To have great poets there must be great audiences too"? Being Walt Whitman's, it is the utterance of a very late oracle, and it is a romantic figuration, still coveting for literature the primitive, the oral, occasion. The age when everything is printed, and everybody can read, is the age of literature meant for the eye, and the study; and though a true work of literature, in prose or verse, is indubitably meant for the ear too, it is for the ear of the imagination responding to the eye, and it is physically sonorous only in the final act of authentication. It is therefore quite feasible to have the poet both come and go before the audience appears. It is the critics who will find and prepare the audiences—who are simply the readers—finding them first among the veteran readers in their private leisures; and if the critics are ever to find the audiences "en masse," as Whitman required, then it will be later: it will be in the schoolroom.

Archibald MacLeish

THE MUSES' STERNER LAWS

In the thirties the war in Spain posed a question which many Americans found it difficult to answer: the question of the responsibility of artists and poets in the face of the corruption of human values, the perversion of human intelligence and the enslavement of the human mind involved in the rise of the police state. Today that question is, if anything, more urgent than it was in the thirties. The police state, though checked in most of Europe, flourishes in Spain, from which it has spread into South America, and rages in Russia from which it has overrun all eastern Europe and the vast extent of China, with the result that civilization has been replaced by police governments in a great part of the earth and individual freedom of mind and conscience, without which civilization as we have known it is impossible, is really secure only in a shrinking area centering politically and economically around our own republic.

More menacing still, the kind of mentality which inflicted the police state on other peoples has made its appearance in American public life and even in the Congress of the United States, revealing itself in the demand, familiar in Soviet Russia and Nazi Germany, that the State should extend its controls to the intellectual and moral life of its citizens: to matters of opinion and belief.

Artists and poets who were able to satisfy themselves before the second World War that they had no responsibility for the sickness of the world find themselves today
facing inquisition into their private lives conducted in
the name, at least, of the government of the United
States. And the whole problem is raised anew.

If it is to be discussed anew—and more effectively than
it was in the thirties—one point should be made at the
outset: nailed to the iron door. The question of the relation of any artist to the time he lives in is a question
not for his time but for his art to answer. Whatever duty
he owes as artist he owes only *because* he is artist. If his
art requires nothing of him in relation to his time, his
time, in so far as he is artist, requires nothing. A despotic
government many compel him to think one thing rather
than another, to substitute for his own convictions the
assertions of the regime, but the moment he accepts
that compulsion he is no longer an artist: he is a functionary of the state.

What ought to be discussed, therefore, is not a sup
posed conflict of responsibilities, the one owed to a
man's art, the other to society. What ought to be discussed is the obligation of art. Does art, by its nature,
impose on those who serve it a duty of any kind with
reference to the public world of happening and event?
Or is the nature of art such that the artist, the poet, is
freed from any such duty—even from the duty acknowl-
edged by the generality of other men? To put it in
literary terms, are those critics right who, pursuing their
reasons back through the mirrors of Mallarmé, discover
loyalty to the art of poetry in loyalty to the inward self
alone? Or was Dante right, and Tu Fu and Shakespeare,
to whom loyalty to the art of poetry was loyalty not
only to the inward experience of the self within the self
but to the outward experience of the self within the
time?

The literary generation in which a man lives may

change the fashion of his answer to that question but it will not change the question. To Coleridge the responsibility of the poet for the world of happening and event—"the close connection of poetic genius with the love of liberty and genuine reformation"—was taken for granted. But Coleridge's reasons were reasons which derived from his conception of the art itself, for to Coleridge "truth operative and by effects continually alive" was "the mistress of poets." With us, though we live in an age not unlike Coleridge's in which liberty is under attack from the same quarters and under very much the same pretexts, the close connection of poetic genius with the love of liberty and of genuine reformation is not taken for granted. Far from it. But the reasons are nevertheless reasons which derive from the art as we see the art. For we believe with Andreyev that life, in the modern world, has "gone within." We believe in consequence that the world of poetry is a world within. And in the world within, the crisis of liberty, the agony of a civilization, though they may throw shadows on the roof of the cave, throw shadows only.

It is, in other words, our modern conception of the proper place of poetry which creates the peculiar modern problem of "the responsibility of the poet." Why we choose to shut poetry up within the inward cave in a time in which the outward world is a world vast, tragic and enveloping to such a point that no human being can ignore its presence or escape its consequences is a question for the psychologists. They may perhaps inform us why we have agreed that our arts may not participate in the encounters of our lives at a point in our history when the encounters of our lives are most desparate. The question for the rest of us is simpler though still difficult enough. The question for the rest of us is whether this modern conception of the limits of the art of poetry is well considered.

It is not, needless to say, an escapist conception: a new aestheticism. Our generation has been pretty well persuaded by critics like I. A. Richards and by philosophers like Suzanne Langer that the arts are instruments of understanding and that what they enable us to understand is our human lives and the world of feeling and of sense in which we live them. We accept the necessary and organic relation between life and art and are even ready, for the most part, to include within the proper concern of the arts the reflection, in the private cave, of the world of public and even political experience.

We agree that what a poet, an artist, feels and may therefore, in the Aristotelian sense, "imitate" in his art may include his sense of the sorry world he lives in. But when we come to the consequence of feeling—even the consequence of feeling in the art itself—the modern barrier erects itself. To feel as poet is not, in our vocabulary, to feel as participant, even though the emotion felt is that savage indignation in the face of injustice and cruelty which moved Swift to unforgettable utterance. The poet with us, the artist with us, must not be enlisted in any cause—even the cause of human liberty —even the cause of man. Which, perhaps, is why Yeats ended his version of the epitaph for the great Dean with those passionate and angry words:

> Swift has sailed into his rest;
> Savage indignation there
> Cannot lacerate his breast.
> Imitate him if you dare
> World-besotted traveller; he
> Served human liberty.

World-besotted we may not be, but neither are we capable of the imitation of Swift. Our conception of the art of poetry forbids it. The duty of the poet, as we see it, is to live within the cave and feel whatever moves there: not to judge or choose; above all, not to judge or choose in such a way as to affect the world outside.

But are we wise—this is the question we should consider—are we wise to see the poet's duty so? Is it only *to feel* that matters in the art of poetry? Was Shaw right for once when he announced that "the main thing in determining the artistic quality of a book is not the opinions it propagates but the fact that the writer has opinions"? Is it truly unimportant in the art of letters what opinions you hold so long as you hold opinions: unimportant in the art of poetry what feelings you have if only you have feelings? Would Tu Fu have been the poet he was if the long misery of his later years, the starvation in the villages, the conscription of the children, the millions dead, had filled him with a gloating, leering satisfaction? Would Dante be revered as a poet if the few images of human virtue he met in his life-time were jealously plunged into the pit of his hell?

The truth, of course, is that we are mistaken in our first assumption. What the art of poetry demands of those who truly practice it is not merely feeling but a *kind* of feeling. Poetry like any other art exists within and by virtue of the human condition. Its ineradicable postulate is man. A poet, an artist, must not only be capable of feeling, he must be capable of feeling as a man: of feeling as Keats felt, whom Professor Lionel Trilling has finely called the last image of health in the long sickness of Europe. The poet's labor is to bring his experience of life, his whole experience, to focus and understanding—but to *human* focus, to *human* understanding. That "universal" of Aristotle's which poetry "tends to express" and without which it is not poetry but something else is a *human* universal. Indeed the central thought of Aristotle's doctrine is precisely that. As Butcher paraphrases it, "imitative art in its highest form, namely poetry, is an expression of *the universal*

element in human life.'' Understanding of that fact is
a precondition of the practice and the criticism of every
art and above all the art of poetry. A material impossibility—Aristotle again—may exist in terms of art but not
a moral, a human, improbability—a violation of human
expectation and understanding. It is only in its relation
to "the universal element in human life" that a work
of art exists as a work of art. Unless its truth is human
truth it has none.

The implications for our generation are obvious.
Loyalty to the art of poetry cannot be taken to justify
a refusal of the human world of tragedy and choice. On
the contrary it is precisely loyalty to the art of poetry
which most ineluctably imposes the acceptance of that
world upon us. For though no external power, neither
government nor institution, state or church, may justly
tell a poet WHAT he is to feel, his art itself will tell
him HOW he is to feel. He is to feel as man. And to
feel as man is to accept the consequences of feeling. As
Swift accepted them. As Milton accepted them.

Whatever in the world of happening and event affects
the universal human element affects the poet in his
quality as poet. He can no more be indifferent to those
evils which destroy the common humanity than he can
be indifferent to human destiny itself, for human destiny
is here in issue. Slavery—above all that worst of slaveries
which constrains the minds and consciences of men
against their wills—the slavery which police governments
have imposed in other countries and which the police
mentality seems intent on imposing here—slavery is a
disaster about which those who feel as men can feel in
one way only. And, feeling so, they have no choice, as
men or poets either, but to accept the responsibility
their passion has imposed. Tu Fu's art did not compel
him to write bitterly, and at the risk of his life, of the
conscription of the little boys. Tu Fu's art required him
to live his life awake and the rest followed. He was

unable, *being poet,* to escape the vision of "the bones behind those weeping eyes."

It is true enough that a poet, an artist, serves his art and not a cause. He goes his own way with his own will beside him and his own truth to find. But on the great issue, on the issue of man, his truth and the truth of history are one. Or, if you prefer it that way, his truth becomes the truth of history. This, I think, is what Yeats is saying in that curious poem addressed to the men of the nineties, the men of the aesthetic revolt, in which, after years of devotion to the Irish Nationalist cause, and at a time when he was writing political poems which Dowson and Lionel Johnson would have damned, he affirms his constant loyalty to his art.

> I have kept faith, though faith was tried,
> To that rock-born, rock-wandering foot . . .

What Yeats is saying in *The Grey Rock* is that "the Muses' sterner laws" demand something more than the Muses' stricter regulations, so religiously observed by his companions of the nineties and the Cheshire Cheese. The Muses' stricter regulations—the drawn blinds, the denial of any passion that has more life in it than death —all this had been well enough for those gifted creatures who "met their ends when young"—and for Yeats young with them. But now the world has changed. Which is to say that Yeats is older. And poetry, which had once been that mirror of the Lady of Shalott which cracked from side to side if you turned your head to look at the actual water-lily, the actual plume, has become, by mere necessity, a way of knowing and understanding and facing whatever a man is obliged to know and understand and face, from that cold heaven of Normandy, cold heaven of despair, to the petty, bitter, degrading squabble with official Dublin over Hugh Lane's pictures; from "that dolphin-torn, that gong-tormented sea" to the ghosts of Casement and Parnell and all the indignation at the heart.

Dowson and Johnson and the men of the nineties had been loyal to the rock-born, rock-wandering foot in what they had *not* done: they had "kept the Muses' sterner laws": they had never given loud service to a cause that they might have a troop of friends. But Yeats, though he had served many causes, the cause of Ireland among them, had been loyal also. For the Muses' sterner laws are not merely the laws of exclusion. They *include* as well. And it is in what they include that they are sternest. They tell the Muses' servants not only what they must forego, but what they must accept as well, if they are to be admitted to that excellent discipline. What they must accept is a whole life, the outward as well as in the inward, "that dead young soldier in his blood" as well as "the pale unsatisfied ones" appearing and disappearing to the mind's sight in the blue depths of the sky.

Francis Biddle

THE BLUR OF MEDIOCRITY

Russell Kirk's *The Conservative Mind*—"a prolonged essay in definition"—examines the philosophy of British and American conservatives for the last century and a half, from Burke to Santayana. He lists half a dozen principles of conservative thinking: belief that a divine intent rules society; affection for variety as distinguished from uniformity; conviction that civilized society requires orders and classes; persuasion that property and freedom are inseparable; faith in prescription (the customary right growing out of agreements of many generations), tradition, and "sound prejudice"; and a distrust of change and innovation.

These attitudes are found in greater or less degree in these conservatives: Burke, with his uncalculated loyalty to the past, and his hatred of abstractions, who so greatly influenced John Randolph of Roanoke; John Adams, the truest of the Federalists, who too put practical considerations above theory; the Romantics—Walter Scott and Coleridge; John C. Calhoun, who, before Lord Acton's famous aphorism, had written that "irresponsible power is inconsistent with liberty, and must corrupt those who exercise it"; Macaulay, Fenimore Cooper, "belligerently American, unsparingly critical of Americanism"; the New Englanders, fighting a losing battle for the place of sin in the universe; J. Q. Adams, who, like a true New Englander, felt that "his relationship to the Omnipotent was a matter of contract"; Orestes Brownson who finally embraced Roman Catholicism when he came to realize that Protestantism could not sustain liberty, because "it is itself subject to popular control"; Nathaniel Hawthorne, who impressed upon an already skeptical nation the dogma of original sin and the devil within us. So different in temperament were their English contemporaries, Disraeli, with his "baroque imagination," Cardinal Newman, with his insistence on authority as against private judgment—true liberty was to live within the "compass of God's ordinances"; J. F. Stephens, who believed that force, not discussion, bound men together; Sir Henry Maine, the great legal historian and scholar.

Finally, by the beginning of the First World War, it was surprising that a bored and luxurious society, with great wealth and great poverty, without true leisure or "modest private security," could produce the most substantial body of philosophic and literary criticism in American history. Irving Babbitt, Paul Elmer More, and George Santayana are representative of this group: Babbitt, who insisted that in our time the task of the humanist was to remind society of its spiritual reality; More, deeply conscious of the decay of humanistic intellectual discipline; Santayana, "a blend of aesthetic Catholicism with skepticism" and his "cosmic urbanity," who was convinced that liberty and prosperity could not be enjoyed at the same time.

Disregard of conservative principles, steadily increasing since the French Revolution, has brought about, according to Mr. Kirk, the present "consumptive society, so near suicide . . . the conflagration of unchecked will and appetite." His picture of American society is not attractive:

A society dominated by hazy sentimentality and concrete appetite, waking to knowledge of its own awful strength, ready to patronize or to lord it over the rest of the world, afraid of responsibility, impatient of admonition . . .

Its contribution to the future civilization is "cheapness, the cheapest music, and the cheapest comic-books and the cheapest morality that can be provided." Tocqueville's famous prophecy has, he believes, come about—"an innumerable multitude of men, all equal and all alike incessantly endeavoring to procure the petty and paltry pleasures with which they glut their lives." This is the picture, I believe, of America today in the minds of many Europeans, to whom the difference between such a levelling economic imperialism, as they think it to be, and the military imperialism of Russia, offers no choice to insure the humanist culture of the West, and results in negativism. It is not a true picture. Yet there are elements of truth in it which cannot be disregarded.

Tocqueville's prophetic insight, his rare combination of an aristocratic instinct for quality with a sensitive understanding of the wretched condition of most human beings gave him an objectiveness in approaching this new adventure in democracy, which was still held in contempt by most Europeans, which raised the scope of his understanding criticism to a level which other philosophers of American society have never reached. Kirk calls him "the best friend democracy ever has had, and democracy's most candid and judicious critic." Lord Acton said of him that he was always wise and right, and "as just as Aristides." The tyranny which Tocqueville dreaded, the new tyranny of the democratic process, was the rule of mediocrity, under which men are kept in perpetual childhood, which "gives to all their passions a sort of family likeness" (Lord Bryce was to find the same likeness a half a century later). The "virtuous materialism" thus established enervates rather than corrupts the soul.

Tocqueville accepts the growth of democratic institutions as inevitable, ordained by a divine Providence. Yet the despotism innate in democratic power must be resisted, and its causes understood: the tendencies to over-simplify, to centralize and to standardize.

When we examine the content of most conservative thinking, the vagueness of its substance and the confusion of its ideal emerge with greater emphasis, set against this extraordinary Frenchman's analysis. Put very simply, most of other conservative thought dates. Take, for example, Mr. Kirk's summary of conservative principles. The assertion that conservatives believe that divine guidance must rule a civilized society implies that liberals are excluded from sharing such a faith, and indicates that those who would preserve the society which they have enjoyed, in most cases as members of a privileged group, assume that God is on their side without taking the trouble to discover whether they are on his. They distrust the skeptical, in essence the critical approach which the liberal welcomes, because it challenges the authority which the conservative admires as long as it is exercised by members of his own class. But the liberal does not reject faith in divine guidance but believes that faith is a matter of individual judgment, and has no place in a democratic state of which an essence, culled from the bitter experience of religious wars, is that State and Church should function each in its sphere, and that what is God's should not be rendered to Caesar—at least the American essence. For even if belief in divine intent rules society—which may be doubted in the contemporary world—the discovery of that intent remains a human task, necessarily involving human disagreement.

Nor do I believe that affection for variety as distinguished from uniformity is an attribute confined to the conservative heart. The marrow of the liberal faith, of the individualism which Mr. Kirk so dislikes, was the freeing of the individual from the bondage of authority and misery which had been his usual lot without much variance along the generations. That at least was the ideal of the men who fought the Revolution and wrote the Constitution, even if their successors have not achieved a closer reality. "Those who won our independence," wrote Mr. Justice Brandeis a quarter of a century ago, "believed that the final end of the state was to keep men free to develop their faculties; and that in its government the deliberative forces should prevail over the arbitrary. They valued liberty both as an end and as a means."

The conviction that civilized society requires orders and classes I am disposed to leave to the conservative. It really comes down to a preference. And in contrasting the present state of American society with, let us say the England between the outburst of the Terror in Paris in 1792 and the first Reform Bill in 1832, the England that Burke did so much to preserve and to restrict, it must be remembered that the scales will tip in the direction of the individual making the comparison. Is it a better world for the workingman, for the vast class of the people, even if it is streaked with vulgarity and mediocrity, than the world of the Middle Ages, of Chartres Cathedral, of the Virgin, not the Virgin of Henry Adams but of the peasant who created the glory of Her image because the life that would come with Her in Paradise would forever replace the thin, grovelling human life that was his on earth?

I cannot put our world against any other period and say flatly men were then happier, the essence of life was richer and more beautiful. But such a reflection need not deter one from recognizing the tendencies toward uniformity and mechanism which threaten us today. And even if they result from the levelling processes of modern society, the equalitarianism which Mr. Kirk so generously detests, I am not prepared to admit that the extreme poverty and extreme riches of an earlier world, the very basis of the class society which Mr. Kirk's Conservative would have us restore, is a price worth paying.

I suppose all this is a matter of degree and of the choice at any given time and place; so that other principles of the conservative, which can be grouped together, faith in prescription and tradition and a distrust of change, could be more easily defended in contemporary America, for instance, than in Egypt or India, where tradition has stood still for many thousand years, and the ancient glories have long ago departed, while the conservative traditions ineluctably remain.

The men whom Mr. Kirk discusses are an extraordinarily diversified and interesting group. Yet sometimes their dish of conservative thought tastes curiously flat, without much spice or variety. The eighteenth century philosophy of a class society, built on a world which has long since disappeared, against the background of a secured leisure and an accepted hierarchy, dates like some smooth performance of *Candida* or *The Cherry Orchard*. It has the nostalgic unreality of so much of contemporary American intellectual conservatism, of T. S. Eliot, that "partisan of a graded society," of Allen Tate, of Peter Viereck, who seem to have little to offer to nourish or cultivate the wasteland which surrounds them.

They can see the forces of an unlimited industrialism at work in a civilization caught in a mechanical spin; but they can suggest no substitute of philosophy or of symbols, blaming democracy for men's sins against the spirit, hating the "barbarian nomads," as Eliot calls them, largely because they have ventured to overrun those preserves which in the world they would like to reconstruct were reserved for the elite. Unless you blame democracy for the discovery of modern power, to equate it with the destructiveness of that power is like thumbing your nose at the Universe because you don't like it.

This confusion becomes more evident when we consider the development of political conservatism in the United States. It has become identified with the business interests and, as Babbitt shrewdly pointed out, aims to conserve property for its own sake, and not like Burke as a support of personal liberty. The identification of business man and political conservative has long since become so complete that it is hard to remember any conservative statesman in the true sense since John Randolph or John Quincy Adams. And the business mind, cautious of speculative thought, suspicious of political change, disliking theory, is by no means conservative where business is concerned, but notoriously daring and imaginative.

So that if the mad rush of the modern world, uprooting the long established traditions and prescriptions of a settled society, was what Burke and Randolph recognized as the threat of their times—and how much more today —paradoxically the Conservative, the American business man, is responsible for it, developing and encouraging speed and change without the control of any moral standard or political principle. Conservative leadership in terms of those restraints has disappeared from American public life, as can readily be seen if we compare the late Senator Taft to J. Q. Adams.

Of course the conservative instinct, now particularly needed, has not disappeared, nor have those symbols which, better than any definition, express its soundness and its depth; the symbol, for instance, of the land, particularly in the South, where for so many men a relation to the land is no longer possible. Yet the needs and the faith to which the symbols gave content have changed, some disappearing, many not yet readjusted; but the symbols have not altered and so have become unreal and can no longer move men to sacrifice.

A purpose to which the conservative—the instinctive yet thoughtful conservative—is particularly fitted, is to recreate those symbols which reflect his own faith. This was strikingly illustrated by the way in which Americans reacted to the coronation of Queen Elizabeth II. The Queen was far more than a token of royal prerogative, indeed she was not that except in the outer trappings: she was the link with a splendid past, a bridge between the tradition of a thousand years and the new world of shattering readjustment; she held her people together and stirred their pride and love and sense of humility as no words could have done. Property seems to be the only symbol which American conservatives of the twentieth century can offer a spiritually hungry people—property, raised to the dry religion of free enterprise as the only way of life.

If the conservatism of the eighteenth and nineteenth century dates when it is applied to the United States of the Reconstruction and two World Wars, it has a core of human common sense that liberals of today would often benefit by following: that change for the sake of change has no virtue; that gratifying a "moral" impulse by unloading it into a law is an example of that sort of mischief (I have in mind, of course, the Prohibition Act, but it would not be unfair to apply the approach to most regulatory statutes, carefully weighing their workability before becoming too enthusiastic); that the roots of men run deep and far and must not too readily be cut; that the unrestrained play of the free market may be no longer useful to all aspects of our American World (in its name do we have to turn over the immense educational and cultural resources of television to exploitation by that market, as we have turned over radio?); and that better democracy is today more important than more democracy.

The end of the true conservative as well as the liberal should be the development of human beings. I do not think Burke would question that end, much as he hated the idea of absolute individual liberty. The contemporary liberal should also know something more of the past, particularly of his own past; and if he cannot be moved by the theological acceptance of original sin, he can certainly accept the healthy reality of evil, now clothed in the psychological garment of the ego and the id, that source of instinctive if uncurbed energy, and realize, unlike Emerson, that evil is a very potent factor, without abandoning any more modern theory as to its nature and causes. And the liberal can afford even more than the conservative to go back to some of the beliefs of his eighteenth century progenitors—caution and a shaft of skepticism should temper his too easy enthusiasms in a world which remains irrational even while he must seek to make it follow reason; and both liberal and conservative may come to realize that freedom does not mean irresponsibility; and to insist that a striving for equality of opportunity need not conduce uniformity.

Allen Tate

MORAL ACTION IN ART

It may be said at once that art being a form of conduct, it must necessarily have moral implications, but that its end is not the inculcation of morality. Its end is to be art, just as the end of man is not morality but the complete man. Beyond these commonplaces nobody seems to know much about the relation of art and morals, though I dare say other persons have expressed them more searchingly. What we must be vigilant about is the delusion that the relation of art to morals is a "problem," and a problem that can be solved. Art is not a branch of mathematics; it has no problems. It has mysteries; they are of an order somewhat inferior to the mysteries of religion, but they are no less permanent.

What we are confronted with in a work of literature, and I suppose also in the other arts, is human *action* translated into *being*—morals moving towards metaphysics. And that is why we get into trouble when we try to get our ethics from works of the imagination. Even if all men could agree on the moral soundness and depth of a given poem, it would still be dangerous to appeal to it as a sufficient guide to conduct. Action as it appears in a poem has been given another kind of reality which is no longer in motion, though it may *seem* to move: it has arrived at the reality of being, the end for which the poem exists. If we imitate its action, we are imitating an imitation, as some persons are said to have been, when, after reading *The Divine Comedy* a few months, they decide to enter the Roman Catholic Church.

The further any abstractions about art get away from poems and other works of art, the more useless they become in what I take to be the primary purpose in discussing poems, paintings, sculptures, and buildings; and that is, to enrich our understanding of the enormous varieties of being that the arts provide, and that, without the arts, no one man would be capable unaided of discovering.

What I shall undertake, therefore, is a comparison of two short passages of poetry, the one written early in the fourteenth century, the other about twenty-five years ago. Both passages deal with the same thing—the submission of the individual will to another will, and both affirm the necessity of submission. But the passages are very different in scope. In the earlier lines the individual will is related to the entire universe of being; in the later, one human will wishes to be absorbed into another human will. The passages are by Dante and Hart Crane.

It is usually convenient to make one's point by showing that some other writer tried but failed to make it; for this purpose, Matthew Arnold is always ready at hand. I suppose Arnold's touchstones have done more harm to the right reading of poetry than any device ever resorted to by a critic. For the touchstones are the shortest conceivable way of wringing all the being out of poetry and making it look like moral action. For years I had been puzzled by Arnold's use, as one of his touchstones, of the famous line by Dante: "E la sua voluntade e nostra pace." I not only didn't agree that the will of God is our peace; I didn't think that the line was poetry. Now that I do agree that our peace is in the will of God, I still don't think that the line *taken alone* is poetry. After I had read Dante I was more puzzled than ever by Arnold's failure to quote the entire terzina of which

"His will is our peace" is the first line. I could only surmise that Arnold shied away from it because the wonderful richness and complexity of the full image had so blinded him that he could no longer see it. Here is the complete terzina in Binyon's translation:

And in His will is perfected our peace;
It is the sea whereunto moveth all
That it creates and nature makes increase.

I don't want to get trapped into the so-called problem of poetry and belief, because I should never get out of the trap. What I do want to emphasize again is the standing menace of under-reading, of which not only Arnold but all the rest of us are constantly guilty. The great image of the will of God as the creative sea extends our experience into a mode of being that we had not enjoyed before, however humbly we may have accepted the doctrine of submission. Are we to conclude that the image of the sea so beguiles us that we slip into believing in submission? I think not. Which came first to Dante's mind, the doctrine of submission or the image of the sea?

There is no way of finding out. But this much can be said: the doctrine of submission as such cannot be poetry because it is in motion; it has not reached any one of several possible ends. One end might be, for religious persons, contemplative prayer. But as poetry it has got to reach another sort of end altogether; it must have to come to rest in a particular mode of being, and one of those modes is Dante's creating and receiving ocean, a figure of incalculable depth and richness. May one just imagine, assuming that we think of poetry as an inculcation of morality, a simple and very literal man who, having read Piccarda's speech, goes as fast as he can to the sea and jumps into it because he thinks that is the way to be at one with the will of God?

Some lines from Hart Crane, a simple and literal man, present the gradual advance of intoxication in a series of very brilliant images. (The poem is called "The Wine Menagerie.") Through alcohol the poet arrives at a certain intensity of vision in which he feels that Self has been liberated from *the self*. This is the stanza:

New thresholds, new anatomies! Wine talons
Build freedom up about me and distil
This competence—to travel in a tear
Sparkling alone, within another's will.

R. P. Blackmur has written one of his fullest and best essays on these lines. I am about to engage in an under-reading but in self-defense I should plead that Crane makes it inevitable. We must not be deceived by the complex imagery, for Crane has *under-written* his poem. Before I go further I wish to give my hand away. I have a strong impression that most modern poetry, however complicated the imagery, is under-written. It is under-written because it leaves out the horse, and tries to use magic to make the cart move. It is half-poetry. It is sometimes called the poetry of sensibility.

The only thresholds and the only anatomies that we are likely to know are those that God has already given us, if we have the wit and grace to find them; and the magic of sensibility will not produce new ones. I am not being pious about this matter. I am trying to discern an objective distinction. There is a radical obscurity in Crane's lines because magic itself is obscure. It is not a "formulable essence," and in so far as it is an "operation" at all it attempts to violate natural law. With Crane, we are not concerned with natural magic; Crane is using propitiatory magic, merely material means for spiritual ends: the mere intensity of sensation disguised as a spiritual good. Baudelaire and Yeats knew something about this, Baudelaire through hashish, Yeats through Madame Blavatsky; and both knew in the end that it was no good. If the other will—in which Crane wishes to travel—is like his, it would scarcely be worth the trouble to travel in it. What we have here, of course, from another point of view, is the standard romantic self-pity (the tear), and not the submission of the will but its destruction. Crane, like most men today, was a self-made angel trying to cheat the condition of man.

One of his conditions is his rational condition. It seems that in nothing that man makes can he afford to ignore it. Dante knew all about self-destruction; Crane put forth images of self-destruction under the illusion that they were images of an intenser spiritual life. An art so ignorant of what it is doing may often achieve great power in the eyes of those who can see around it: Crane's poem is powerful. But it is an art that in the long run will destroy itself; as Crane destroyed himself, for his suicide was his last act of magic. I am not repudiating my praise of Crane. He was probably as great a poet as a magician can be.

John Crowe Ransom

SYMBOLISM: AMERICAN STYLE

The prudent and pious reader is embarrassed if you
say: Symbolism. He knows that nowadays he will have
to reckon with it—but there is no clear-cut description
in what he can read about it in advance. He is apprehen-
sive of not making the response to it that is expected—
because the advance notices do not seem to connect the
symbolic effects with his own familiar needs. Perhaps
the truth is that a bold symbolism, if and when it really
stirs the soul and casts a new light over life, is one of the
varieties of religious experience, though an apocalyptic
one, not an orthodox. It is not easily imposed upon the
common reader even if he is used to literature, for it
goes beyond the conventional range of literary experience, which he thinks has been sufficient for his needs.
Perhaps there is a dialectical need for it, to fill a gap and
complete a series of literary effects. But he will ask if
literature, with its scrupulous feeling for reality, must
submit to as many forms as there are theoretical possibilities.

Suppose we take from the confusion of symbolic doctrine a few of the aims that have been professed, and
look at them a moment singly, even if there may be
some overlapping. We shall find that in every one
there is a departure from the literary canon; that is,

from the familiar canon which for convenience we would call the Aristotelian.

I. It is said that the symbolic art-work intends to have its existence purely in language, and must on that level satisfy the reader if he can receive it, not permitting the usual ulterior "meanings" which obtain in common language. Though language is generally regarded as a mere "medium" of experience, it is a medium which is said sometimes to escape from control and realize a life of its own. But language is exclusively a human activity, and even this kind of language will come within human experience, and in fact for greater honor it is said to make the human experience especially "humane" or humanistic. It meets with resistance from the old-fashioned reader, whose interest is likely to be in language of another and easier kind. How do words remain words and yet repudiate their function as "signs"? The answer would be: When they become symbols. But that seems circular. For what are symbols?

II. The symbolist promises to perform an act of free or absolute creativity, and realize an art strictly for art's sake. He will therefore abandon the usual preoccupations of writers, and their readers; such as their concern about the success of the animal life, or even the higher life which is involved with morality, and social and religious adaptations. But this does not seem intelligible, or possible. How can he forget his passionate attachments? And what, for that matter, can a free creation be? Having no determinate form nor direction—it aims only at freedom—how would it achieve any character at all, and miss being nonsense and whimsy? And what would ever push it into action in the first place?

III. A third version. The symbolist would like to heal the ill-famed split between the subject of knowledge and the object; the one that Descartes is said to have brought about, or at least to have published and forced upon the modern consciousness, which has been troubled ever since by the ambiguousness of knowledge and the impossibility of absolute truth. When language manages to make no reference to the fixed objects—after having made too much to them under the "imitation" theory of the complacent eighteenth century writers—and to make none to the feelings of the subject—after referring to them too much in the period of the Romantic revolt —then the hateful dualism may be said to be extinguished at last; by artists who in the temporal succession are the post-Romantics. But surely symbolism must start with existing words, and these are the signs of their objects, and indirectly of the feelings caused by the objects. How will the words be made to dissociate themselves from the sense of the objects and the responses to the objects which are the feelings? And why should they do so?

IV. We will try one other version. The words of the symbolic work are, indeed, those which have served as the names of the objects, and they continue to do so. But now the objects are not held in their old relations to one another; they assume new relations. These must be other than logical relations. But they are said to be very powerful relations, so that the symbolic work has "unity" to an astonishing and perhaps mystical degree. A new and tighter world, though having somewhat the same original constituents, replaces the old world. And perhaps this version seems more credible, and more intriguing. Thus it is said that a highly favored relation will be that of paradox, the relation which holds opposites together. All the same, we are likely to fear that the trick will turn out to be on the specious side, and grow tiresome; for we will look for the new logic which really reconciles the opposites, as the old logic scarcely allowed, and we shall be disappointed if we find them only juxtaposed physically! Can it be claimed that if they are held together long enough their opposition will be "resolved"?

These are some of the smartest descriptions of the symbolic language. But, in less challenging forms, symbolism has long been coming into repute with liberal intellectuals; it rates a good deal better than as merely a latest extravagance of language or *avant-garde* effect. Able philosophers have risen to its defense, such as Santayana, and Whitehead. Perhaps symbolic may be said to have become, in its most modest usage, the adjective which describes all those languages that are not logical and scientific yet are intensely humanistic. More recently, at least in this country where his work had to wait for translation, there has been the German Cassirer, along with his able champion, our Mrs. Langer. Cassirer's "symbolic philosophy" takes very high ground, and Mrs. Langer writes a book about "Philosophy in a New Key," and now another which might be said to begin upon the study of art as "Aesthetics in a New Key." A sobriety attaches to the profession of philosophy, however, which is likely sooner or later to tame symbolism, and lop off its pretensions sadly if it has any.

And what of symbolism in action, as it works in literature? After all, it would seem indecent if we stopped with a theoretical presentation, especially if we have followed up every theory with a theoretical counterpunch and knock-out. Symbolists did actually succeed upon the Romantics, as the authentic post-Romantics, and very shortly. The interesting thing is that they were our own highly original American writers, not only theorists but creative artists too. They anticipated the French *Symbolistes* later in their century, and the full-scale arrival of symbolism nearly everywhere in this century. They filled a period of literary history with which we can scarcely have had a good acquaintance, since it was not well studied. But now we may find it written up to the length of a remarkable book, which is sympathetic yet sophisticated and critical too: *Symbolism and American Literature,* by Charles Feidelson, Jr. (Chicago, 1953).

The present essay is deeply indebted to Mr. Feidelson's book. It is a very important literary history, and he is the master of a knowing and fascinating dialectic.

Emerson was the great originator of symbolic theory; after the German idealists, of course, though he seems to have been an original, and to have sprung from his own national background. Emerson used all the symbolic advertisements which I have noted, and more, in his re-iterative yet fertile style. He was reinforced by Thoreau, Alcott, and others. The creative writers of eminence were Whitman, Hawthorne, Poe, and Melville.

Among these, Walt Whitman was the rugged and imperturbable one. He had a fine though not fastidious literary instrument at his command. It enabled him to represent himself engagingly as "tramping a perpetual journey" across the length and breadth of the then United States, encountering the ever-fresh New World scenery, and the "natural persons" whom he loved and miraculously became for the moment before he moved on. But he never stopped. The logic for this kind of composition is that of an eternal serial or cataloguing process; he defied loudly the ancient stopping-places to which the old kind of poetry might have tempted him, with its stuffy dogmas, respectabilities, and fulfilments. Yet he is zealous at declaiming "the word *en masse*," and the words "American" and "democratic," and in spite of his magnificence Mr. Feidelson has to dismiss him in this poetic aspect as a corrupted symbolist, in fact a sociologist.

The best symbolic achievement of Whitman's, says Mr. Feidelson, is "When Lilacs Last in the Dooryard Bloomed." It is the poem where Lincoln's coffin goes on the train from Washington to Springfield, mourned wherever it passes through the teeming American scene. The key-symbols are the lilac which stands for the new birth in the spring of the year, the drooping star which stands for death, and the bird whose song embraces

birth and death indifferently, and so inspires the poet
that he becomes the bird; and now his vocation is a
proper and symbolic song, in which death and life are
indistinguishable. I think Mr. Feidelson might have
been a little more resistant here. Is not this disposition
of death a little easy? Poets in older modes might have
coveted for the occasion such dramatic properties as
lilac and star and bird. (Hardy might have said of the
dead man, "He was a man who used to notice such
things.") But are we to find consolation in a verbal
equation?

We obtain acute judgments of the achievement of
Hawthorne (who was a timid symbolist), of Poe (who
was one perversely and in defiance of his logical theory
of composition), and of Melville. In Melville's *Pierre*
we find a well-furnished and most substantial anticipa-
tion of Gide's curious and intricate play of symbols in
The Counterfeiters. But *Moby Dick* is the great masterpiece, and I fancy that the interpretation which Mr.
Feidelson has for it is novel, and pretty final too. This is
a symbolic work whose symbolism is about the symbolic
passion itself, and its final vanity; for even as a symbolist
Melville carried his critical habit about with him. (Melville and Mr. Feidelson are alike perhaps in having an
attachment to symbolism which drives them towards but
not quite to the act of "intellectual suicide.") Ahab
voyaging over the seas is the type of all symbolists, and
the White Whale which he pursues is that final heavenly
yet inhuman Vision of Truth that symbolism seeks. But
in the event, the whale destroys his pursuer. The ship
and crew vanish beneath the dark waters, which have
not yielded up their secret. Only Ishmael, the sympathetic but not quite committed companion and reporter
of the voyage, is tossed up alive, perhaps to make other
voyages if he dares. But it is not without significance, I
should think, to notice that the naturalistic plot of
Moby Dick is in the straightest narrative style (i. e., an-

swering to the logic of a real action), punctuated only by stops for the heavy symbolic comment of the reporter or the author. It was on that understanding alone that I gave it my own first reading when I was young. But if it had not worked I should wonder who would read *Moby Dick* even when old. Savage as he is, the whale is more comfortable for the reader than the ineffable symbolic Absolute which he stands for and the reader is supposed to yearn for.

A symbolic work appears to have its existence partly in "literature proper" and partly out of it. One may easily suppose that it aspires to exist entirely out of it.

Coleridge's ideas about poetry will come to mind at this point. They are both old and modern. Coleridge is counted on rather heavily by some symbolists because he regarded the poet as a creator next only to God, and did not stint himself in paying tribute to the power of the Secondary Imagination. I think they may not always be aware of the stern restriction which he imposed upon the imagination even at full flight.

In that most famed and involuted sentence of Chapter XIV in the *Biographia Literaria* he represents the power of the imagination as "first put in action by the will and understanding, and retained under their irremissive, though gentle and unnoticed, control"; then as revealing itself in "the balance or reconciliation of opposite or discordant qualities"; and after this beginning, names at least ten different pairs of opposites; one for example being of "judgment ever awake and steady self-possession, with enthusiasm and feeling profound or vehement," while another pairing "still subordinates art to nature." I believe it is accurate to say that the understanding (to us, the faculty of logical order) is responsible for one of the terms in every pairing, and keeps ever awake and in its duty, in order to be ready to restrain the imagination if it tries to be free.

Yet Coleridge was thinking of "poetry," not symbolism, whose emergence into history was waiting upon its agents, the Americans. I should like now to offer another consideration, which seems to find something essentially symbolic in the language of literature itself, especially and spectacularly in poetry. Symbolism has trouble defining itself, but so does poetry. What is that strange *je ne sais quoi* which distinguishes poetry forever from prose, and is grasped instantly by some intuition, though few if any of us can rationalize it, or render it by logical definition? Throughout the history of poetic theory the closest critics have been content to define it negatively, by what it is not. That is to say, poetry is virtually represented as arising when the prose shakes itself freer and looser by a series of transformations which can all be isolated and identified, but only as specific breaches in the prose logic. Nor has anybody yet spoken with authority to tell us what is the hidden use that makes us cherish the resultant with so much passion. The breaches are quite demonstrable; they are the poetic "figures" or tropes. But so beneficent is the positive and creative power which they generate that they have been licensed or authorized since poetry began. Reputable philosophers and scholars have categorized and listed them, first the Greeks, then the Romans adding to the list, then the workers in the modern European languages; until there had been reared a monument of industry, a list running in Shakespeare's time to several hundreds of entries. All that is pretty well gone by, in our time; the poets being so experienced in their tradition that they can tell for themselves, without consulting the Rhetorics, what is permissive in this art; or, if this is what they want to know, what is not permissive.

The bolder and more positive-looking tropes are such as synecdoche, metaphor, paradox, prosopopoeia (or personification). With them it is as if the logical sign of the prose were replaced by a new sign, which could easily be called a symbol, the magical agent itself. Per-

haps these particular symbols are specially easy to con-
strue, but they may be according to the type of all
symbols that are really practicable. The new sign or
symbol contains in its total meaning the old sign, plus
something new and foreign which frees the language
and makes it swell with meaning. It will never get back
into its tight logic again; the modern apologist of poetry
is sure of that, and declares it incessantly. The symbol
will not give up its increment of meaning. The logician
can find the logic of the structure beneath the centrifugal and Gothic detail, still working if he looks for it;
provided the law of Coleridge is still being adhered to.
But the *je ne sais quoi* is there too. This is the "divine
part" by which the humanism of our species insists upon
being complicated. And the difference between the complete symbolist and the ordinary poet is that the symbolist is capable of losing himself in his expansive
symbols, but the poet is trained by his tradition to keep
them under control.

In his postscript Mr. Feidelson offers this summation:
"Symbolism is humanism but a critical humanism." I
take it that this will hold for Melville and the most intelligent symbolists. They must symbolize. But they are
prepared to find in symbolism the locus of "error, confusion, darkness"; so they will watch out. We could not
ask for a fairer judgment than that.

Robert Evett

PROGRESS IN MUSIC

If western music were, like most of the other arts, supported by a really long tradition, the issue of present and future progress in music would perhaps be less important. If, for instance, there were extensive musical pieces dating back to the time of Euripides, or even going back a thousand years, music as we know it would seem less new. The fact is that only a few fragments have survived the Greco-Roman era. Even the music of the Middle Ages, which can be reconstructed and performed, was left by its composers in such a vague and fragmentary form that the authenticity of its modern interpretations can never finally be proved.

The supreme accomplishment of the Middle Ages in music was the development of a notation, a system of committing sounds and rhythms to the page in writing; all music composed before the perfection of this system is at least partially lost. The development of large, elaborate forms has been predicated on the notational system, which was usable as early as 1400, but very cumbersome. Refinements in style and technique followed refinements of notation consistently, but the earliest really sophisticated styles are not much more than four hundred years old. Because of this, music is the infant of the arts, a recent arrival, hundreds of years behind literature, painting, sculpture and architecture. The classical period of music is not Greco-Roman antiquity: it is the late eighteenth century, and Mozart is its Virgil.

The lack of a long tradition seems to make musicians, especially composers, inordinately jittery about the future. Music is alone among the arts in that its relatively brief history has, in the main, been one of clear and obvious progress. Some musicians feel that the progress reached its zenith in the music of the High Baroque, especially in the work of J. S. Bach, and that subsequent changes have been less progressive in character. Others trace an unbroken line of progress from the Gregorian Chant to the present day, and see that line continuing, unchecked and at the same greatly accelerated speed, into an apparently unlimited future.

We are accustomed to using the word "progress" ambiguously, applying it to either general or personal improvement. To recognize progress in the development of an individual talent is easy; it is more difficult to recognize in music generally. To accept trend as a phenomenon in and of itself progressive is to follow Hegel into that curious (and rosy) view of evolution which considers practically everything a step in the right direction, and which puts all artists at the mercy of historical processes. Arnold Schoenberg, who tended to think of music history as a general onward-and-upward movement, felt that progress was a divinely inspired thing, that the composer who set his own taste higher than the gift of God would end up, like Jonah, inside the whale; Schoenberg preferred to prophesy at the gates of Nineveh.

I suppose that the first criterion of progress is some kind of recognizable improvement. The word "recognizable" here is, of course, dangerous, since not everyone is capable of recognizing a change for the better. However, change is easily discernible, and few would be naïve enough to assert that a chronological accident had made the music of Rossini or Weber superior to that of

Mozart or J. S. Bach. The comparison, of course, is unfair at the outset, since Weber and Rossini were not composers of the first rank. The worth of the historical view
of progress must be tested by comparing the output of
the best composers of different periods.

This issue is generally side-stepped. We like to say
that we like Beethoven and Mozart equally in different
ways, that Mozart is subtle where Beethoven is sublime,
and so on. There is certainly no question that, in his
major work, Beethoven introduced a kind of passion and
grandeur not to be found in earlier music; at the same
time, he introduced a kind of coarseness, an obviousness,
an element of the gross, which music could have done
without very nicely, and which had to supersede the
subtleties of the eighteenth century if the new style were
to have the effect for which it was intended. Beethoven's
achievement, while not the first of its kind in music, is
a superb illustration of the composer-*qua*-Shiva, destroy-
ing as he creates.

Since Beethoven's time, the destruction of the past has
become a part of the working process of those musicians
who feel that they are helping things along to make
progress in music in a progressive way. Wagner and
Liszt, for instance, expanded harmonic language while
making a frontal attack on form. Schoenberg, whose
work was aimed, at least in part, on the destruction of a
whole system of harmonic and melodic conventions
while building up another system of tonal relationships,
frequently relied on the most rigid of antique forms. If
the evolution from Liszt through Schoenberg is progress
in the Hegelian sense, it is a strange brand, since it goes
backwards and forwards at the same time.

In that these composers and, especially during the past
fifty years, a great many others, have added enormously
to the technical resources of music (and, in some instances, actually extended the aesthetic frontiers of the
art) they have provided that recognizable improvement

which, in spite of the destructive element in their work, could be used to support the historical view. In that their innovations have, in many instances proved to be only an *embaras de richesse,* impeding their work, the innovations would tend to seem actually regressive. The most pathetic example of this auto-frustration is probably that of Schoenberg, whose heart, as he constantly reminded us, was off in *Verklaerte Nacht* a-chasing the deer, while his head was contriving a system to put an end to all such nonsense. The compromise at which he finally arrived, of writing alternately in old and new styles, was one man's tragedy. But his thinking, brilliant and logical as it was, has provoked a catastrophe in the musical art and in the work of dozens of smaller composers. Schoenberg's metaphysics relieves the composer of personal responsibility; it makes him a vessel through which the music simply flows, whether he likes it or not.

It is not Schoenberg's technique which makes this true. Such composers as Alban Berg and Luigi Dallapiccola, to whom Schoenberg's method is subject to their own personal wills, have found their personalities in Schoenberg's technique. Schoenberg himself did not wish to have his method imitated by people who did not understand it, and, unfortunately, this irresponsible imitation is epidemic in the world at present. However, without the onward-and-upward view, composers would not feel the need—indeed, moral responsibility—for adopting styles and methods developed by others, styles which they themselves find abstruse.

The act of musical creation is one of the most personal, private occupations that a human being can undertake. The kind of music anyone writes, or whether he writes at all is, finally, his own business. To assume, as Schoenberg did, that change in musical method is divinely dictated, is to make God party to some outrageous practical joke. To assume that historical processes inexorably dictate change is to dispose, once and for all, of the spiritual nature of music, reducing it to a mechanical operation.

I would suggest that any real progress in music is a private matter, something that evolves in a lively musical mind and constitutes a development of the resources of that mind. Personal advancement takes on general significance only insofar as it becomes part of the experience of the musical community, stimulating and shaping the thought of other minds. Because of this, a responsible composer will find or assimilate into his technique only those elements which he needs for his work; and these elements may as well be drawn from the past—perhaps the remote past—as the present. A revaluation of the past can inaugurate a tremendous personal evolution.

Paul Hindemith, a composer who totally rejects the notion of progress as an historical process, gives particularly eloquent testimony to the case of progress as a personal and private affair. Hindemith's early music sounds like Brahms, and not like very good Brahms, but the elements of his own style are there. Between the end of the first World War and 1922, the main elements of Hindemith's style crystallized. From that date until the early thirties, that style was in a process of continuous refinement, as Hindemith assimilated the *methods*, minus the manners, of the past.

The perfected style, as we find it in *Mathis der Maler*, has not changed noticeably in twenty years, and it will never change, because Hindemith knows exactly what he is doing and why. A composer as solidly rooted as Hindemith has no more need to change style than Bach or Mozart would. Hindemith is eclectic in the literal and best sense of the word, since his knowledge of the past is so exhaustive that every successful technique ever employed is part of his equipment.

Bela Bartok was eclectic, too, in a rather more limited way. His major influences were Beethoven, Liszt, and the folk musicians of the Balkans. It is probably the folk music which sustained his equilibrium during the Central European musical upheavals of thirty years ago. Again, his evolution was a personal one. It produced a rich, distinguished style, impossible to imitate, but with only a few technical eccentricities (most of them harmonic and rhythmic) which could be of use to other musicians.

To list the composers, from Debussy to Peter Mennin, who have built personal styles on a careful analysis of existing music with a view to preserving existing traditions, is to account for the stylistic richness of this century so far. The lack of a common practice in twentieth century music can be considered a weakness, and in that it encourages charlatanry, it is. But the lack of stylistic orthodoxy encourages the maximum development of the lively mind. Exponents of the historical view of progress feel that our great stylists are outside the mainstream of the art, have divorced music from its mission and its meaning, and are a thoroughly pernicious crew. The stylists tend to believe that the road from Beethoven to Wagner to Schoenberg leads straight to hell. This reminds one, of course, of the old Brahms-Wagner feud, which Wagner seems to have won. At present, there are two camps, armed, neither of which is willing to yield. On the matter of progress, however, there seems to be one point of agreement, which is that progress, whatever it may really be, can not come out of a literal imitation of antique styles.

In *The New Year Letter*, Mr. Auden reminds us that every aesthetic discipline carries with it a sin, peculiar to it, to which its exponents are especially prone. The composer whose predilections are conservative is constantly in danger of losing himself in the past; of losing himself so completely that his own development never occurs. One of the delights of a pre-perfected style is that it poses no real problems to the composer; if he follows the simple instructions on the label, he is bound to confect something fairly palatable.

If eclectic composers, like Hindemith and Bartok, may be considered progressive in that they have adopted the techniques of the past but developed personal styles from those techniques, what is the position of a man like Stravinsky? During the past thirty years, Stravinsky has worked in several distinct styles, most of them clearly appropriated from the eighteenth century. But Stravinsky never sounds like an eighteenth century composer. In a work like *The Rake's Progress*, Stravinsky approaches the style of Mozart so closely that at times one chord progression, or even one note could produce a completely antique effect. Yet the dryness of the scoring, the slight alternations of harmonic and rhythmic usages produce a sound which is peculiarly, recognizably Stravinskian and of our century.

Aaron Copland's music poses the same problem. Three works, written within a few years of each other— *El Salon Mexico*, the *Piano Sonata*, and *Appalachian Spring*—are totally different in materials and effect, but they are all obviously the work of the same composer. Again, there is a harmonic and rhythmic consistency which Copland brings to his material by which he is able to transform that material into his own. Stylistically, Copland and Stravinsky seem to be skating on the thinnest possible ice. They have helped to give the word "eclecticism" a pejorative meaning, which is perhaps unfair. To be more conservative is surely to succumb to that sin peculiar to eclecticism, but to have drawn style *from* style, as they have is to have established personality and to have progressed in the personal sense.

Anonymity is an abyss into which it is very easy to fall, and one of the easiest ways to do this is to imitate currently fashionable styles. For the past twenty years, there has been a large, miraculously growing body of American composers, conservatory trained, passionately conservative, and motivated solely by the desire to conform to existing fashion. These are the composers who are not embarrassed to write like Stravinsky one year, Hindemith the next, Bartok the next, and Schoenberg the next. In most instances, their work is technically very good, but badly timed and otherwise undistinguished. A composer who has no convictions of his own serves only one function, which is to get in the way. Our best young composers, men like Robert Palmer, David Diamond and William Schuman, have suffered professionally from their refusal to join the noisy crowd on the bandwagon, and even better established men, notably Roy Harris and Walter Piston, have been hurt for the same reason. If there is any single phenomenon impeding a general progress in music, it is the effect of fashion on musical style.

Compared with the fashionable imitators, those few real innovators working at present deserve our respect. But there is a sin peculiar to *their* discipline, too: the assertion of individuality at the expense of standards.

For many years, most of the important experimental work in America has been carried on in New York by the composers associated with John Cage. This work, at its outset, was distinguished by a revaluation of Occidental standards. Cage hoped to introduce certain Oriental values into our conception of music. This involved experimentation with percussion, rhythm, and form.

In effect, this experimentation has produced two different sets of results. Lou Harrison and Alan Hovhaness have adjusted the rich, percussive sonorities to the traditions of the West. Cage himself and Morton Feldman have almost finally divorced themselves from Western traditions. Cage has written music in which radios are the performing instruments, so that the composer has no control over the sounds produced. Feldman has composed pieces on graph paper, in which no notes are written, so that the performer makes up the music as he goes along.

The fact that his music has, conceptually, some relation to the improvisatory practices of India, does not, in itself, constitute an improvement in Western music. One suspects that, because it is less controlled, it is inferior to the Indian original. The fact that Western music can be written down accurately has made its evolution a special thing, and if the element of control is removed, everything peculiarly Western about the music is destroyed, even if familiar instruments are used. And Western standards cannot be imposed on a music which disregards its basis. While it would be unfair to suspect Feldman's sincerity, one can only assume that what standards he has are of his own making, and that no matter how elaborate his rationale is, he has arrived at a musical anarchy. A composer to whom originality and innovation supersede purely musical values must be guilty of husbanding his own talent badly.

The total accomplishment of musical innovation in the twentieth century has been depressingly small. The Italian Futurism of forty years ago has disappeared, almost without a trace. Atonality, as it was thought of forty years ago, has proven to be little more than an extension of Romanticism. Its best apologists not only employ the forms of the past, they constantly compare their music with that of the past, assuring the listener that, once the difficulties of idiom are surmounted, the music will have much the same effect as that of Beethoven or Brahms, as if that in itself is desirable. One might point out that, if the effect is to be the same, the evolution of an elaborate new technique is scarcely necessary. And, if the aesthetic standard is to remain the same, there is no reason to assume that technical change constitutes general progress.

Inversely, real technical innovations, such as the split-

ting up of the gamut into quarter-tones or the evolution
of a music without notes, innovations which strike at the
root of the Western aesthetic, are not progressive if one
assumes that Western music as such is capable of further
development. Real and important as these innovations
are to their creators, their general application is terribly
limited by the contexts in which they must occur.

If great changes of technique or style are generally so
ineffectual against the broad, traditional aesthetic standards of music, one may well wonder why anyone bothers
to tamper with common practice or to alter existing
methods in any way.

The most valid reason is surely that of purely private
need, the need of becoming oneself musically. As he
develops, any lively composer will, sooner or later, come
face to face with a blank wall, a dead end into which his
technique and his preconceptions have led him. Until
he has reached this point in his career, no matter how
brilliantly or rapidly he has advanced, he cannot have
attained that individuality which distinguishes him from
everybody else. He must either find his way out of this
situation or relax into oblivion and anonymity.

It is at this point that he must develop what Hindemith calls "the crown and glory of technique," which is
style, and no matter whose shoulders he is standing on,
what influences have gone into his style, what new technical resources it may require for its realization, or what
thinking has conditioned his choice, the result will be a
new sound, called modern not because its component
parts are original in themselves, but because they have
been regulated to fit the needs of a single, special individual. Having arrived at this happy condition of being
himself, he will show what the theologian calls "the outward signs of an inward grace," not because he has been
given this grace, but because he has had the courage to
fight for it, to conjure it out of his own mind, spirit, experience and imagination.

Frequently, a generous composer, with missionary instincts and abundant good will, will attempt to lead other composers, especially young or unformed ones, through the whole process of development, including the last stage. The unfortunate thing about this is that lively people are difficult to lead. Like horses, they must be broken before they can be made to submit to the will of the master, and once this is realized, there is no further hope for them. I suspect that people of real talent have been destroyed by overzealous teaching, but the small number which survives the process of indoctrination is heartening.

A gifted composer must, ultimately, find himself through his own resolution. This is why musical progress, in the general sense, has only a superficial meaning and might better be called a change in common practice, based on the idioms and techniques of some powerful figure and enjoyed by a coterie of composers who have not yet been able to assert their individual wills on what they know. Real progress is a private affair, concerning only the individual composer and his art.

Herbert Read

PRIMITIVE ART AND MODERN MAN

The relations between primitive and modern art are as old as the Eiffel Tower—exactly, for the Eiffel Tower was built to commemorate the Universal Exhibition of 1889, and at that exhibition there were numerous anthropological objects which attracted the attention of the artists of Paris, above all, of Gauguin. "It is great," said Gauguin. "In the Java village there are Hindoo dances. All the art of India can be seen there, and it is exactly like the photos I have. I go there again on Thursday as I have an appointment with a mulatto girl." Van Gogh wrote to Emile Bernard:

There is something I am very sorry to have missed at the Exposition, that is the collection of dwellings of all the races. . . . So could you, since you have seen it, give me an impression of it, and especially a sketch with the colors of the primitive Egyptian dwelling. . . . In one of the illustrated papers I saw a sketch of ancient Mexican dwellings, they too seem to have been primitive and very beautiful. Oh, if only one knew about those times and could paint the people of those days who lived in such dwellings—that would be just as beautiful as Millet: I don't say as far as color is concerned, but in character, as something significant, as something in which one has a solid faith.

This is eighteen years before Picasso painted *Les demoiselles d'Avignon,* and note what Van Gogh is saying (and what Gauguin and Emile Bernard were thinking at this time)—namely, that primitive art is beautiful, and that it is beautiful because it is primitive—that because it is primitive it has something which is significant, something in which one can have a solid faith.

Until that time, and indeed till long after that time, anthropologists and ethnologists had been completely blind to the aesthetic appeal of the objects which they piled up in rich confusion in their museums. Their favorite epithet for the description of such objects, throughout the nineteenth century, is "crude," and "crude" I suspect they remain for most anthropologists, who are not accustomed to give any scientific status at all to aesthetic values. Frobenius, towards the end of the nineteenth century, was probably the first anthropologist to use the word "art" in connection with primitive peoples, and he did not lay much stress on it.

Robert Lowie, as late as 1925, is probably the first anthropologist to recognize, in his own words, that "the aesthetic impulse is one of the irreducible components of the human mind . . . a potent agency from the very beginnings of human existence," though he quotes Jochelson, whose work is unknown to me, as having previously admitted this fact. But what I wish to emphasize is that the whole of this revaluation of primitive art —its very recognition as art—was due to artists, and not to scholars and scientists, who, in spite of their more intimate knowledge of the material in question, remained obstinately purblind to its aesthetic qualities.

All this is matter of fact, and perhaps not very important. What is more interesting and debatable is the motive underlying the recognition of the aesthetic value of primitive art more than sixty years ago. Why did artists in 1889 find primitive art not merely beautiful, but also significant—"something in which one has a solid faith?" That, I take it, is the real problem.

I think there is little doubt that the answer to this

question lies in the artist's revolt, conscious or unconscious, against the industrial civilization which, by the third quarter of the nineteenth century, had become such a hideous reality. In the case of Van Gogh and Gauguin, European civilization was a "dismal swamp," corrupt beyond redemption. Gauguin deliberately turned his back on it, and went to Tahiti to seek the primitive reality. To a certain extent he found it, and this is how he describes it:

A delight distilled from some indescribable sacred horror which I glimpse of far off things. The odor of an antique joy which I am breathing in the present. Animal shapes of a statuesque rigidity: indescribably antique, august, and religious in the rhythm of their gesture, in their singular immobility. In the dreaming eyes is the overcast surface of an unfathomable enigma.

In the case of Van Gogh the reaction was less conscious, more introverted, and the end was madness. From the asylum in St. Rémy he wrote of his *horror of life,* but he also wrote that he considered the artist's duty was to think, not to dream, and he said of Bernard's and Gauguin's paintings: "the thing about them is that they are a sort of dream or nightmare—that they are erudite enough—you can see that it is someone who is mad on the primitives . . ." and that gave him "a painful feeling of collapse instead of progress." But his own concentration on the visual was an escape from the civilization around him—as he said himself: "it is really at bottom fairly true that a painter as man is too much absorbed by what his eyes see, and is not sufficiently master of the rest of his life."

Van Gogh died just after 1889 which I have given as the year in which the relations between primitive and modern art began, so he does not really come into question. But Van Gogh is the father of that movement known as Expressionism, and the Expressionists were to become, twenty years later, the most consistent representatives of a primitive style in modern art. By a primitive *style* I mean a mode of expression more or less directly influenced by primitive prototypes. Emil Nolde, like Gauguin before him, actually visited the South Seas, and there was the direct impact on other Expressionists, such as Schmidt-Rottluff, Pechstein and Kirchner, of Frobenius's publications, and of Carl Einstein's *Negerplastik*, published in Leipzig in 1915.

To return to France: I would like to suggest that there was no break in development between the discovery of primitive art in 1889 and its direct translation into cubism from 1907 onwards. Gauguin went on painting until 1903, and his works, of course, gained in influence after his death. By 1904 we know that Vlaminck was taking an interest in primitive art, and Vlaminck infected Derain with his enthusiasm, and Derain infected Matisse. Both Matisse and Derain began to collect Negro sculpture before 1907. Then came *Les demoiselles d'Avignon* and a series of paintings, by Picasso, Braque, Derain and others, which grew increasingly geometrical in style, and finally, in other hands, emerged as cubism: cubism analytical and synthetic, and then abstract and uncontaminated by any representational element.

Meanwhile another development was taking place which was to have its repercussions on modern art. About the same time that Gauguin was discovering primitive art, Freud was discovering the unconscious. I have no documentary evidence of the first contact between art and psychoanalysis, but I suspect that it took place in Munich between 1908 and 1910. There is some research to be done on this question, but I think it would establish that both Kandinsky and Klee had some knowledge of psychoanalysis before 1910, and certainly the group of artists who assembled in Zurich on the outbreak of war in 1914 and established the Dada group were familiar with some of Freud's ideas. This group was presently taken up by a trained psychiatrist, André Breton, and from the interpretation of primitive art, psychoanalysis, the poetry of Rimbaud and Lautréamont, post-Hegelian philosophy and I know not what else, the movement known as Surrealism was born.

The surrealists from the beginning took a serious and indeed a scientific interest in all forms of primitive art, and in Paris at any rate there was a close understanding between the surrealist artists, the psychoanalysts, and the anthropologists. The general effect of this was to reveal a common basis, in the unconscious, for those irrational forms of art in which the contemporary, no less than the primitive man, felt impelled to express himself.

These historical considerations are perhaps unduly pedantic, but the scope and complexity of the relations between modern art and primitive art are not fully appreciated. I hope I have shown that it has not been a superficial flirtation; that on the contrary there has grown up, over a period of sixty years, an intimate connection which, on the one hand, has led to a revaluation of ethnological material, a great portion of which has now been rescued from the scientific lumber-room and elevated to a worthy place among the creative achievements of mankind; and on the other hand has given to the modern artist a new mode of expression which he finds in accordance with his emotional or spiritual needs. And that brings me to my last point.

I might be criticised for using the word *"Angst"* (anguish) in this context, and for suggesting that the similarities which exist between certain types of primitive art and certain types of modern art are due to a common psychological condition. Let me try to make my meaning clear. It seems to me beyond doubt that the trend of modern art away from representational realism and towards some degree of abstraction or symbolism is but a reflection of those philosophical and religious trends which, themselves no doubt determined or at any rate intimately related to economic trends, have led mankind into a state of religious unbelief, of psychological imbalance, and social unrest. If there is one word which succinctly defines the universal condition of mankind today, it is the word *insecurity*—mental insecurity, social insecurity, metaphysical insecurity.

I am not going to suggest that the same or a similar word can be used to characterize primitive man. This term is far too inclusive for our purposes, and we need some classification of primitive races before we can venture to generalise about their metaphysical characteristics. But there exists that general division to which I have already referred—that between primitive races whose art is naturalistic, and primitive races whose art is geometrical or symbolic. It is roughly, as I have said, the distinction between paleolithic art and neolithic art, between what is usually called bushman art and what is usually called Negro art. At this point I would quite sincerely ask for the anthropologist's guidance, because it does seem to me that we lack any thorough correlation of types of religion and types of art. I am assuming, however, that such a correlation would reveal a parallel between religions of fear, terror, propitiation and retribution to which would correspond arts of symbolic or geometric tendency; and between religions of ritual and sympathetic magic based on a belief in the beneficence of nature and the gods to which would correspond a naturalistic or representational art.

If such a correspondence does in fact show itself throughout the history of mankind, then it is very easy to explain the return of the modern artist to forms of art similar to those we call "primitive." The reason lies in mankind's return to a "primitive" state of mind. To call the state of mind of a contemporary existentialist "primitive" is perhaps paradoxical; but when the existentialist (and we must remember that he represents the up-to-date Christian theologian as well as the up-to-date atheist philosopher)—when the existentialist begins to talk about the anguish or uneasiness which overcomes him when he faces up to the problem of man's cosmic predicament, he is merely using elaborate linguistic signs to describe the same feelings which overcome primitive men, but which they can only express in emotive symbols. Similarly, the modern artist, not being an adept in philosophical verbalization, is reduced to expressing himself in concrete symbols—that is to say, in works of art that are the objective correlate of his inner emotional tensions. Modern man, and the modern artist in particular, is no mere eclectic monkey, trying to imitate for his occasional amusement the artifacts of primitive races; on the contrary, he is, spiritually speaking, in a tough spot himself. The more honest he is with himself, the more resolutely he rejects traditional forms and worn counters of expression, and the more nearly, and the more unconsciously, he finds himself expressing himself in a manner which bears a real and no longer superficial resemblance to so-called "primitive" art.

Robert Richman

It is perhaps one of the main paradoxes, and certainly the most interesting one in the modern art movement, that the basic aim of its leaders was to destroy the masterpiece theory and along with it the concept of the master in their attempt to refocus attention both of the artist and of the critical audience onto the work of art itself. Yet few if any periods in history are marked with more "masters" in any given fifty years, or few gave more adoration to its masters. All of them helped to form the modern theories as they worked at their art; and some few of them, instead of courting notoriety as Picasso has done, actually have tried and preferred to let the work of art and not their special personality be shown and known. To name some of these, without any attempt to evaluate their order or merit—Cézanne, Braque, Gabo, Henry Moore, Picasso, Mondrian, Yeats, Eliot, Henry James, James Joyce, Hindemith, Bartok, Stravinsky, Schoenberg and his school, Frank Lloyd Wright and Le Corbusier.

It is more important to place these artists in their age, in relation to one another, in relation to the springs of art from which they stream, rather than to see them individually or to pass judgment on the excellence and value of their single or several works; for, to begin with, in no age in the history of art—in so short a period as half a century—has the interrelatedness of the several arts been so actual, so inherent, or so importantly marked by a conscious theory of art, not even in the Renaissance, nor in Byzantium. Though this interrelatedness did signify two great periods of art—the Sung Dynasty of China of the ninth to twelfth centuries and the Middle Ages of Western Europe from the late tenth through the thirteenth centuries. In these two great epochs of art, however, roughly 300 years were afforded the slow evolution of Sung or Mediaeval art, whereas less than fifty years were consumed in the swift revolt of Modern art.

In fact, it is precisely these two periods—the Sung and the Mediaeval—to which most of the twentieth century masters turned for part of their theory and a portion of their craft and technique. It is easy to see in modern literature in the English language, the turn to the Middle Ages for theory and practice (Eliot and Joyce to Dante and the Scholastics; Yeats to Byzantium); but it is easier to trace, in the visual and manual arts in England, the return under the aegis of Ruskin and Morris to the Pre-Raphaelites. It is noteworthy that Paul Hindemith and Bela Bartok have turned to the Gregorian Chant and to folk music; and that Hindemith especially has gone back there by the way of Scholasticism. Recently Mr. Hindemith was converted to Roman Catholicism in a way reminiscent of Mr. Eliot's conversion to Anglo-Catholicism. Each seemed in the analysis of aesthetic problems to confront religion, as Mr. Eliot with letters did in *The Sacred Wood* then so Mr. Hindemith with music did in *A Composer's World*. And by this I do not mean to imply a parallel.

Whereas Yeats' use of the Ideal he called Byzantium is explicitly stated in two of his poems—"Byzantium" and "Sailing to Byzantium"—and underlies *A Vision,* the use Naum Gabo, the Constructivist sculptor, has made of Byzantium in his work is hidden in his bloodstream and suggests that certain of his constructed sculptures were born from the impingement upon his senses of the Russian Icons which he saw almost daily in his boyhood and youth, and from the architecture of the village in inner Eastern Russia, where he was born. Since admittedly great artists do not borrow from the art of others or other civilizations, but rather take from it, one may not expect to find their admissions; and I would tend to doubt any direct admission on the grounds that Shakespeare did not know when he stole from Montaigne, specifically because he was more attuned to fusing words and images into poetry than he was to the study of influences of the French essayists on the English poets in the Age of Elizabeth I.

Equally indirect yet also equally important has been the influence of the Chinese, largely the Sung—of scroll paintings, of drawings, and of pottery—upon the work of Cézanne, Frank Lloyd Wright, Henry Moore and Bernard Leach, the English potter. The Sung artists believed that a work of art should grow from the inside, the germ evolving into the large finished form or, as Mr. Wright demands, that a house should grow organically from the nucleus out to the finished landscape surrounding the home. Sung artists also placed primary emphasis upon the excellence of the execution of a work of art—not in the restrictive and polished formal manner—but in the manner of the way in which the brush strokes showed not only a skill in control but a spirit of freedom as well. And the final ideal of the Sung artists was that the materials should delimit the form.

It is in pottery, one of the absolutes of abstract art, and in England, that the modern movement in the arts has had a continuity from the days of William Morris; and it is in the crafts—and again in England—that the influence of the Middle Ages and the influence of the Sung Dynasties meet. The descent is from the theories of Ruskin the philosopher, through Morris the designer, to Edward Johnston the letterer, to Eric Gill the stonemason, to Bernard Leach and the late T. S. Haile the potters. These theories have come full circle in the writings of Herbert Read, who bespeaks Ruskin, the Middle Ages, and the Sung, and whose theories helped to shape the present generation of designers and architects in England, especially the town planners who try to make the new England of the International style blend into the old England of Tudor and Georgian houses, as in the works of Lionel Brett, the architect and planner.

All these Sung influences were deep, and hidden, and major (they merged in the early 1920s with the Mediaeval or echoed it); these influences had to do with the way a man held his pen to paper, his chisel to stone, or his hand to the clay; not only this but how his materials were treated with simple respect and allowed to take shape organically, as dew forms on the branch of a tree, rather than for the materials to be poured into some mold or pattern which had been handed down from the Renaissance without so much as a question being asked by maker or by user whether or not the design of the water pump on the farm, for instance, or the bathtub in a fashionable Fifth Avenue home, or the legs of a very old Singer sewing machine really did have to look like Renaissance grillwork found on the gate of a late sixteenth century Italian formal garden. The concept that form follows function, materials express form, and line follows form—so peculiarly the property of architectural theory since the days of Louis Sullivan's *Kindergarten Chats*—these men in England were learning daily. And they had allowed their fingers to memorize the lesson and to turn the theory into their daily involuntary habits of execution be it the chair of Morris, the lettering of Johnston, the stone carving of Gill, or the bowls of Leach.

Moreover, these influences have shown up persistently and beautifully in the best of modern architects in America, especially in their use of native materials, where Frank Lloyd Wright stands with his mantle on his shoulders apart from and beyond the movement. The Sung ideal imprinted itself forever in Wright's consciousness when he lived in Japan in the early part of the century and learned the importance of materials and techniques to a concept of form, both as they were united in the native module architecture of Japan, which he was to take in the special and privileged way artists must have and was to make into his own, and from the Sung standard as Buddhist Japan had altered and theorized upon it. Moreover a literary and ethical tradition influenced Wright's architecture: the Sung ideals and standards were known and used by Emerson, Thoreau and Whitman: and from their Easternized writings Wright obtained much for his theory and sermons on architecture. In more than one sense, then, Wright is surely Emerson's self-reliant and transcendentally Ideal Man turned practicing architect.

The most salutary of all the uses of the past seems to me to be that which Cézanne made of the Sung standard: it shows itself most subtilely and most beautifully in those late landscapes which occupied Cézanne so much of his time from 1890 to his death in 1906. One thinks of "La Montagne Sainte-Victoire" and "La Montagne Sainte-Victoire, vue du chemin des lauves" in which his stroke is calligraphic and the color areas essentially make of the landscape a new and real creation on the canvas—a created work of painterly art in which nature is not represented but transformed. And the combinations of colors and strokes evoke that sense of imminence behind the visible in nature which the Sung painters made to be synonymous with God. The latter of these two paintings of Cézanne provides the actual link between the "new realism" and "analytic cubism" in that long progression from Manet through Seurat to Cézanne and Gauguin to Braque, even though to look at a Manet on one wall of the gallery and then at a Braque on another would never indicate a lineal descent and certainly not in a mere 30 years. But surely too Cézanne handed on the tradition of French classical painting to the generation who followed him—improved, brightened, and not diminished by the use of Sung methods. And his brush was picked up by Braque, who uses it in the classical manner for a more organic abstract art.

To determine the manner in which the master made use of his tradition had been the occupation ordinarily of the philosophers—of Aristotle discussing Sophocles' use of Homer. But the twentieth century masters have themselves primarily been discussing the manner of using their traditions. In an age such as ours when the major artists were in open revolt against the machine age and the mechanization of life it forced upon us, or when these artists are involved in another variety of open revolt against the authority of national, monarchial or totalitarian governments and regimes, or when the artists themselves are revolting against their immediate forebears—as Yeats threw off the Lord Tennyson—the problem of the artist using his tradition is an intricate one.

In the main, there has been a most conscious use of the Mediaeval tradition, with an emphasis on the doctrine of economy which in art pronounces that the least means shall be used to achieve the greatest end. In the work of Eliot and Hindemith where they connect with the past there seems to be a continuous system of roots, some deep, some near the topsoil yet ever growing far down and back into the past. For Eliot, the main roots go to Dante, the legends of the Holy Grail, Spenser, Shakespeare, Donne, Dryden, Coleridge, Arnold, and James root by root through the succession of centuries from the thirteenth to the twentieth; for Hindemith, the roots are in Gregorian Chant, Orlandus Lassus, Josquin des Prés, J. S. Bach, Mozart, Beethoven, Mendelssohn, Brahms and Max Reger. If Eliot and Hindemith make use of the bone structure and the nervous system of the tradition of European literature or music, Stravinsky and Picasso and the Surrealists took the voluptuous flesh and senses from that tradition of music and painting. One can distinguish this tendency largely in their attitude towards form, as a contrived surface.

The Surrealist painters could take over a Bosch landscape and his gnomic colony without having any more than a mild surface likeness to Bosch; the mystic cult of flesh worshippers which barbed Bosch into his half real, half ritualistic *Millennium* triptych was not the motivation nor the purpose of the Surrealists who copied him. Again the better approach in Surrealism was that of the painter Yves Tanguy, whose imagery was personal but whose methods stemmed from his own French tradition of classical painting—no copy here of Bosch or Breughel or Grünewald. The eclecticism of the poorer Surrealists was merely to use Bosch molds instead of Corot molds; and even though it is evidence of better taste to prefer Bosch to Corot, the Surrealists were still pouring plaster into molds—and only the molds were different. This is the exact opposite of the Sung standard.

In music, it is especially in his neo-classicism that Stravinsky does parallel the Surrealistic. Stravinsky's writing is full of little ideas and mannerisms taken from Pergolesi, reshaped in the prefabricated molds of Mozart, as in *The Rake's Progress,* and dressed with smartly dissonant harmony and sensitive orchestration. In his non-classical work, Stravinsky creates synthetic primitive music as in *The Rite of Spring,* synthetic Mediaeval music as in his Mass which is based on Mauchault's Mass, synthetic Baroque as in the Septet, and synthetic Romanticism as in *Appolon Musagete.* In all of these facets of

Stravinsky's work, the primary accomplishment and unifying element is his concern with surface.

Bartok used primitive rhythms as the foundation of his new and exciting idiom and often of his form, the primitive influences having been assimilated and re-expressed in a music that is integrally primitive in rhythm, autogenetic in line, and thus modern in form and idiom. Picasso on the other hand was equally adroit and expert in painting as though he were an African Primitive, or ancient Altamira muralist in a cave in Paris, or a Degas with elongations and a blue palette; or a Catalonian painter; or a Hellenic linear draftsman; or a Cubist or a Surrealist. To list these is not to denigrate Picasso; it is merely to show one use of the past, and I think an inferior eclecticism. But in his great *Guernica,* all of his various styles and technics were fused into an essentially integrated style and form. The same is true to lesser degrees in his other better works; yet he can turn back to mimicry at once when he is confronted with pottery and unashamedly will decorate a jug as though it were a painter's canvas even if the shape were that of a water bag. However, in more recent years Picasso, in the presence of the ancient tradition of pottery at Vallauris in France, has come to understand form in pottery, to respect it, and to submit his personality to the artifact, all of which is to the credit of this vital and enigmatic master.

We are back again to pottery and the utensils and the furniture, and the house, and the implements of living, as it were, man's everyday art. It is one of the most significant merits of the age to show that the concern for a better poetry or a better music is meaningless unless those who make and design the "everyday art" have similar aims and similar standards. Thus Morris and Ruskin and Alvar Aalto, the Finnish furniture designer, and James Prestini, who turns wooden bowls on his lathe, are brothers in kind in this revival of the Mediaeval and Sung standards—treatment of materials and respect for organic forms both in architecture and poetry, knives and forks, monuments and murals, pots and pans, or tragedy. It was once so in Sung China. And it must always be that this single standard cannot be laid on by hands from above, nor achieved by a legislation nor by any other prescriptive order either from the heads of church or state. It comes from artists working with a singleness of purpose on the lowest level and a single aesthetic for judgment on the highest.

In the best of the art of the past, the singleness of purpose and the single standard of aesthetics for utensils or for poetry was the product not of an academy's rules nor any other such prescription: it flowered from a central philosophy where the oneness was to be chosen from, freely by the fortunate artist as he might have chosen his next breath. The important condition for the artist was that a unity existed between his religion, his government, his philosophy and his aesthetics.

Although in the twentieth century there is not the unity of these four as it would seem there was in the Greece of Plato, or in the Christian Middle Ages of Aquinas, there is today a unity of a special kind: it is in the very philosophic investigations themselves trying to establish what is reality? how does the ideal differ from the real? or the real from the actual? The philosophic systems of Whitehead and Maritain who oppose those of the positivists and their herald, Wittgenstein, seem to have a more direct influence on the major artists today, who also seek to find the answers to such questions as what is real? what is art? what is form? what is illusion in a line, a word, a color, or a shape? In short, what is the bird Brancusi liberated from the cold stone?

The revolutionary change in all design related to architecture and town planning—art in industry, in objects for everyday use, and in advertising lay-out and graphic design—is everywhere apparent. School children recognize and usually like the International style in jet planes as well as in the United Nations Secretariat Building. Much of this is the result of the influence of Mondrian, the painter, and Naum Gabo, the constructivist sculptor. Only a comparison of one of Mondrian's late compositions in primary colors with the flat painterly façade of a Le Corbusier building in Paris—or of *The Column, 1923* by Gabo or his *Spheric Theme, 1937* with the industrial architecture of the nuclear fission plants—is needed to see their influence. But in a reciprocity, unobtainable by agreements yet special to the realm of art, Mondrian and Gabo were also influenced and refined by the best architects and designers—it is as though their own ideas were rayed out to architecture and refined in the process of being reflected back into their special genius. The same interplay exists between geometric abstract painting and sculpture and the well-designed fork we eat with.

This concern for dignity and economy of form, and for cleanliness of line, motivated the "geometric abstract art" of Mondrian and Gabo, Le Corbusier and the designers who work in the International style. As a corollary, there was another type of artist who mixed a deep concern for his materials with a respect for the organic growth of form in art; and Henry Moore, the English sculptor, as much as Frank Lloyd Wright, or Cézanne, or Braque is the master who has evolved another theory of abstract art—it is an "organic abstract art." In one of the finest uses of the Sung standard, Moore abstracts the form from his materials in a manner that is the direct opposite from the contrived surfaces of Stravinsky. The particular shape of Moore's *Reclining Figure, 1946* was determined by allowing the form to evolve out of the large elm log on the pattern of the grain lines of the wood; with modifications and adjustments to chalk on paper, even Moore's drawings have a special grain in their evolution of form.

Of all arts, literature was the most introspective in the half century for indeed there was not only the search for the proper form in poetry or fiction, for the central language, or for the words and rhythms of common speech; but there was a constant and evergrowing written record—a body of critical essays, theories, diaries and confessions—laid before us.

In all of the other arts, there has been a real preoccupation with a theory of art, but it has not rubbed off onto the practice of that art: theorists of architecture or of painting or of music are far outnumbered by the architects, the painters and the composers *per se*. In the literature written in English this century beginning with Henry James and—with the exception of Yeats and Hardy—continuing through Eliot and Joyce, who wove his theory into his fiction, it has been the custom among the first rank of authors in America and in England to compound their creative roles with critical roles.

Of more than unusual interest, and uniqueness otherwise, is the fact that in one artist the three characteristic concerns of all artists in the twentieth century were made carnate. Henry James was perpetually concerned with what he called "the central authority"; that is to say, through whom is the fiction to flow out of the story (the illusion) and into the conscious experience of the reader (the reality)? a debate, as it were, with the whole tradition of the novel. This debate with slight variations of terms and conditions appropriate and special each to his art, Hindemith, Cézanne, Eliot and Gabo each has held on other platforms. In the age of James, no other artist had a more pervading nor more conscientious sense of the role and the responsibility of the artist. None has ever probed further the remote caves and reaches of language as the materials of his art. And all this at a most unlikely time in the history of the arts: in the very teeth of Zola and the naturalistic novel; of Pater or Wilde and art for art's sake; of Howells and the Back

Bay Brahmins; of Hardy and the determinists; and the prophets and priests of the New Science.

The influence of James must surely be felt, even if only by indirection, by whatever literate artist addresses himself to his art. James did not allow his criticism to interfere with his writing of fiction. Nor has Eliot, who under the influence of James, it seems to me, wrote that very special essay "Tradition and The Individual Talent." Eliot has been concerned with language and form really more than with questions of belief; he has always sought to write the most economical line approximating the language of the best in everyday speech. And with *The Wasteland, Ash Wednesday* and *The Four Quartets,* Mr. Eliot has shown concern with the music of each line in these long poems and the same concern for the music of the whole poem: each line seems to generate from the line before and evolve into the next; all lines then relate to each other and to the whole which approximates the form of music itself. Eliot thus broke the back of the English stanza. In his experiment both with the language of speech and with the autogenetic form, Mr. Eliot is facing two of the stalwart antagonists in the tradition of all literature: to keep a conscious control over the language and to force it into a formal contrivance as variegated as the *Four Quartets.* He does this in some of the most singing lines in poetry in English—all this in the metaphysical wrestle with the question of what is reality.

But the real "intolerable wrestle with words and meanings" was not Eliot's but James Joyce's. He took the whole of tradition as his province—the historic and the primordial, the conscious and the unconscious. And all in an attempt to do this: not only to make form equal idea in literature; not only to make materials equal form; but to make materials *be* idea. He had hoped, in the major but lovely failure of the twentieth century—*Finnegans Wake*—to let structure conform to the imaginative patterns, the rational patterns, and the biological patterns which inhere in the mind—consciousness itself, association, recall, memory, reverie; in short he tried to extract out of the very word *conform* the root word *form,* so that neither the extraction nor the word would be noticed, so that the reality we read is coidentical with the reality of Joyce's being as he was actually writing *Finnegans Wake* and by substitution with the reality of Mankind.

THE ARTS IN FRANCE

Henri Peyre

THE FRENCH NOVEL AT MID-CENTURY

There have been few periods when the novel in France was richer than it is today, and the age of Proust, Mauriac, Martin du Gard, after World War I, was perhaps one of them, but there have been many eras when the estate of fiction was much lower. There is much that is significant and even more that is promising in the crop which has matured since 1940. The difficulty is to avoid strings of names and titles and at the same time not to remain too vague in one's generalizations.

World War II and its climate of tragedy and of anguish threw a number of writers, alive or dead, among the uninfluentials. Their works are museum pieces for the young. Duhamel, Romains, Morand, Maurois are among those. Gide is admired for much more than his fiction. Proust towers above the French novel of the century. Next to him, Mauriac, another Nobel prize winner, is respected; but he, like Montherlant, has turned to the drama or that favorite French art-form, the moralist's essay. Among the writers who have had a public since 1930, four are intensely alive today. Malraux, whose novels were prophetic and helped mold, if not events, at least the significance they have assumed for us; Bernanos, to whom the world was a spiritual struggle between saints and sinners, God's grace and Satan's wiles; Giono, who forsook his former manner of a pagan poet and of a preacher of natural life and has become a less ambitious story-teller; Julien Green, whose *Moira* is one of the good novels of violence of the last few years. He, too, seems at present to have been lured to the stage.

A few other novelists, whose audience had gathered very slowly before World War II and who are all over fifty years old, have enjoyed a recrudescence of activity and of fame: Bosco, the author of somewhat artificial, but poetically written, stories of mystery set among Southern French peasants, and Jouhandeau, who has far more stark power and has portrayed, in the ruthless manner of an incisive Catholic, the shabby comedy of little towns and the bitter sorrows of married life. Marcel Aymé and Queneau are the masters of laughter in modern French letters: the first often spoils his gift for story-telling and his fertile inventiveness through a somewhat cheap facility which he seems unable to resist; the second is a humorous and brilliant renovator of the French language.

The younger generation, including the writers now in their twenties, thirties or forties, can only be judged on its promise and a limited achievement, for the war years and the economic difficulties which they left in their wake delayed the maturing of the new talents. A few events impressed these novelists unforgettably and explain their moods, their tone and their hopes: the abject defeat of France in 1940 and her sense of bitter isolation, individual and national; the guilt complex gnawing at the French today, as a consequence of the collaboration with the conqueror which a number of writers accepted; the spiritual anguish and the moral dilemma which preceded the decision of those who joined the Resistance and faced the prospect of torture and slow death. Lastly, the French have lived in a state of inflation, hence of insecurity and lack of faith in their future, ever since 1918, and these conditions are reflected in the mirror of their fiction, for the reader who can interpret them aright.

There are twenty or thirty novelists under fifty who count, and no one can say as yet which of them will rise markedly in stature. Three are well known in this country: Simone de Beauvoir, Sartre, and Camus. The first two are very important novelists, in spite of some limitations which critics have ruthlessly exaggerated.

Next to these, a group of novelists haunted by metaphysical unrest, eager to portray and to cure human misery, could be, conveniently but rather artificially, formed. Genet, the inmate of prisons and the singer of evil and of homosexuality, is the most gifted; Blanchot is the most profound, a sort of Mallarméan creator of fiction; Beckett has been acclaimed as a combination of Joyce and Kafka, and not unworthily of either. Abellio and Rebatet, former collaborators with Germany, have written inordinately long, confused volumes which, however, impose upon the reader their own universe. Gadenne, Marcel Schneider and Henri Thomas are, in our opinion, among the lesser-known ones, the most earnest, most imaginative and most promising of these novelists of inquietude, solitude, and anguish.

A second group should be made up of the story-tellers, who write vividly, sketch characters and contrive a plot with skill and joy, eschew ideas and repress emotions under an incisive and ironical manner which is the tone of the new post-war generation. They have hailed Stendhal and, even more, Laclos, as their models. The most gifted of these novelists are: Nimier and Gary, both are picaresque; Bazin (*Viper in the Fist*), Dutourd (*A Dog's Head*), Vailland (*Drôle de jeu*), and Cabanis (*L'Age ingrat*), more analytical and incisive; Brincourt (*The Paradise below the Stairs* and especially *La Farandole*), more lucidly intimate and tender.

Two other groups at least should be mentioned. Contemporary France, for the first time, has a large number of very gifted women-novelists, ranging from Marguerite Yourcenar (*Mémoires d'Hadrien*), Marguerite Duras (*The Sea Wall*) to Dominique Rolin, Violette Leduc, and the youngest of them all, Françoise Mallet, whose *The Illusionist,* written at twenty, was an amazing first novel, only rivalled by the début, at nineteen, of the author of *The Awakening,* J. B. Rossi. North African writers have suddenly brought an original note to French literature, a note of impetuous vigor, a less refined and less introspective but more buoyant and even more moral talent: Camus is the best-known of them, followed closely by Roblès (*Cela s'appelle l'aurore* is one of the very good recent novels), Mammeri, Mouloudji, Merle, Jules Roy, and a promising newcomer from Tunisia, Memmi (*La Statue de sel*).

To all these novelists, the technique of fiction, once dear to successors of Flaubert, Henry James and Joyce, seems to offer little of interest. They have ably assimilated the lessons of Joyce, Kafka, Dos Passos, and Faulkner. Content is their concern: they are obsessed by man's solitude, the inadequacy of all communication and of language, life's absurdity. Yet they are not nihilists, not even pessimists. Three phrases might sum up their common and intense preoccupation: to denounce bad faith and build only upon sincerity and authenticity; to explode the delusions and conventions of romantic and bourgeois love and accept eroticism or sex as a basis for a new ethics and a truer companionship between the sexes; to reach out to other men, revaluate fraternity and our responsibility to help save the world, through literature. They echo Camus' motto: "We refuse to despair of men."

Wallace Fowlie

MID-CENTURY FRENCH POETRY

At the turn of the mid-century, French poetry is still fully engaged in one of the richest periods of its long history. Its roots are essentially in symbolism and in the achievements of poetry between *Les Fleurs du Mal* of Baudelaire (1857) and the death of Mallarmé (1898). Especially in France the creative spirit has always been fully conscious of its heritage, of its belonging to the past, of its role destined to continue and perfect a tradition.

During the past fifty years, the youngest and the oldest poets have been proud of the fact that the art of poetry has enjoyed an extraordinary prestige. The wealth of modern French poetry and its high quality have jealously preserved this prestige. More than the novel and more than drama, poetry has continued to renew itself. Only perhaps the realm of literary criticism has been productive to a similar degree, and the most vital books of criticism have considered the problems of poetry and poets.

The half-century has been dominated by four major writers, all born around 1870, and who have reached now the status of classical writers. Two of these are prose writers: Proust and Gide; and two are poets: Valéry and Claudel. Their common background was symbolism. They were initiated into literature by the stimulation, the achievements and the manifestoes of symbolism. Each reacted to symbolism in his own way and according to his own purposes. They are the most illustrious members of the oldest generation still writing. The combined influences of Mallarmé and Rimbaud have proved more permanent and more vital than any others in the twentieth century.

The word "purity," a concept with which modern poetry is permeated, is associated primarily with Mallarmé, with the doctrine he expounded on Tuesday evenings for so many years (1880-1898) in his apartment on the rue de Rome. There his most brilliant disciple, Paul Valéry (1871-1945) listened in his early twenties to Mallarmé's conversations on poetry. The leading symbols of Mallarmé's purity: his virgin princess Hérodiade; his faun, more interested in his own ecstasy than in the nymphs; his swan caught in the ice of the lake—all reappear, changed but fully recognizable, in the leading symbols of Valéry's poetry: his Narcissus, the contemplation of self pushed to its mortal extreme; his Jeune Parque and his marine cemetery.

La Jeune Parque, which may well be Valéry's greatest poem, composed during the war years (1914-1917), reflects in no way the event of the war. This poem, with the major poems of Mallarmé, with *Les Illuminations* of Rimbaud and the early prose pieces of Gide, treat so pervasively the theme of solitude and detachment that they create a new mythology of poetic purity and human absence. It is poetry anxious to live alone for itself and by itself. It is poetry of exile, written outside of the social sphere. It bears no relationship to a society or to a world which might be comparable to the bond between the tragedies of Racine and the monarchy of Louis XIV.

After writing his poetry of exile, Rimbaud lived in exile in the deserts and cities and mountainous regions of Abyssinia. The same need for voyage and solitude was felt by Paul Claudel, who has always claimed Rimbaud as his master in poetry, as the writer who revealed to him the presence of the supernatural in the world. Rimbaud's greatest ambition was to move beyond literature and poetry, and this has been realized to some degree by Claudel, whose vocation as poet has always been subordinated to his role as apologist of Catholicism. The entire universe is the site of the Christian drama for Claudel. The form of his *verset* is reminiscent of the rhythms in *Les Illuminations*. He continues Rimbaud's Dionysian turbulence, whereas Valéry, in his more chastened, more classical style, represents, with Mallarmé, the Apollonian tradition.

The second generation of poets were those men born at the end of the century. On the whole, they participated in the experience of World War I much more directly than the generation of Valéry and Claudel. This group of writers, particularly in the years after the war, demonstrated a changed attitude toward the role and the activity of the writer. The poet was for them a far less exalted being than he had been for Mallarmé and Rimbaud. The excessive intellectualism and aestheticism of the late symbolist period were drastically modified and diminished.

The experience of the war and the rise of the cinema were only two of the many new forces which were shaping the younger poets at that time. Surrealism was the most significant literary movement in France between symbolism and existentialism. Its leading spirit and theorist was André Breton who even since World War II has made attempts to revive surrealism as an organized movement. But most of the poets who at one time or another adhered to the tenets of surrealism are today writing poetry that is no longer strictly surrealist.

Breton and Benjamin Péret have remained closest to the beliefs and practices of orthodox surrealism. Péret took part in the Civil War in Spain, and has been living in Mexico since 1952. He was perhaps the best satirist of the group, the closest spiritual descendant of Alfred Jarry, whose *Ubu-Roi,* of 1896, was a major text for the surrealists. Some of the purest of the surrealist poets have died: Crevel, whose suicide was interpreted as an act of heroism; Desnos, a victim of a German concentration camp; Artaud, who spent the last nine years of his life in an insane asylum; Paul Eluard who appears today a greater Resistance poet than Aragon.

The miracle of Eluard's work is the extremes it contains and the ease with which he moves from one extreme to the other, from the poet's solitude, from his deep and secret intimacy, to his sense of communion with everyone, to his civic hope. His solitude is his generosity. His sense of the collective comes from what is most individual in him. He is the poet of love, in one of its highest forms, love which will not allow a man to remain within himself.

Several important poets who wrote during the decade of surrealism and have continued to write since that time, had no formal connection with any literary school. Jouve in recent years has grown into a poet of great influence. His universe of catastrophe is described in poetry of a lofty Christian inspiration. Since 1940, St-John Perse has lived in the United States where he wrote *Exile,* one of the profoundest statements on the war. Jean Cocteau has written poetry intermittently throughout his career. He remains one of the most gifted poets of his generation, even if the signal success in his other genres: theatre, cinema, criticism, has somewhat detracted from his position of poet.

Henri Michaux has enlarged the domain of poetry. The character he has created, Plume, is the type of innocent who never escapes the violence and the cruelty of the world. He is innocent but he is tormented by a sense of guilt. A comparison of Plume with the characters of Kafka has often been pointed out, but there is a greater struggle in the Kafka characters than in Plume who accepts whatever happens to him as part of his fate.

Prévert is probably the most widely read of the French poets today. But more important than his poetry is his writing for the cinema. *Les Visiteurs du Soir* and *Les Enfants du Paradis* are two of his outstanding successes. René Char, born in 1906, is one of the best poets of the south. He first allied himself with surrealism and has always retained in his subsequent poetry the boldness and profusion of imagery one associates with surrealism. He was maquis captain in Provence at the end of the war and has written movingly in his poetry of his war experience.

The third and youngest generation of poets writing in France at the turn of the mid-century is more dramatically allied with action, with the war and the Resistance, than the poets of the other two generations. Sartre defined the new literature as being "engaged," and this term applies to the poetry of this generation so directly concerned with actual circumstances and events. The greatness of Jouve (who chronologically belongs to the previous generation) brilliantly illustrates this use of the immediate event in poetry. Pierre Emmanuel has written generously of his admiration for Jouve and of the influence which Jouve's poetry has had on his own. One of Emmanuel's noteworthy achievements is the vigor he has given to poetry of a well-defined subject matter. His mingling, for example, of the Orpheus theme with the redemptive power of Christ is in one of his early works, where the mystery of man is not separated from the mystery of the exterior world.

The ambition of this youngest generation has been, in general, to recall the poet to reality, after the long experimentation of poetry with language, with the symbol, with the hieratic role of the poet. The new writer has felt a greater desire for communication, for immediate communication with the reader. On the whole, he is less subjective than the earlier poets. He appropriates the common basis of world events and world problems for his verse.

Existentialism, as a literary movement, has not developed any poets, with the possible exception of Francis Ponge, on whose work Sartre himself has written a long essay. Ponge's first important publication was in 1942, *Le Parti Pris des Choses,* a work of great rigor and objectivity, and one completely lacking in any subjective lyricism. Although Raymond Queneau, born in 1903, has written principally and prolifically in the domain of the novel, he is also a poet. His central preoccupation with language, with what he considers a needed revolution in language, places him centrally among the poets. His influence is wide, exceeded only by the more massive influence of a writer like Sartre. By advocating the reintegration of the vitality of spoken language, each book of his is a "stylistic exercise." In the freedom of composition he practices, he is often reminiscent of surrealism with which he was in fact at first associated.

These, then, are some of the most representative of the three generations of French poets writing in the early fifties. During the tragic years of the war and the German occupation of France, the poets reached a larger audience than usual. At the grave moments of history, humanity is wont to turn to its poets in order to reconsider man's fate, to understand more profoundly the relationship of man with the universe, and to enjoy the poetic word as the expression of the ideas by which men live. There are signs in it of impatience and haste, but its poetry has in common with the poetry of the two preceding generations the visible influence and even domination of the same gods of modern French poetry: Rimbaud and Apollinaire, especially, and then the less visible but always present influence and examples of Baudelaire and Mallarmé.

Herbert Read

THE CHALLENGE OF BOIMONDAU

From time to time during the last several years there has been news of a new "communitarian" movement in France founded by Marcel Barbu; but it has usually been rumours of difficulties and dissensions, and we have lacked the evidence for any proper discussion of the subject. Now the community itself has published a handsome illustrated volume of 150 pages which gives the story of the foundation of Boimondau, its history year by year, and all the relevant facts about its constitution, organization, membership and production. It seems to me to be a document of the greatest significance.

Boimondau is a word made up from the first syllables of the words Boitiers Montres du Dauphine, the Watchcase makers of Dauphine, which is the industry carried on by the community in the town of Valence. The community was founded in 1940 by a small manufacturer, Marcel Barbu, who had established a factory in Besançon and tried without success to run it on co-operative lines. Having failed as a benevolent capitalist, he closed down his factory and went to Valence, resolved to build from the ground upwards. He went out into the streets to recruit *fellow-workers*, men who were to share his responsibilities from the beginning. They soon had a small workshop going, and in spite of the war it prospered. But Barbu, who is described as a "messianic" figure, soon got into trouble with the Germans, and at the beginning of 1943 the whole factory had to go underground. Barbu fled to Paris, where he was soon arrested; but the headquarters of the community was transferred to a farm in the district known as the Vercors, where a "collective" was established. There the community remained, suffering considerable privations, until the Liberation. From April 1943 it was led by Marcel Mermoz, a comrade who had spent more than three years in prison and concentration camp.

Mermoz obviously acquired a strong personal ascendancy over the group, and when the factory was reassembled in Valence after the war, Mermoz was made "chef." Barbu in due course returned from the concentration camp, to find himself replaced. As a matter of fact, it was not entirely a question of personalities: a principle had always been involved, but never decisively settled until Mermoz took matters in hand. The messianic Barbu wanted a "movement," with headquarters in Paris, nationwide propaganda, even political candidates. Mermoz and the majority preferred the local "cell," believing that trust and the necessary self-sacrifice could only be established face to face. If they were successful, other workers could benefit by their experience. They took as a motto a sentence from St. Exupéry: "Force-les de bâtir une tour, et tu changeras en frères: mais si tu veux qu'ils se haissent, jette-leur du grain." (Make them build a tower, and you will change them into brothers; throw corn to them, if you wish them to hate one another.) Barbu retired from the community, but unfortunately they could not agree on terms of compensation. Barbu sued the community for 10 million francs, but the case seems to have been settled out of court for a sum of about 8 million. It is only fair to add that with his money Barbu founded another communitarian experiment, "la dité Donguy-Hermann."

A worse crisis came in 1947. The franc was devalued and the Boimondau factory was suddenly faced with a complete breakdown of their sales organization. They had no financial reserves, and the banks naturally refused to make them a loan. They still had their farm and some of them were able to work on a subsistence basis there; but the majority were out-of-work, with no unemployment pay, for more than four months. There was only one deserter. At the end of the year of 1951 the community had one of the most up-to-date factories in the world, with an annual production of half-a-million watchcases. They now subscribe to "la Securité Sociale" and "les Allocations Familiales," and with this form of assurance believe that they can survive any future economic crises.

Meanwhile the communitarian idea has been spreading in France and Switzerland and there are now about eighty communities of various sizes adhering to a Fédération des Communautés de Travail, with headquarters in Paris. A periodical, *Communauté*, serves as an organ of information, but propaganda, in the political sense, is foreign to the movement. They believe in deeds, not words; in example, not conversion.

The foundation deed of the Boimondau community is a long document of thirty-six articles: it was drawn up and accepted at the beginning of 1944. Most of the articles would be found in the rules of any co-operative undertaking. I shall only draw attention to certain original features in the Boimondau organization.

In the first place, there is no community living. The workers live a normal family life wherever they can find accommodation in the town of Valence. But all the families in a district are organized into a district group, and there is a joint council of district groups. There are two other groupings—by professional grades, and by social activities. All three groups elect representatives to the General Council; the General Council elects a management committee and a tribunal, and appoints a "chef de communauté" and an assistant or adjutant.

The community does not regard its members as merely "workers": every aspect of their lives is a community concern—their health, education, amusement, and above all their morale.

There is a General Assembly of the whole community, whose decisions must be unanimous, but its power is purely legislative: it has no executive function. Executive power rests with the chief, elected for a period of three years by the Assembly.

All the members of the community, husbands, wives and children, are entitled to a share of the proceeds of the community's activities: it is recognized that each member of the community has a *social* function as well as a *professional* function, and each function is duly rewarded. It is specifically laid down in the articles of association that each "compagnon" (the name given to a member on admission) shall take an active part in the social and intellectual life of the community. Companions should make an effort to adapt their private lives to the moral sense of the community at large. Religious beliefs are encouraged, including a belief in disbelief. All production is held in common, and can only be sold either for reinvestment in production or on dissolution of the community. There are no private shares in the capital of the community.

Details of the earnings of the individual members of the community have not been published, but there is no question of equal pay, except in the case of identical professional and social services. Since intellectual attainments and a wide variety of social functions are allotted points for pay, there must be quite a large divergence in receipts, but this does not seem to have given rise to any trouble. Trouble, indeed, is anticipated and settled by the machinery of the General Council; and there is always the Tribunal to adjust quarrels.

Two characteristics of the Boimondau community would seem to be in conflict with the traditional principles of co-operative communities: the hierarchical organization (particularly the vesting of final authority in an individual) and unequal "pay." Pay is not, of course, the right word for what is in effect a division of profits, but that is not the point. These communitarians believe that "equal pay" would be very unequal justice. A community is responsible for the well-being of all its members, and the fact that the community does not live under one roof, sharing food and other necessities and amenities, by no means relieves the community from full responsibility. Allowances must be made for children, and the mother who looks after her children at home is serving the community as much as the woman who works in the factory. But Boimondau goes much further than such obvious adjustments for service: it rewards "social values." If a companion learns a foreign language, the community as a whole is so much the richer, and that "value" must be rewarded; and if he can play football for the community, that too is a value and should be rewarded. Musical gifts, ability to teach economics or philosophy, to work a cinema projector or organize a dance—all these are community services with their appropriate awards; the more freely such services are recognized and rewarded, the stronger and happier the community will be. Anyone can improve his or her position by becoming a more useful member of the community; and it is the community itself that decides the relative value of the various social services.

As for the appointment of a "boss," and of the various "chefs" (chefs de sections, chefs de groupes, chefs d'équipes, chefs de foyers)—that seems to the logical French mind to be required not only by day-to-day workshop efficiency, but also by the full enjoyment of life. If one of these units does not like its chef, it is a simple matter to get rid of him; the chef of the community itself can always be replaced at the end of his three years' period of service (a minimum period to ensure continuity of policy).

Critics (particularly from the left) will be eager to point out that a community like Boimondau, competing with its products in a capitalist market, dependent on banks and insurance companies for its tokens of exchange and economic security, is far from being the realization of a new social order. But that is not the point. Unless we remain satisfied with Utopian aspirations (or believe that we already live in the best of all possible worlds) we must ask: what are the immediate and practical steps towards a better society? In other words, is Boimondau, and the other communities in France and Switzerland which it represents, a step in a new direction, away from totalitarianism no less than from capitalism? Perhaps only time can show, but there is an unusual air of confidence about the Boimondau community. Their ideal is "faire des hommes"—to make human beings—and they know that their worst danger is the success that would threaten them with "l'embourgeoisement."

Joseph Frank

AN EXISTENTIALIST IN THE UNDERWORLD

Jean-Paul Sartre's monstrous treatise—running close to six hundred pages, and titled *Saint Genet, comédien et martyr*—is certainly one of the strangest books ever to be written by a reputable philosopher. Kant, it is true, once wrote a short book on Swedenborg—but only, as he jokingly remarked, because someone had persuaded him to purchase a complete edition of Swedenborg's works, and he decided not to let the investment of time and money go to waste. Moreover, Kant's purpose was to show that Swedenborg's delineation of the geography of the supernatural was—as the title of his book proclaimed—the dreams of a spirit-seer. Jean-Paul Sartre's book is about a far more outlandish figure than Swedenborg: Jean Genet, ex-jailbird and self-confessed thief, pederast, prostitute and stoolpigeon. Genet's sumptuously obscene celebrations of Evil, in a prose whose preciosity recalls Proust and Giraudoux, have made him, since the end of the Second World War, the rage of Parisian literary circles. And Sartre's intensely, sometimes comically serious discussion of Genet is a dazzling display of dialectic, ending with what Sartre calls "a request that Jean Genet be well treated."

How can we explain Sartre's choice of so strange a subject? It would be a simple matter to allude to his taste for paradox, which, in truth, runs riot in the present book. One might also refer to Sartre's personal friendship for Genet, and his admiration for a literary talent which developed under impossibly adverse conditions. Nor should it be forgotten that, at least since the advent of Surrealism, it has become a French literary fashion to revere a figure like the Marquis de Sade and to recommend the total liberation of the instincts as the recovery of man's true liberty. None of these explanations, however, nor all of them together, seem to me entirely adequate. The truth is that Sartre has been preoccupied in recent years with the problems of an Existentialist ethics; and in the figure of Genet, he found a pretext for developing certain ideas on Good and Evil that have not hitherto found expression in his theoretical writings.

Despite the book's huge bulk, and Sartre's jaw-breaking vocabulary, his basic idea about Genet is very simple. Genet's work is a gigantic glorification of vice and crime. a willful inversion of all normal ethical standards. Sartre believes that Genet, as a child, was caught in an innocent boyhood theft; this was a traumatic experience that determined his life. Choosing to accept the role assigned him by society, Genet assumed this burden of guilt and turned it into a positive mission. "I was a thief"—Sartre imagines Genet saying to himself—"*I will be The Thief*; it's my profession of faith, it will be my martyrdom."

Once this choice was made, Sartre proceeds to unravel its implications by "existential psychoanalysis." This specially patented Sartrian method assumes that *every* aspect of a life, down to the minutest detail, is symbolically linked with the choice an existant makes among his own possibilities; even "the world" of the existant surges into consciousness as a structure of meanings determined by this choice of himself. And this leads Sartre into a veritable delirium of symbol hunting, an orgy of psychic code-deciphering that makes Freud look like a neophyte and Jung like an amateur. It is difficult, in a brief quotation, to give any adequate idea of Sartre's grotesquely far-fetched interpretations. But some notion may perhaps be derived from his remark that Genet is a passive pederast because "surprised while stealing *from behind,* it is his back which blossoms when he steals, it is with his back that he awaits the discovery and catastrophe." Similarly, if Genet uses argot, Sartre breathlessly interpolates: "To speak argot is to choose Evil, that is, to know being and truth but to refuse them for the sake of non-truth . . . that is, to choose the relative, parasitism, failure."

The consequence of these analyses, which unhappily take up most of the book, is to dissolve all the motives for Genet's actions into a symbolic repetition, in one form or another, of his original crisis. Sartre always concentrates on the *meaning* of Genet's acts in this symbolic framework, and, as a rule, carefully avoids considering them from any other perspective. *"In reality"* Sartre writes, in an incautious moment, "Genet steals because he is a thief and because he has no other means of existence; *in the imaginary,* he steals to make himself a thief." By interpreting Genet's crimes as if they were only performed for purposes of "the imaginary," Sartre skillfully glosses over their more sordid results. And whatever their effects, their ultimate cause is not located in Genet himself (a subject who, according to Sartre's ontology, exercises his liberty with every action and at every moment); the trauma of his childhood experience is always to blame.

"If, in this whole affair, we wish to find the true guilty parties," Sartre argues, "let us turn toward the decent people and ask by what strange cruelty they made a child a scapegoat." By implication, therefore, Genet is completely absolved of any responsibility for his misdeeds; he is the victim of an inescapable determinism. This is indeed a strange conclusion for a philosopher who, in *L'Etre et le Néant,* argued that liberty is synonymous with the *pour-soi* (or human consciousness). A writer in the new *Nouvelle revue française* recently remarked that "Sartre has a philosophy where liberty has never played so large a role, and a politics where it has never played such a small one." The same might be said of Sartre's philosophy and his notion of moral responsibility.

For Sartre's whole conception of Evil, as developed in *Saint Genet,* shifts moral responsibility from the wrongdoer to Society. The original ethical sin, according to Sartre, is the splitting of Good and Evil; this is caused by the "disquietude" of the spirit, which is in a state of "permanent revolution." "But this disquietude terrifies us: we try to suppress it by checking the spirit in its course and expelling its mainspring of negativity." We identify Good with what *is* already; Evil with change; and we project this Evil, which is part of our liberty (another term for spirit), on those outcast groups and individuals who then symbolize and objectify all our temptations. To recover true liberty we must arrive at a "synthesis of Good and Evil"; and on this ground, Sartre passionately pleads with us to "listen to the voice of Genet, our next-of-kin, our brother." But if "Evil is projection," as Sartre argues, then clearly it is *Les Justes* (the decent citizens) who are responsible for its existence; not the criminal but the judge is guilty.

Since Sartre's conception of Evil is totally social, it is no surprise to have him tell us that "the abstract separation of these two concepts [i.e., Good and Evil] simply expresses the alienation of man." Sartre always uses the word "alienation" in a Marxist sense, and when this alienation is removed by the classless society, presumably the miraculous synthesis of Good and Evil will also be accomplished. But what is to become of the "disquietude" of the spirit? Will man cease to be afflicted with the *angoisse* before his own liberty that is at the center of Sartre's Existentialism? Certainly this would seem to be implied. In the ideal order, Sartre himself admits, "the prescriptions of ethics would become social reflexes." And so the happy, unalienated worker can then take his place in the ranks of those whom Sartre, in *La Nausée*, politely calls *les salauds*—the stinkers; those who conceal from themselves the fundamental contingency and absurdity of all moral duties and of existence itself. Sartre is thus caught once again, as he has been increasingly in recent years, between his Marxist sympathies and his Existentialist convictions, between the vision of a just and stable society and his view of the spirit and human liberty as negation and disquietude. On the plane of theory, these two facets of Sartre's thought exist as an unresolved antagonism. On the plane of practice, however, Sartre has provided himself with a neat little escape hatch.

In a revealing footnote, where Sartre emerges for a moment from behind his Hegelian armor, he states bluntly that "this synthesis [of Good and Evil], in the present historical situation, is not realizable. Thus every morality which does not explicitly declare itself *impossible today* contributes to the mystification and the alienation of mankind." And, a few sentences later, he makes these ominous remarks:

Action must give itself ethical norms in this climate of insurmountable impossibility. It is in this perspective, for example, that we must envisage the problem of violence or the relation between means and ends. For a consciousness that would live this agony (*déchirement*) and finds itself, at the same time, forced to will and decide, all the splendid revolts, all the cries of refusal, all the virtuous indignations, would appear like outmoded rhetoric.

These sentences go a long way to explain Sartre's present collaboration with the Stalinists (or is it Malenkovists?). He conscientiously suffers his *déchirement* over their immoral actions, but indefatigably reassures himself that, at the present time, all morality is impossible anyhow. Naturally, he continues to belabor all opponents of the Communists as despicable violators of human dignity. And when someone like Albert Camus dares to protest against Communist atrocities, he dismisses this as "out-moded rhetoric." After all, was it not Sartre who argued that one of the primary ontological structures of the human consciousness was *mauvaise foi*?

Kermit Lansner

RECENT FRENCH PAINTING

The dominance of abstraction, in all its forms, is the most striking feature of recent French painting.

At the moment, the most consistent painters are those who have made a program of abstraction. The younger ones are involved in its philosophy and contentious about its logic. They have no truck with subject matter and regard painting as a spiritual pursuit which consists in the arrangement of forms and colors. This group is the nearest thing to a movement in Paris today, although it has none of the searching originality which distinguished the major movements of modern art.

The work of these painters, if we can imagine some ideal canvas which will sum it all up, is flat and neat. The straight line and ruled curve are everywhere in evidence, bounding, geometrical forms. Occasionally the clean organic shapes which Arp often uses appear. There is little expressiveness of line and no cultivation of the riches of material so dear to the French tradition. The best of this painting is impressively monumental, and several of the painters have begun to work large—in preparation, I suspect, for the decoration of public walls. Although the aesthetic of abstraction implies an unlimited range of possibilities for new ideas, any large exhibition of this painting seems remarkably uniform, as if it were the product of communal enterprise. Magnelli, a Florentine, is the strongest painter who works in this style; Pillet, Dewasne, Vasarely, Poliakoff and Deyrolle are a few of the others who follow this program of abstraction.

Although the work derives from Cubism, it owes much to other abstract styles which are foreign to France. Consequently there has been a healthy renewal of interest in such painters as Kandinsky, Mondrian, Malevitch and Klee. Of the work of the modern French masters, the large canvases which Leger painted in the twenties are most closely related to the paintings of this group.

A great fluidity and delicacy can be found in the art of Hartung and Schneider. They both handle space in Cubist fashion, but their inspiration is more emotional and their execution more spontaneous. They use a variety of generalized calligraphic motifs, some like fragments of penmanship exercises which were once common in grade schools, brushed on with softness and precision. Their color is suave and luminous and they have been able to paint small pictures which combine the suggestion of carefully constructed space with a personal immediacy which is lacking in the more formal abstractionists. This is a subtle art of organized transience.

Holding the center of French painting is a fairly large group of painters who have veered to neither of the poles of abstraction. They remain deeply involved in the French tradition and still retain their attachment to the subject, attenuated as it may be, as well as their passion for fine painting. Most of these men have been known for some time as they worked through the influences of Picasso and Matisse. They stand now as the first names in French painting behind the aging masters, having attained, these past few years, to some firmness of style which promises to persist. There is nothing radical about their work to eyes which are accustomed to modern painting. It has a substance and finish which results from the attempt to combine abstraction with impressionism. In particular, these painters have concentrated upon the creation of light through color. Their designs are carefully fragmented; small areas of color are juxtaposed to create the illusion of intense light. Abstraction is used as one approach among several and these painters have not been put off by the charge that they are illogical in combining traditions.

Bazaine constructs his paintings as if they were mosaics; brilliant bits of color are arranged in larger patterns of vigorous rhythms. Manessier and Singier paint pictures of haunting luminosity in which volume and composition in depth are sacrificed to the delights of color and paint. Esteve and Le Moal must be mentioned, while Pignon, long regarded as one of the most promising painters, remains closer to the subject which he paints with a strong sense of composition.

Well into middle-age, Tal Coat has passed through the usual influences. Now, painting in Cézanne's own country, he has reduced its technique to the barest indications of color and stroke. It is hard to believe that he can long remain in his present style which attempts to abstract the essence of landscape by the mere suggestion of mountains, trees and rivers. His paintings have several overtones. They are reminiscent of some of the watercolors of Cézanne and of fragments of Chinese landscape painting; and were they not tied to the subject, of the lyrical improvisations which Kandinsky painted around 1911. Masson, who has been a minor virtuoso during the past thirty years has also turned to nature; his figures, and landscapes are seen through a diaphanous haze of Renoir colors.

I have only spoken of an art which is calm and ordered, however diverse it may be. There has been little in French painting since 1945 which is comparable in spirit to the extremity, violence and anguish which have characterized much of the literature of contemporary France. Though the influence of Picasso can be seen at every turn, it is primarily his techniques of construction or certain mannerisms which have been followed and rarely the powerful expression of his later styles. There are a few small signs that a painting of extremes is beginning to attract attention in Paris.

During the past few years there have been several shows of work which has little precedent in the French tradition. No catch-all phrase can suggest the different manifestations of this painting; no aesthetic has been developed for it. At the moment it includes the work of Dubuffet, vehement images related to the art of children and the insane, laid on with great thickness of matter and paint, as well as the work of a young painter like Riopelle. At first glance his paintings seem to be similar to those of Jackson Pollock. But they are not made up of a maze of lines of high, glistening color, but of a profusion of strokes and daubs, earthy encrustations which cover the canvas from side to side, rising and falling upon the surface as they form into many smaller patterns. Other painters have used Klee-like motifs; some have used the canvas as a stop for a vehement gesture in paint.

This kind of painting defies both the tradition of craftsmanship and the ordered arrangement of the abstract artists who are primarily interested in the construction of the picture. It is too early to predict what influence this type of expressionism will have upon French art.

Most of the painters I have mentioned are in their forties and fifties. They were born under the sign of Cubism and grew up in the shadow of the masters who created the major style of modern art. Picasso, Braque, Leger, Delaunay and the others were in their early thirties when they painted some of their most impressive pictures. When we compare the age of artistic maturity of these two generations it is evident how long and difficult has been the struggle of the younger men to achieve the confidence of style. Small wonder that there is little which is strikingly new about their work.

Norman Demuth

MUSIC IN FRANCE

It is characteristic of the French composers born late in the last century that they have moved with the times. Consequently, Marcel Dupré and Claude Delvincourt are as up-to-date as could be desired. The former has excelled in organ music of an individual character, while the latter has to his credit, *Lucifer,* a Mystère (to text by René Dumesnil) which, with Honegger's *Jeanne d'Arc au bucher* and Milhaud's *Bolivar,* ranks as one of France's greatest dramatic works. Delvincourt is Director of the Paris Conservatoire and a man of inspiring energy and enthusiasm. Severely wounded in the 1914 War, when he lost an eye and suffered other injuries, he played an heroic part in the Resistance Movement during the last war, when he spirited away to the Maquis all the students leaving the Conservatoire who were earmarked for slave camps in Germany; this he did right under the eyes of the Gestapo. He was a hunted man for some long time. Such heroism on the part of a musician can make other musicians feel proud, and at the same time, humble.

Similar musical enterprise can be found in the lighthearted works of Jacques Ibert whose *Diane de Poitiers* and *Escales* are achieved with the acme of polish and refinement. If one wishes that Ibert would be a little more serious sometimes, that wish is qualified by the thought

of the wit that would be missed. At the other end of the
scale, the somewhat austere approach of Georges Migot
exercises a restraining influence, for Migot concentrates
mainly upon alla capella choral works of some magni-
tude.

Wit is also found in the works of Jean Rivier whose
musical blade is one of the finest steel and polished to a
dazzling brilliance. Rivier is a composer whose music is
not particularly serious, but is impelled from a serious
point of view. His Symphonies, however, are serious
works, direct and harmonically acid. Impelled by counterpoint, his symphonic and chamber music is highly
and skillfully developed. His *Ouverture pour un don
quichotte* reveals a thematic spontaneity which is astonishing in its variety. Rivier is a man of strong views and
detests superficiality on the one hand and too much
emphasis on musical construction on the other.

Opéra-comique has benefited from the works of Marcel Delannoy and Edmond Bondeville. The former has
also composed a magnificent Symphony and two enjoy-
able Concertos. His first opéra-comique, *Le Poirier de
Misère,* was on a sinister and cynical subject, but *Ginevra*
and *Puck* are true to type. Delannoy has widened the
vista of opéra-comique in various ways. He is a master of
lyricism and his works have all the stuff of opera in them.
Bondeville in his two works *L'Ecole des Maris* and
Madame Bovary reveals a mind not so concerned with
any new expressions as with the desire to provide first-
class lyrical entertainment. He is Director of the Opéra,
and, as in the case of Delvincourt, administrative duties
interfere with his leisure for composition.

Last among the group is Henri Martelli who adopts a
classical approach to twentieth-century problems. Impelled by pure polyphony, his music is well-wrought and
sensible. His Wind Trio and Sonata for Two Pianos express elegance in terms of counterpoint. Martelli eschews
sensuousness, but his music is not in any way repelling

and players can find much to interest them, and to enjoy.

Whatever direct influence Debussy, Fauré, and Ravel once exercised on young French thought has long since gone by the board. The French aesthetic is now sturdy and more cosmopolitan, although it maintains its essential qualities. The counteracting influences were Stravinsky and "Les Six," these being counteracted in turn by Albert Roussel, who, emanating from Vincent d'Indy, brought French symphonic thought to its present high state of excellence and removed all flippant tendencies from the generality of French thinking. D'Indy established the classical formal concept and Roussel, the technique. This came about very quickly. Today the Conservatoire students all reveal Roussel's uncompromising approach to harmony and his clarity in counterpoint. French music is no longer necessarily "délicieux" and its symphonic concept can take its place with that from any other country so far regarded as "superior." In many respects France still expresses *le dernier cri*.

Selection is invidious and space limited, but one would single out in the first place Henri Barraud, Henri Tomasi, and Tony Aubin. The first is head of the music department of the French Radio and the second a conductor of some note. Aubin is an isolated figure as he is almost the only one to show direct ancestry from Franck. He conducts the Radio orchestra and teaches at the Conservatoire. His *Symphonic romantique* and Scherzo, *La chasse infernale* show that he is endowed with a well-developed symphonic sense. All three are hampered to a certain extent by their routine tasks but they probably work better as a result.

Next one would point to Pierre Capdiéville for his radio-drama *La Tragédie de Peregrinus*. He was a pupil of Vincent d'Indy and the integrity of his Second Symphony emphasizes his pupilage. Manuel Rosenthal, one of the few pupils of Ravel, bears no traces of his musical ancestry in his works. *François d'Assise* and *Jeanne d'Arc* are written upon an altogether different aesthetic. Henri Sauguet is remembered by his extremely lengthy opera *La Chartreuse de Parme* over which he spent seven years, so it is said. Unfortunately, these seven years were among his formative ones and it is possible to follow Sauguet's development as the opera progresses. He is more worthily represented by the ballet *Les Forains* and the *Symphonie expiatoire*. The facetious composer of the era is still Jean Françaix whose music is superficial and facile; but it is fair to say that he has many admirers. His oratorio *L'Apocalypse de Saint Jean* proved that he is not suited to large forms, but there will always be a place for works like the ballets *Beach, Le Roi nu,* and for orchestration such as he made of Boccherini in *Scuolo di ballo,* even if that place is not one of great importance.

It is not unkind to say that one musician, at any rate, finds Jean Martinon more acceptable as a conductor than as a composer. Martinon is sometimes confused with Jean Martenent, one of the few French composers influenced by Bartok. Martenent works upon a large canvas and thus does not make things any easier for himself. His *Orphée,* in three movements, reveals the surprising fact that there is much in common between the French and Hungarian *goûts*.

André Jolivet and Olivier Messiaen headed the group "La jeune France," the name being taken from Berlioz. Jolivet has written the first Concerto for Ondes Martenot and Orchestra, in which he portrays the gradual emergence of sound from chaos to cosmos, and to the final silence of the spheres. This is as may be; the work is a full-scale concerto and one finely contrived.

To dismiss Messiaen in the few lines available is well-nigh impossible if justice is to be done him. He is one of the few living composers about whom a book could be written with no fear that it would be out-of-date before publication. Not that Messiaen is by any means at the end of his tether, but he has already covered more ground and shown himself to be more original than any other French composer. There is, therefore, already enough material to fill a book.

One has often regretted that music today does not often arouse the old frenzies of anger and enthusiasm. Messiaen proves the exception, for even though his aesthetic and style have become recognized, performance is reminiscent of the scenes which were regular events in the twenties.

Messiaen has created his own musical language and has perpetuated it in a book. It is not systematic, for it is in no sense arbitrary, but it is a specialized technique and as such demands the consideration of all musicians. He is a mystic, devoutly religious, and a lover of nature—over and over again he takes his impulses from birdsongs. At first glance his works appear too rarified, but realization comes as a revelation, and once one has fallen beneath the spell, one never goes back. His harmony is all perfectly logical and reasonable, although the congregations at La Trinité felt otherwise at one time—Messiaen has been organist at that church for many years. The *Turangalila Symphony,* in ten movements (an interval is allowed after the fifth), caused a riot when first performed in France. Two performances by the BBC and a study of the work convinced me that this will prove to be the greatest work since *Le Sacre* and *Wozzeck,* greater, in fact, than the former.

This is an utterly inadequate summary of Messiaen's work. Suffice it to repeat that he is the most original composer now living. His technique is so far from being systematic that it allows full play to all emotions.

The French have always been fond of coteries from the days of the Lullyistes v. Ramoneours to the present time. "Les Six" have long since attained their object.

Milhaud and Honegger are now household names; the former continues to pour out music in a ceaseless stream, much of it extremely fine.

"La Jeune France," already referred to, had the furtherance of new music in the true sense of the term as its main aim. Today there are the "Dodécaphonistes" or followers of Schoenbergian systematic composition. They are presided over by René Leibowitz. Many of the original members have disavowed the aims and objects, but those remaining include Paul Dessau, Pierre Boulez, and Antoine Dukamel. Serge Nigg, the most distinguished of the band apart from its president, separated himself from the others quite recently, as he discovered that Schoenberg was divorced from humanity.

Then there are the "Progressistes" who follow the cultural philosophies of the USSR in which music must have social significance and be comprehensible to one and all at the first hearing.

"La Zodiaque" is a coterie founded to combat all other coteries. It disavows all systems, fashions, and, in fact, all the "-isms" and "-alities" that have ever existed. The members include Maurice Ohana, Stanislas Skrocatchevski, Sergei di Castro, Pierre de la Forest Divonne, and Alain Bermat. Finally, this is the group devoted to "Musique concrete" who concern themselves with sonorities. The principal advocates are Pierre Schaeffer and Pierre Henry. The system is extremely complicated and to this writer utterly useless.

It would not do to ignore two members of what is known as "L'Ecole de Paris," Tibor Harsanyi and Marcel Mihalovici. The former is the more immediately approachable of the two, but this does not imply that his music is easy to assimilate. His Concertstück for Piano and Orchestra is outstanding. Mihalovici has composed many magnificent works which are heard all over the Continent, except in England.

William Becker

FRENCH THEATRE: THE NATIONAL GENIUS

The American interest in French theatre has usually re-
volved—especcially since the war—on a desire to be in
touch with new plays. Immediately after the Second
World War France seemed to be the only country in the
world making a reasonably significant contribution to
dramatic literature. Today, one can no longer satisfy
quite such a selfish desire, for the French theatre has
reassumed a traditional existence in which new plays are
both less prominent and less necessary. The present
visitor will find a brilliant theatrical activity—but one
which must be loved more for its own sake than for what
it might export to Broadway.

Consider just the established major talents of the post-
war period. Anouilh is now apparently dedicated to
writing the same one play over and over in various
forms of fancy dress. Montherlant has not written a new
play in many years, though his older plays are revived
and strike one as more stiffly untheatrical than ever.
Sartre, since his wholehearted commitment to the CP,
no longer belongs to the ranks of responsible intellectuals. Camus has still not fulfilled his early dramatic
promise. Obey's very real theatrical genius is being dis-
sipated in the increasingly unreal and perfunctory
mythicism of his material. And Cocteau seems simply to
have evaporated into his own shimmering emptiness.

One must, of course, realize that judgments so severe as these can only be made from within the French context: any other country would rightfully be prostrate with gratitude to have such a roster of names writing anything at all. But French theatre, like French cuisine, tempts one to assume the gourmet's finickiness with his appetite; and both can be plentifully satisfied—by the fare at the Comédie Française alone.

If one is inclined to be harsh with the established talents, one generally learns from the French themselves to be enthusiastic over the newest ones. Nevertheless, during a recent visit, I found the only two new plays that were attracting serious attention to be pretty poor stuff. Both were first plays by well-known novelists whom the French regard as deeply *sérieux*. And oddly enough, neither author is a native Frenchman, though both write in French. Julien Green is of American origin, and his play, called *South,* suffers (like his novel *Moira*) from a thoroughly unreal perception of the American background against which it is set. In France where few people know or understand the issues of the Civil War, *South* has been a major success: the French like to think that Green perceives life "purely" and for them an American setting is as abstract or indifferent as anywhere. To an American, such indifference, especially to a fact as rich in reality as the Civil War, is not only impossible, but quite undesirable; and Green's "pure vision" seems a preposterous irrelevance. Yet *South* did not seem to me more false than Samuel Beckett's *Waiting for Godot*. Beckett is an Irishman whose exile in France has led some people to compare him to Joyce; a not less invalid analogy would place *Waiting for Godot* alongside Kafka's *The Castle,* for Godot is never identified and never arrives. The play is not just plain bad; but with its tedious and fancy metaphysical dialogue, it is *faux bon*—which is, perhaps, worse.

But if Henry James was right in supposing theatre to

be the most characteristic expression of the French national genius, it is only proper that the subsidized national theatres should represent that genius most compellingly. (I speak now of the *dramatic* theatres, for the Opéra is poor, its ballet intolerable, and the Opéra Comique a public disgrace.) There are now three such theatres: the two *salles* of the Comédie Française and the recently formed Théâtre National Populaire which plays at the Palais de Chaillot. The TNP is not yet in a class with the Comédie: it is too new, too exclusively the projection of a single personality, and too much beset by internal difficulties. It has been the center of much public criticism; and one begins to sense that the very thing which made the TNP possible—the forceful genius of its founder and leader, Jean Vilar—will probably prevent it from surviving in its present form. The company, I gather, has never been good throughout, and recently a sizable group of the leading performers has quit. This internal dissension was apparently political: Vilar is deeply identified with the Communists (he directed *Danton's Death* with Robespierre, played by himself, as the pure hero, and converted Danton into an epicene bourgeois decadent, whose mouthings about revolutionary ideals were meant to be taken as hollow irony). The public criticism, however, seems mainly chauvinistic: Vilar is one of those rare Frenchmen with an understanding of German theatre and literature (Giraudoux was another), and of the nine plays presented during its first few seasons, the three most successful were by Brecht, Kleist, and Büchner, whereas the one Molière was generally considered to be badly staged and performed. One now hears it argued that the TNP is neither national nor popular (it was created partially as an experiment in taking the classics to working-class districts, and plays a good deal of the time in town halls outside Paris). The criticism is probably true, but misses the real point which is that Paris theatre has always been deficient in giving expression to foreign dramatic literatures, and that only such a distinct departure as Vilar has provided could serve a venture of this kind. It would have been idle and also impossible to compete with the Comédie. Thus it is quite useful that conditions—the unwieldy Chaillot platform-stage, the uneven company, the necessity of touring—have forced Vilar to adopt a style as distinct from the Comédie's as his repertoire. It is a style, much like Tyrone Guthrie's, based on a spectacularity of stage grouping and movement: Vilar is fond of large processions, of a stage full of moving actors constantly forming themselves into new patterns, of a hammy pictorial dramatism at the climaxes—the sort of directorial touch which is often less effective for being so evidently a directorial touch.

If the TNP is essentially a director's theatre, the Comédie is the very apotheosis of an actor's theatre. No other institution of the kind in France or England can rival it, not Stratford, nor the Old Vic, nor in fact any of the private companies now at work, with the possible exception of Jean-Louis Barrault's. I recently saw more than twenty plays at the Comédie, and only one small curtain-raiser seemed to me mishandled. One realizes in watching the Comédie troupe how much Barrault's style owes to his training there; for the mimeticism which he has made internationally famous is actually one of the greatest current glories of the Comédie as well. One sees also that there is a kind of gimmickry about Barrault's miming, that it remains extrinsic and unassimilated, whereas at the Comédie, mimetic control is a discipline more than a device, and is meant to contribute richness to a balanced style, not to create special shock effects like the highly self-conscious mannerisms of Barrault. In the end, one is likely to find that the Comédie's more subtle and integrated way, while less startling, is actually more finished, and will wear better. As a traditional theatre, the Comédie is not subject to great variations in its repertoire; but one should note that the current style and the current repertoire do amount to a reciprocal process of discovery, for both rely heavily on the great Latin tradition of comedy and performance: some of the best productions in the present repertoire, for example, are of plays by Feydeau, Musset, Marivaux, and Pirandello. And it is entirely right that the greatest benefit from this process should accrue to the works of Molière. One is not ever likely to see Molière more brilliantly represented than in the Comédie presentations of *Tartuffe, Le Misanthrope,* and *Le Bourgeois gentilhomme.* Nor, in fact, is there richer theatre to be had.

Parker Tyler

THE FRENCH FILM

To consider the French film is to consider, by and large, our most sophisticated cinema—and by "sophistication" I mean all that the word implies: the French can get away with a technical sloppiness or cheapness by sheer élan and the kind of impudence and laissez-faire that comes from consciously careless superiority. Gérard Philipe, an actor of exceptional charm under any flag (his most distinguished film role was the hero of Radiguet's *The Devil in the Flesh*) acts in Racine at the Comédie Française, as does Jean Marais, also a film star. One detects in Philipe's semi-grotesque barker, who introduces and supposedly relates the fables of *The Seven Deadly Sins,* an authority that comes of a width of professional as well as of private and social experience. I suppose it will not sound pretentious to say that cinematic techniques and literary sources notwithstanding, the chief ornament of the French film is the French face with its deep and dauntless look into all the places of human nature.

The Italian contributions to *The Seven Deadly Sins* ("Avarice and Anger," combined, and "Envy") are curiously unsophisticated, whereas even the "Sloth" of the French, a little fantasy almost *betise* in its tricky obviousness, has a knowing air that Rossellini's rendering of Colette's shrewd vignette, "Envy," misses. One might call it style, except that style is the most difficult element of a film work to achieve, more so than in other arts, and for this reason its problem discourages serious commerce with artistic premises in films. It is as though the French start by assuming this handicap, and since no one—except perhaps, sometimes, Cocteau and Renoir—strives for style, a certain style appears from the conscious lack of effort toward it. Maybe, indeed, this is the specific definition of French sophistication. The short-short verve of "Gluttony," its point like a pinprick of the intelligence, the easy and open, yet quite dry, sentiment of "Pride," and the Zolaesque lyricism (yes!) of "Lust" are all done with the Devil's knowledge of mankind. Yet as we know from the Eighth or Unknown Sin tacked on at the end, the Devil is no longer to be taken so seriously as the traditional conception of sin demands. The Eighth Sin, if you please, is "belief in evil appearances." It is typical French *blague* and a joyous commentary on evil itself as an ethical "style." The whole film is obviously without relation to evil except indirectly.

Gérard Philipe also plays the hero of *Fanfan the Tulip,* a kind of folk hero temperamentally allied to D'Artagnan and the medieval figure of the Fool. The work is something of a spoof on romantic adventure costume-films and as such must any audience with brains take it. Yet, were *Fanfan* not a certain assertion of volatile spirits, it would be intolerably corny and coarse. The nation of Molière persists in loving self-interested, simple-minded scoundrels and in this creamy little piece we have a subjective fantasy of Sganarelle's. Perhaps the only vulgarity is unthinking repetition but the French are far too amused not to be amusing. Their euthanasia-based crime film, *Justice Is Done,* turned into a complex trial film, brilliantly put together, and though there was something un-French in the piously accented concern for "justice" via the jury's verdict, it was simply more *sensible* than any trial film I know about.

Something far from sensible, as art, and only paradoxically so as social observation, was the climax given
the film *Forbidden Games,* about which I wrote on an
occasion when I did not know how radically the novel's
ending had been changed for the screen. In the novel,
the little boy is killed by falling off the church roof
while trying to steal a cross big enough to suit a cow's
grave. The little girl then successfully completes the
theft and, burying the little boy's corpse, plants the cross
at the head of his grave. Such a climax makes aesthetic
consonance with the preceding development of the
story. The film's ending, on the other hand, is a piece of
"interested" arbitrariness. Could the French makers
have been thinking of the mass audiences of Britain and
America? I complained of the film's moral pessimism,
which wrought sentimentality out of its archetypal
tragic drama. I now complain of its perversity and of
what may be also the avarice of its makers. Avarice may
not be a deadly sin in France but perhaps, there as elsewhere, it is a deadly virtue.

Cocteau's "myth movies," the last of which was the
full-scale philosophic statement of *Orpheus,* have distilled a kind of perfume of modern techniques in literature, theatre, and film. *The Strange Ones* had as its
theme the first sprouts of theatricalism in the adolescent: the rank, dramatized narcissism of a race of aes-
thetes whose one "action-plot" is incest. The art of this
film is dominated by the love-death legend conceived as
a playground in which the aesthete consorts with his
bourgeois neighbors also condemned to the ghosts that
Freud made flesh. Cocteau's quasi-Surrealist style, born
of promiscuous wit rather than artistic necessity, made it
easy to render the bourgeois tempest-in-a-teacup, *The
Storm Within,* valid and moving. The gypsy picturesque-
ness that crept into that movie's matriarch is not facetious but a perfectly sound social observation. It was just

high *blague* (and part of the incorrigibly sincere and
desperate tenderness of modern French sensibility) for
Cocteau to have declaimed at the end that his gypsy
"has no home on earth," so "the caravan moves on!" Of
course, he means the White Goddess in her contemporary diurnal aspect. This is first-rate mythifying. It
is much better than the total effect of *Orpheus,* where
Cocteau encased his sophisticated modern magic in the
popular happy-ending formula of the mass art. So doing,
he parodied his own play. Perhaps Cocteau's game of
wits with a commercial art has led him to overestimate
his prowess. *Orpheus* contained a bad misstep. It was a
fine-art boner. Perhaps in Paris one can successfully conceal the old-fashioned devices of ghoulish melodramas,
of which the "mystery house" is one and the "merciless
vampire" another, because the French themselves possess
an ironic dimension on such things, having absorbed
Eugene Sue and the Grand Guignol into the cultural
consciousness. But in sheer objectivity, *Orpheus* was an
attempt to substitute sophistication wholesale for art
retail. *The Seven Deadly Sins* is a kind of chamber art,
and there sophistication is, as it should be, modestly
retail.

THE ARTS IN ITALY

Mark Schorer

THE FICTION OF GIOVANNI VERGA

In 1840 Giovanni Verga was born into a Catanian family of the upper-middle class with at least legendary aristocratic antecedents in a dim and distant Castile. As a boy he spent the summers in the southern village of Vizzini, where his father had another house, and as much of the winters as were made difficult in Catania by political upheaval or the plague. The division between the city and the village, between the *borghesi* and the *contadini*, was to be the great division in his literary career, as it was in his early life. At fifteen he knew that he was to be a writer, and when his schooling was finished and his father was ready to send him to the university for the nearly conventional degree in law, the boy proposed that the money be used instead to subsidize the publications of his completed *"romanzo storico"* called *I carbonari della montagna*. All legends of the fathers of literary men to the contrary, this folly was pursued—in four volumes. Yet it was a folly that committed Verga to his splendid fate: he found himself a published writer, and after his father died in 1863, he promptly removed himself to the north of Italy, where all stylish writers lived. Florence and Milan took their toll and paid their price for fifteen years as the young Verga moved into his first and false literary success.

In the period between 1867 and 1876 he published a

series of books with precisely suggestive titles: *Una pec-
catrice, Storia di una capinera, Eva, Tigre reale, Eros,
Primavera ed altri conti*—all works that one might expect from a highly gifted young Sicilian who was trying
to be a smart north Italian writer in the somewhat inert
years after the Unification. These are novels of northern
manners, of sexual intrigue in a world of fatal females
and icy.dandies as Verga observed them. It is interesting
to note that the early hero, a young Sicilian drawn in
the image of Verga, gradually gives way to the northern
gallant, *freddo e duro*. Always reticent about his personal affairs, Verga yet permits us to speculate on the
probability that this transformation developed to a degree in himself. There is the evidence of at least three
stories written in his maturity and published in the volumes otherwise devoted to Sicilian peasants: "Caprice"
and "The How, When, and Wherefore" in the *Cavalleria* volume, and "Over the Sea" in the *Little Novels*.
These stories return in a softened, reminiscent mood to
intrigues between ladies of fashion and a Verga-like
hero, indeed, in two of them, to Verga himself, Verga
referring to his own stories of Sicily, and thereby bridg-
ing that chasm between the high and the low that was
presently to be positively leapt across in the career itself.

In the early work, he attempted to write in Tuscan,
and the attempt, for all the popularity that some of these
novels achieved, was a failure: the style as much a matter of the outsider listening and reading, as the situations were of the outsider looking—neither more sharply
nor fully than an outsider could. At any rate, he was no
more satisfied with the attempt at literary migration
than we may assume that he was with the attempt at
social migration, for suddenly, in 1874, as if in imaginative exasperation with the manner that he had developed
and the matter that he was still to exploit, he burst out
with *Nedda*, the true promise. This Sicilian *Tess*, with
its abrupt shift in subject matter, expelled at a blow

every affectation of syntax and figure that he had cultivated, and the story, told swiftly and baldly and with a
certain brutality, takes its stylistic color from the dialogue of its peasant characters. Yet two more works in
the old manner were to follow, and then, in 1876, after
the beginning of the author's own return to Catania,
four years of silence, and then the revolutionary triumph
in the *Cavalleria* volume of 1880, which brings to its ful-
ness every promise of *Nedda* in new style, new method,
new subject, and which was to alter the history of Italian
fiction.

Verga left an account of the origin of the style:

> It is a simple story. I had published some of my early
> novels. They went well: I was preparing others. One day, I
> don't know how, there came into my hands a sort of broad-
> sheet, a manuscript moderately ungrammatical and a-syn-
> tactical, in which a sea captain succinctly told of some
> vicissitudes overcome by his ship. Seaman's talk, without an
> unnecessary phrase, short. It struck me, and I reread it: it
> was what I was looking for, without exactly having known
> it. Sometimes, you know, a sign, an indication, is enough. It
> was a revelation.

The essence of the new method, which is a certain kind
of objectivity, is touched upon if not adequately accounted for in a prelude to the story of "Gramigna's
Lover":

I believe that the triumph of the novel, that most complete
and most human of all works of art, will be reached when
the affinity and the cohesion of all its parts will be so complete that the process of the creation will remain a mystery
. . . the hand of the artist will remain absolutely invisible,
and the novel will have the effect of real happening, and the
work of art will seem to have made itself, to have matured
and come forth spontaneously like a natural event, without
preserving any point of contact with its author; so that it
may not show in any of its living forms any imprint of the
mind which visioned it, any trace of the lips that murmured

the first words, like the *fiat* of the Creator; let it stand by itself, in the single fact that it is as it must be and has to be, palpitating with life and immutable as a bronze statue, whose creator has had the divine courage to eclipse himself and to disappear in his immortal work.

And for the third point, the new subject, and the new subject not only in the general sense of the Sicilian peasant, but of the particular special interpretation that Verga was to throw over the life of that figure, "Caprice," another story in this volume of 1880, gives us the first clue:

When one of those little beings, either more weak, or more incautious, or more egoistic than the others, tries to detach himself from the group, in order to follow the allure of the unknown, or out of desire to better himself, or out of curiosity to know the world, then the world of sharks, such as it is, swallows him, and his kin along with him.

This is a clue that is to open an incipient theory of social history outlined in the introduction to *I Malavoglia,* Verga's greatest work, published in 1881.

After that came the *Little Novels,* then *Mastro-don Gesualdo,* and on these four volumes Verga's reputation rests, for as there was little of final importance before 1880, so there was even less after 1888. Years of effort went into a story of Sicilian aristocratic life, *La Duchessa de Leyra,* which was meant to continue the novel series and of which nothing came. The work that he brought to completion is minor. Mostly there was silence, twenty years of it, until he died in 1922, immortal, and in a sense, unknown.

For the drama of Verga's literary career finds no corollary in the sluggish history of his reputation. Neither in Italy itself nor in Europe at large nor in the United States has there at any time been one of those rushes of renewed interest that are the commonplaces of nearly all great literary reputations. In Italy Verga is safely canonized in every literary history of whatever complexion as the greatest Italian writer of fiction after Manzoni, and is respectfully permitted to slumber in that greatness; yet one may surely wonder whether the neo-realism of the post-war Italian novelists, whose work is among the most important in present-day Europe, would have been even possible without the example of this early master of nineteenth century *versimo*. In France, he is regarded as an imitator of Zola and, in at least one late work, *Il marito di Elena*, of Flaubert. In the United States, when he is remembered at all, and with even less justification in fact, he is taken for the librettist of Mascagni's opera, *Cavalleria rusticana*. D. H. Lawrence, who has done more than any other one man to bring the works of Verga to us, is in part responsible for this final indignity, since he wrote in the preface to his translation of the volume that contains this story, "Everybody knows, of course, that Verga made a dramatized version of *Cavalleria rusticana*, and that this dramatized version is the libretto of the ever-popular little opera of the same name." Four years after the publication of his superb story, Verga adapted it to the stage in a slightly sentimentalized version; and six years after that, two others (Targioni-Tozzetti and Menasci by name) carried the vulgarization on to the point at which we have it now in Mascagni's opera. Yet of the five translated volumes that have been published in the United States, three are by Lawrence: *Mastro-don Gesualdo* in 1923; *Little Novels of Sicily* (*Novelle rusticane*) in 1925; and *Cavalleria rusticana and Other Stories* (*Vita dei campi*) in 1928. To the group has been added Eric Mosbacher's badly needed new translation of *I Malavoglia*, under the title *The House by the Medlar Tree*. This supersedes the only previous translation into English, made under the same title in 1890 by Mary A. Craig. One may say this even though Mr. Mosbacher saw fit to cut

Verga's text, without any indication that he did so, by at least a hundred pages. The motive would seem to have been manufacturing economy only, for the portions that have been deleted seem generally to involve subsidiary characters, and the central story of the decline of the Malavoglia fortunes remains. If something has then been lost in social richness and coherence, Mr. Mosbacher gains enormously in stylistic fidelity over Mrs. Craig, who did only a little cutting but whose translation is genteel and tepid, quite false to the downright original. It was in an introduction to the Craig version that the novel was honored by the praise of William Dean Howells, who called it "without reserve . . . one of the most perfect pieces of literature that I know."

Howells continues: "This poet, as I must call the author"—and so must we—has two great classes of characters in *The House by the Medlar Tree:* the products "of conscience and order," and the "children of disorder." Among the second he numbers the unheroic hero whom he calls "the merely weak . . . poor 'Ntoni Malavoglia." ". . . goodness brings not pleasure, not happiness, but it brings peace and rest to the soul, and lightens all burdens; the trial and the sorrow go on for good and evil alike; only, those who choose the evil have no peace." This is Howells' attempt to bring this dark, this quite non-Christian novel, nearer to those "smiling aspects of life," which he himself preferred in fiction, than it can legitimately be brought. For Verga's view of human experience is at once more desperate and more analytical than Howells' comment suggests, and this view is made clear enough in Verga's own introduction to this novel, a rare statement from the novelist which, unfortunately, no translator has yet seen fit to publish with the book that it illuminates.

It is at least an apparent irony that Verga's two tragic novels should be founded on a theory of progress; but the irony evaporates when we understand that his novels

—and he projected five at various social levels—were to be concerned with the *victims* of progress, the conquered, and that the whole series was to appear under the collective title, *I vinti*.

Human society is a river that begins with low, denying springs and ends in a great, fulfilling torrent. At every point in this stream, some individuals feel that it would be desirable to be farther upstream, and the friction of their efforts to get there causes the whole to swell. The incessant wave that the total effort creates drowns many of the very individuals who are making it, and they are tossed lifeless—*i vinti*—on the shore. Verga makes the corollary in class structure quite explicitly: at the bottom, the simplest material needs (*Medlar Tree*); next, money (*Mastro-don Gesualdo*); next, social power (*La Duchessa*); next, political power; finally, total domination. At every stage, some individuals grow uncomfortable within the limits of that stage, they begin to yearn for some undefined move, begin to feel "*la vaga bramosìa dell'ignoto, l'accorgersi che non si sta bene, o che si potrebbe star meglio.*" And the first to feel these impulses are destroyed. It is a mark of Verga's modernity that, while he was still charmed by the idea of progress, he wished to write of it as "*Il cammino fatale,*" and it is surely a part of his greatness that, while he wished merely to observe, he made true tragedies out of this fatal modern idea.

The House by the Medlar Tree has two heroes, an old grandfather who knows only "the religion of the family" and tries to keep the oysters on the rock, and a young grandson who, still wishing to preserve that ideal but being "more egoistic than the others," has been touched by the vague desire for the unknown, the beyond, and hopes to make the oyster-life better. He brings about the devastation wrought by the sharks of the world, and is himself destroyed, and in his destruction, ruins most of his family. At every stage, he who wishes more for his family is at the center, and at each stage he loses them more: first their boat, then their house, then pride, at last all but the name: *ill-will*. And with that only, another grandson is left to fight his way up the stream.

All around the story of the Malavoglias is the closely woven life of the town of Aci-Trezza, a fishing village just north of Catania, lying under Etna, and in the minor characters Verga presents his several other stages in life's stream: in the corrupt priest, the political druggist, the rich landlord, the miserly entrepreneur, every scheming wife and daughter, the sad sharpies: each moved by his kind and degree of ambition, each drowning someone and all really drowned. And these are the people who figure in the separate episodes of the *Little Novels of Sicily*. The situations, in fact, echo the subsidiary situations of the novel, and nearly all of the characters seem to have their prototypes in the larger work. This is not to suggest that these stories do not have their own integrity, each its own, and the integrity of each really pointed by Lawrence's superb translations; it is only to suggest that when Verga came back to write of Sicilians, he wrote out of a whole imaginative experience.

Imagination is compulsive. It accepts a subject, even an interpretation of a subject, and it finds that a style is decreed. Or it finds the style that it wants and is then able to explore the subject that it most needs. The young Verga, a Sicilian trying to imitate Florentines, becomes an Italian who thinks in Sicilian. The young migrant, both sentimental and moralistic, becomes sensuous and moral when he finally confronts what he knows (nor merely believes) to be *la verità*—which is only to say that which he does know. The objectivity on which he prides himself is in fact a deeper assertion of the personality of the author than any he has been able to assert before: the true pity that lies in the observation itself, not in the comment, not in the colored word. And how it shines in this work of the early eighties! As we read of these people who do not know what history is, even their own (no notion of the battles in which their sons are killed, no notion of that greater Italy of which in 1863 and 1864 they are already a part); who do not know that those very *faraglioni* outside their harbor, among which their boats are destroyed in storms, have for generations been said to be the rocks that the blinded Polyphemus hurled at Odysseus; who accept without question or wonder the Homeric sunrises in which they live and cannot question the sunset toward which they aspire since they do not know what that sunset is—as we read of all this ignorance, we know where we are: in the midst of our own.

Howells may have found some peace here; but it is hard to find today. What an American writer today can find here is an apparent loosening up of the forms of fiction through a certain kind of concentration which is in fact that sense of responsibility to meaning that decrees a form. What an American reader can find here, as Howells pointed out, is the full quality of a different life from his, but lived within the same truths—although different truths from those that he saw. Even the tourists in frivolous Taormina, looking a few miles south to Verga's *faraglioni*—even the tourist who does not know what armies fought at Syracuse or what people built the temples at Agrigento, who has not read Verga, or Homer either, must feel that, under the golden air, lies an island, labor a people heavy with an ancient fate. This is Verga's great evocation—*i vinti, i vinti!*

Paolo Milano

SILONE THE FAITHFUL

A foreigner in Italy, if he is interested in literature, will soon discover that Ignazio Silone is better known and more honored abroad than in his own country. After his first surprise, he may find this fact not too hard to explain—at least superficially. After all, Silone lived in exile for a very long time, and, though he has been back in Rome since 1944, his novel, *A Handful of Blackberries,* is the first book he has published since his homecoming. Besides, haven't Italian literati been more than a little envious of Silone's world-wide fame? And wasn't his political stand, as an anti-Communist socialist, bound to be unpopular in his country?

True as this all may be, it is far from essential. Silone's position today is a very meaningful but a solitary one, not only at home but in the world, and as much in literature as in politics. The following remarks may serve to explain this situation.

Silone believes in politics. Both in principle and in practice; after the war, he actually sat as a deputy in the Italian Parliament. His is a rare attitude among the writers of today, who, everywhere, are either "estranged" or "engaged." Either they have withdrawn deliberately from public life, watching over their own "metaphysical" privacy, or, in a kind of voluntary rush into self-abasement, they are ready to pursue alien aims. Silone, on the contrary, is neither alienated nor committed. He does not think in the least, as a Marxist would that politics should rule over literature; no, he is convinced that politics should be so directed as to make literature free, because a certain kind of *political* life is the premise of all art. In our society, the writer's freedom, if it isn't to become an illusion, must be *earned,* even in the hard, most unpleasant way. If nothing more, the writer's concern with and for society should be a reflex of self-defense and a form of his love for the independence of his quest.

Silone is also a socialist—and surely a *socialist* novelist in the 1950s is an almost anachronistic figure. He does, however, take the long view of socialism. He considers socialism the modern form of Christianity, the present expression of man's eternal hunger for justice, which, as Christianity once did, can look forward to centuries in the future. Retreats, heresies, successful distortions and temporal compromises may well have the upper hand for long periods; yet, inevitably, the deep-rooted motive, the living thread will always reappear. Russian Communism, viewed in Silone's historical perspective, may well prove to have been an immense, ill-taken detour.

Finally, strictly as a novelist, Silone refuses to be "literary." Not only does he dislike psychological or experimental writing, believing, as he does, in plain communication; but he also feels that a narrator should respect and adopt the ancient modes of the popular mind, for there lie the roots of human discourse.

In a way, and this is not the least of his wonderful peculiarities, Silone has been writing the same book again and again for years, much as a painter portrays the same landscape for a lifetime. Silone's novels, his few stories and his non-fictional work betray a compact and stubborn unity of inspiration. Back in the thirties, *Fontamara*, his first novel, was little less than a revelation. The impact of Fascism on an Abbruzzean village was shown to be, on the surface, the insertion of an extraneous body, though, substantially, a more violent form of an immemorial oppression. The figure of the *cafone* made its appearance in literature. The *cafone* is the destitute peasant, of Italy and of everywhere, whom the Powers constantly exploit and History by-passes constantly. Two-thirds of mankind, the "absent" majority, were distinctly visible in the microcosm of *Fontamara*. But the book was no political tract: irony, a heavy peasant irony, kept the representation on balance and the vital spirits alive.

Silone's next two novels (*Bread and Wine* and *The Seed Beneath the Snow*) offer a variation of the essential conflict. Here, the day-by-day calvary of peasant life sets the background against which not Fascism but professional anti-Fascism is to be measured—the emptiness of its party-lines, of its underground networks below and of its slogans from above. The hope kept alive by the insulted and the injured, against violence on one side and abstraction on the other, rests on an almost Tolstoyan covenant between simple friends. Here politics turns evangelical again, and the seed is ripening in new catacombs.

A Handful of Blackberries takes us back once more to a familiar village in the Abbruzzi—but in 1946, in the troubled times that followed the end of the war. The Great Deceiver, now, is the Communist Party, with its bureaucracy, its emphasis on obedience and its distrust of the peasantry's moral instinct and of its political spontaneity. Since the *cafoni* are right but they are steeped in their folk-ways and dreams, and the Party is wrong but ruthlessly "modern," *A Handful of Blackberries* is a satire rather than a drama. Neither realistic nor symbolic, it is not even a novel in the ordinary sense of the term, it is a long apologue. Its characters are few and exemplary; their size is heightened and their vicissitudes are told in a leisurely, proverbial manner. The subplot, for instance, (the love-story of a Communist functionary who breaks with the Party and of a displaced Jewish girl who stands courageously by him), is literally a romance, and has its moments of sheer melodrama. As the ancient humor of its long-winded talks remind us at every step, here is a folk-tale. It should be read and enjoyed accordingly.

Since Silone first began to write, quite a few things have happened in literature and in history. In Italy, several writers have appeared, (I am thinking less of the "neo-realists" as of such original talents as Carlo Levi and Elio Vittorini), who could tread on new ground because Silone had first broken it for them. He was the carliest to step "beyond Eboli."

On the world-stage, the *cafoni* have made themselves felt lately, from Indo-China to Morocco and from Kenya to Venezuela. On the other hand, the East-German riots against the Russian occupants have recently made an old prediction of Silone sound very pointed. Fifteen years ago, he wrote that the day might dawn when the workers themselves would discover that "Marxism is the opiate of the people."

Silone can wait. If his fellow-Italians are slow in granting him plenary recognition, time is on his side. And the foreign reader would be ill-advised if he took a cavalier view of *A Handful of Blackberries,* dismissing the book, nostalgically perhaps, as a belated echo of those "populist" novels so eagerly acclaimed in the thirties.

Silone is now at work, and a return to Silone may well be in the cards. One thing is certain: such a swing of the pendulum could not possibly be a purely literary affair.

Nicola Chiaromonte

AMBIGUITIES IN ITALIAN LITERATURE

In the farthest and most resplendent regions of the
South, there operates a hidden Ministry for the defense
of Nature against Reason: a maternal genius of unlimited power to whose jealous and unremitting care is
entrusted the sleep in which those people are sunk.
Should such a defense relax for a moment, should the
sweet and cold voices of Reason be heard by the sleepers,
Nature would be thunderstruck. This incompatibility of
two forces which are equally great and, contrary to the
optimist's view, unreconcilable; this frightfully secret
defense of the territory of Nature, with its songs, its sorrows, and its dumb innocence; this, not the ruthlessness
of History . . . is the cause of the conditions in which
this land lies, of the pitiful defeat in which the expedi-
tions sent out here by human reason invariably end.
Here, thought can only be the slave of Nature, and its
gazer. A critical examination is no sooner attempted, no
sooner does a tendency take shape to correct the celestial
conformation of these regions, to see water in the sea,
chemical compounds in the volcanoes, insides in man,
than death swiftly comes to the offender. . . . The immobility of these regions has been attributed to other
causes, but they are not the true ones. It is Nature that
regulates the life and organizes the sufferings of these
people. Here economic disaster has no other cause. The

long succession of kings and viceroys, the unconquerable array of priests, the multiplication of churches like amusement parks and of hospitals and prisons as well, stem from this. Here where Nature, once the mother of ecstasies, has taken refuge, Human Reason, everything in reason that is dangerous for Nature's Empire, is doomed.

This passage, I translated from a successful and significant book, *Il mare non bagna Napoli (The Sea does Not Touch Naples)* by Anne Maria Ortese, which received a Viareggio Prize. Miss Ortese's remarks about the struggle between Nature and Reason in the South could well apply to the moral and cultural situation of Italy as a whole. If Nature is taken to include the common denominator of social, religious, and cultural beliefs by which, statistically speaking, the majority of the individuals in a community finally abide, and if by Reason one does not intend only theoretical thought and practical enterprise, but, more generally, the principle of consistency in life and thought, then the war between the two, with Nature winning most of the battles, is certainly not a peculiarity of Southern dereliction and inertia. It dominates the Italian scene, and it is particularly visible in the narrative literature of today, when practically everybody claims to be a "realist," that is to convey a definite experience rather than a literary mood.

In Italy, literary traditionalism is, of course, part of nature. To the sensibility of most Italian readers and critics, an accomplished literary form still is the most convincing proof that the writer is dealing with reality. Hence, for example, in Miss Ortese's book, the critics have highly praised the two short stories, while tending to dismiss the straightforward descriptions of Neapolitan life which constitute the real merit of the volume. The joke is that the short stories (one about a poor shortsighted little girl who puts on a pair of glasses for the first time, and sees a world which, as her aunt puts it "one had better not see," the other about a melancholy spinster who on Christmas day, nurtures for a moment the hope of getting married, but cannot quite get excited about it, and finally dismisses it) are nice pieces of writing, while the descriptions are often-marred by "neo-realistic" emphasis, which does not prevent the short stories from being sentimental anecdotes, while the journalistic accounts are pieces of passionate and forceful writing.

Speaking of the struggle between nature and reason, a case in point is the excellent novel by Giese Rimanelli, *Tiro al piccione* (*Pigeon-shooting* was the term used by the partisans during the war to designate their ambushes against the Fascist Black Brigade, whose insignia was the Roman eagle: the "pigeon"). This is the first good literary account of the Resistance war seen from the Fascist camp. It tells without any fuss the story of a seventeen-year-old boy who, in 1943, sees in the German trucks that roll north through his home town going north just a chance to escape from the family, an uneasy love affair, and tedium. In the north, he ends up by enlisting in the Black Brigades; not because he believes in the Fascist cause, but just because there is little else to be done. Ambushes, massacres, cold-blooded killing, terrorism, plus a love affair with an army nurse, are what the young man gets in the way of "sentimental education" and "reason."

He is in a constant state of disgust, and yet he goes on, simply because he has found a couple of comrades there, and killing (or being killed) on one side seems to him very much the same as killing (or being killed) on the other. What is revolting to him is "nature," not an idea: the inhumanity and senselessness of a fratricidal struggle into whose causes he does not care to inquire. What irritates him about the Fascists is their incapacity to see that they are defeated anyway, so that their cruelty becomes doubly senseless. On the other hand, what makes him suspect that the partisans' cause makes some sense is the fact that they are obviously on the winning side. This is as far as his reason goes. As for his nature, it tells him that making love is better than killing, friendship more satisfying than enmity, peace more desirable than war; above all, that all men have a mother, hence the mothers' point of view is the only universal one.

These, and especially the last one, are classic tenets of Italian "natural" morality. In ordinary times, they might not mean much; but in moments of upheaval and mechanized ferocity, they appear as the most precious heritage of "nature" precisely. When everything else is shattered, they remain, and they are effective, people actually abide by them. It is to this morality that Rimanelli's here finally surrenders when, after the Fascist rout, he goes back into the folds of the family—the prodigal son, which is as it should be.

The reader, however, feels somewhat frustrated, as if all that had happened in the meantime had been a bad dream rather than a tragic experience. Artistically speaking, the young man who, one night blindly decided to take his life into his own hands, was real, a hero of our time. The prodigal son returned home is just "normal." What next? There are signs in the book, that the young man is drifting in the direction of the Communist religion. But one knows that, in any case, this is a secondary issue, since the real catharsis of the drama has already occurred the moment the harassed hero has embraced his mother and sat at the family table.

Together with Miss Ortese's book on Naples, the jury of the Viareggio Prize brought to the attention of the reading public an account of the retreat from Russia, *Il sergente nella neve* (*The Sergeant in the Snow*) by Mario Rigoni Stern. It is the real story, told in the first person, of the endurance, the sufferings, the calm courage, of a sergeant of the Alpine troops and his comrades from the moment of the Russian counter-offensive on the Don, which broke their lines, to their arrival to safety after a month of terrible marching through the frozen steppe and several desperate battles to break through encirclement by the Russians. An extremely honest document: Sergeant Rigoni, his soldiers and officers are very attractive individuals, in addition to being sturdy and courageous soldiers.

The book is also a straightforward testimony in favor of Italian "natural" morality and humaneness. Rigoni has great sympathy for the Russian people; he understands that he is waging an unjust war on them, does not like it, but, of course, has no choice but to perform his duty as scrupulously as he can. The march, the suffering, the sticking together as the army disintegrates, the hopeless battles, are all parts of a job that has to be done. Inhumanity isn't.

What happened to Rigoni in the Russian village of Nikolaievka could have happened in precisely that way only to an Italian. Rigoni and the remnants of his battalion had been fighting the whole day, and it had been a massacre. Only twenty of them were left, with no ammunition. The Russians were all around them. To try to get some food, Rigoni knocked at the door of an *izba*. The door opened. Inside sitting at a table there were Russian soldiers, eating; women were serving them. The Russians were armed; Rigoni was armed too. He remained on the doorstep, frozen; then he announced in Russian that he was hungry. One of the women gave him a plate of soup. He ate, said "Thanks," and turned about to leave. The Russians did not budge. The woman who had served him took him to the door. Near the door, Rigoni noticed some beehives: he asked the woman for some honey to take to his comrades. The woman gave it to him and the Italian invader left. "For once," he comments, "circumstances had led men to act just like men."

Natural morality, which war, and history in general,

violate for their own abstract motives, had asserted itself. To an Italian, such occurrences are the equivalent of a religious revelation, in fact they are even more convincing. However, he knows that while they are both the expression of an eternal truth, they are also exceptional. Real life is absurdly impervious to "natural" morality. For Sergeant Rigoni the unfortunate soldier of the Russian campaign, reality seems to have been limited by two orders of facts: one was his battalion, kept together by the peculiarly strong *esprit de corps* which characterizes Italian Alpine troops. This meant that particular job of war that had to be done by him and his comrades. The other dominant fact was nostalgia for the native mountain village. The rest, war in general, its causes, the ideological conflicts connected with it, and even the Italian army at large, were just abstractions to be best ignored.

This finally makes of his book, for all his honesty and realism, a piece of regional, if not sectional, literature. In fact, the reactions and the behavior of a Neapolitan infantryman would have been very different from Rigoni's. The natural morality, however, would have been very much the same although felt and practiced in a different fashion. The Neapolitan, that is, might have been sloppy, hysterical and cowardly, whereas Rigoni was efficient, level-headed, and courageous. But to him, too, war would have been just a violation of the natural order and inquiry into its causes a matter for highbrows; moral problems would have ended with the distinction between the "humans" and the "inhumans," and reason would have been either a question of practical expediency and ability, or else a scholastic notion.

Such a human and yet subtly disappointing (as if we were denied the whole truth), limitation of the intellectual and moral horizon, and of "reality" itself can be noticed even in a sophisticated writer like Mario Tobino. He is the author of several books, among them a long story on life under Fascism, *Bandiera Nera (Black*

Flag). He has also written an excellent volume of memoirs about the war in Lybia, in which he participated as a Medical Corps officer. There Lieutenant Tobino had some bitter experiences of the weaknesses of the Italian character, and he does not mince his words in denouncing them.

As a civilian, he is a psychiatrist, in charge of the women's section of an important insane asylum near Lucca. In *Le libere donne di Magliano* (*The Free Women of Magliano*), Tobino recounts in the form of a loose journal his experiences with his patients, or rather he describes a number of them one by one, not as diseased individuals, but as strange, and sometimes quite touching, characters. Particularly successful is the portrait of one of these women, Lella, who had waited on him with passionate care for ten years, in relative freedom, and one day was sent back to her cell because it was discovered that she was hoarding in a crazy way all sorts of things, including money. Questioning the justice of the decision, Doctor Tobino gives his own interpretation of Lella's character, as motivated by an unbounded need for devotion. As long as she could show one of the doctors her exclusive love by serving him, she behaved quite sanely. Her troubles, the mania for hoarding and even stealing, started with the arrival to the asylum of a woman doctor in whom she saw a rival. At that moment, Tobino maintains, she was left without a God to serve, and she started stealing, and giving the money she stole to her brother. Human sympathy is what we all need, and humility in the face of what we do not understand; then, even madness can appear "natural." Could there be a nicer attitude for the harassed director of an insane asylum? Certainly not. Yet, in some way, for a writer and an intellectual who contemplates the monsters of madness, the appeal to sympathy, and the ability to describe the insane as "character," do not seem to be adequate answers to the problem.

If realism is the ability to render things as they are, without any literary embellishment, morality, or catharsis, then the most realistic piece of writing that has appeared recently in Italy is a non-literary document published by the magazine *Nuovi Argomenti,* edited by Alberto Moravia and Albert Carocci: the *Memoriale dal carcere (Memoirs from Jail)* by Saverio Montalto. It is the story of a man who killed his sister and wounded his wife and his brother-in-law, written by the man himself not for a literary magazine but for the judge of instruction. The man was a Sicilian town clerk, whose sister was seduced and then unwillingly married by a local small-time Don Juan. From that moment the nightmare that will lead to crime begins for Montalto. The acquired family starts torturing him as the inferior creature who succeeded in insinuating himself in a sphere where he does not belong. Not content with moral torture, they extort money from him, force him into debt and fearful subjection.

This is not enough: they coerce him to marry into the family, so that he can be more completely at their mercy. At the same time, his sister is continually beaten up by her husband, and treated as a servant by the rest of the family. Until, with an anguishing fatality that the reader senses from the beginning, crime comes, an outburst. The merciless narrowness of Italian provincial life has never been rendered with such raw power as in this attempt by a murderer to reconstruct the atmosphere, rather than the motives, of his crime.

Neither a realist nor a surrealist, Tommaso Landolfi occupies a place by himself in contemporary Italian literature. He is a self-conscious, extremely literary writer, yet there is simplicity as well as truth in his pages, since he is motivated not by literature but by an authentic mood. The mood is a despondency so complete that it takes up a romantic tinge. Despondency, the total inability to see any purpose in life, is, of course, contradicted by the very fact that one goes on living. It is the consciousness of this fact that is the source of Landolfi's special kind of irony. His novel *La biere du pecheur* is a kind of aimless rambling, from descriptions of weary love affairs to a couple of first rate accounts of the author's only real passion, gambling.

Gambling is to Landolfi the most senseless, devilish, sinful passion of all. That is why it is also the most irresistible and significant. Yet, if it were made to seem serious, it would lose its true meaning, which is aimless automatism and conscious self-deception. In this, gambling is the symbol of all other passions, including love, and life itself; dreary and comical at the same time.

Other narrative books have appeared recently in Italy that would deserve some attention. Those that have been chosen here should, however, give the reader a sufficient idea of the complexities, and the limitations, of the "realistic" trend that dominates contemporary Italian narration.

Kermit Lansner

ITALIAN PAINTING

From the end of the eighteenth to the beginning of this century, there was little in Italian art which can now hold our close attention. It does not compare—nor does the work of any of the other European countries—with the painting and sculpture of France; either in its intensity, intelligence or imagination. Nineteenth century Italian art was unadventurous and provincial; at its best (among the *Macchiaioli* of Florence) it was rarely more than pleasant.

In that remarkable burst of invention which touched all of Europe about fifty years ago, Italian painting came to life again. The discoveries of the Parisian painters, beginning with the Fauves, now seems entirely natural in light of the continuous tradition behind them. Much stranger and more dramatic was the sudden development of new art movements in other countries. Italy, in particular, oppressed by memories of the past, covered with monuments of former glories, politically immature, seems to have lacked at that time any of those characteristic signs of modernity which were well developed in France. Suddenly she moved into the vanguard of experiment in art. Futurism, looked at now, seems to have been a summary achieved in one bold step of those many things we mean when we speak of the modern spirit. It was one of the first of Italy's peculiarly modern experiments—Fascism being another. I mention them together not because there was any real sympathy between the two, but because the garish, if superficial, melodrama of both now seem so outdated.

The pictures of the Futurists are familiar enough although they are not shown as frequently as those of other schools. But the 1949 show of Italian art at the Museum of Modern Art, the comprehensive retrospective at the Venice Biennale some years ago and, recently, several smaller exhibitions in New York of works by Balla, Severini, Russolo, Carrá and Boccioni remind us again of the importance of their art. The central dogma in the program of the Futurists was the glorification of motion: "Everything is moving, everything is running, everything is whirling . . . moving forms are multiplied, deformed like vibrations through the space in which they pass." This controlling idea was applied to subject matter drawn from the most contemporary aspects of their environment. The Futurists had little use for the standard themes which were always present in the works of other painters—although these served, in fact, as vehicles for the most revolutionary discoveries of new forms by the greatest among them. Thus the peculiarly modern subjects: factories, automobiles, trains, mechanized war. They also had the idea of changing the spectator's point of perception, thus affecting his psychological relationship with the picture. They wanted to "place the spectator at the center of the painting" which would become a "synthesis of what one sees and what one remembers." This intention was one aspect of the larger doctrine of simultaneity which was developed. Each of these ideas was present in the other schools of modern art in one degree or another, but none combined them so skillfully as the Futurists nor expressed their doctrine so forcefully. The influence of the group is still felt although it was never as strong as that of the Cubists and other French artists.

By 1915, a little more than five years after it began, the movement was finished. Boccioni, to my mind the most gifted both in painting and sculpture, died in 1916 while the others returned to more conservative styles and never again, with the exception of Carrá, achieved the success of their Futurist works. They remained fine painters but were no longer important ones. Many explanations have been offered for the sudden dwindling of the Futurists. It seems probable that this fate was inherent in the program of the group itself and the demands they made upon the resources of painting.

Besides the Futurists there was another group—composed mainly of three painters—which was of equal importance in modern art. The Metaphysical School was Italian in origin and fulfillment, though its influence can be noted in the atmosphere of innumerable works by mediocre artists who followed. The obsession with motion so characteristic of the Futurists is absent from the paintings of the metaphysicals. De Chirico's canvases are bathed in a mysterious silence which is strangely eloquent. Although this painting relies for its emotional effect upon the combination of perception and memory—or association—it uses other means than the flamboyant skills of the Futurists. Yet, like their work, it has a modern patina upon a modern substance. It is an art immediately felt as contemporary, but not fully integral to our immediate concerns, even slightly deviant from the strongest current of recent art itself. It is expressive of the longings of the modern spirit rather than of an immediate reality.

Morandi, who lives in Bologna, is far less known than De Chirico or Carrá but he is now regarded by many as Italy's foremost painter. Driven by a passion for plastic perfection, Morandi works a very small area which he has cultivated for thirty years. A few jugs, vases, bowls are painted and repainted. His work has the silence of the metaphysical school, but the strong serenity is his

own. One knows that he is a contemporary but feels
that he might have painted these same still-lifes at any
time; and this very absence of the modern flair which
distinguishes the other painters seems to have allowed
him to continue in the same spirit for years—like
Cézanne whom he admires.

The decline of invention in Italian painting coincides
with the rise of Fascism. The older, famous painters,
driven by their personal needs, returned to less adven-
turous styles, the younger ones were unable to generate
new ideas. It seems likely that this diminution in power
would have happened in any case, but political restric-
tions reinforced the decline. Sympathetic contact with
other countries was discouraged and artistic energies
which could only flourish by concentration upon the
problems of art were often led off into irrelevant enthusiasms.

The most conservative tendencies of the period were
embodied in the group called the *Novecento*. Although
some among them became the official artists of the day,
it would be a derogatory simplification to assume that
their program was decisive in Italy. The *Novecento* was
not a coherent movement. In fact it was only a loosely
connected association of artists whose common bond was
a distaste, or an inability, for the unsettling advanced
art of the century. Whatever the more permanent effects
of Fascism upon painting and sculpture, it did not
smother them completely nor, until late in the game,
attempt to exercise a thoroughly rigid control. During
the twenties and thirties there were many painters,
some of whom have been treated to retrospectives and
reconsiderations in an attempt to work out a continuity
in Italian art; and their styles were as various as their
notions of what painting might be. But they looked to
the past. Precedent was found in the long tradition of
Italian art and, in several instances, in the local dialects
of the regions from which they came. The best work of

the period had little of the bombast of Fascism; the imperial pretensions of the government do not appear in the still-lifes and landscapes of Tosi, the lonely figure of Casorati or the quiet glimpses of city and family life which Rosai painted. Scipioni, co-founder with Mafai of a "Roman School" in the late twenties, used an expressionistic, rhetorical style, but it is personal and romantic rather than public.

What is missing in all these painters is either the inspiration of new ideas or the original fusion of old ones. Campigli, in Paris, managed to develop a charming but repetitive style based on various models from antiquity, but de Pisis, working in the same city, did not go farther than a great facility with the techniques of the Impressionists. Only Magnelli continued to break new ground, though his work has little felicity about it.

Since the end of the war, Italian painters have felt the full force of the major achievements of the art of this century. At the successive Biennales each country has hung, in number, the best works of its artists. These were eagerly studied and assimilated. The vigor of the Italians who had continued to work for many years without benefit of the most original ideas of the time flourished in their attempt to catch up with the rest of Europe. It is a sign of the living pertinence of modern art that it immediately held these men who had been isolated for so long. Painting in Italy during the past decade seems then like a hurried recapitulation of styles which have been long familiar to most of us. The central idea of abstraction, deeper and more inclusive than it had been in the days of the Futurists, dominated a number of subsidiary styles and even the reactions to it seemed like echoes of movements which had taken place in Paris twenty years before. Again Picasso dominated everyone. Influences from his more recent and even from his older periods inspired painters of widely diverse purpose and talent.

Combined with the tendency towards abstraction was a reluctance to put aside the powers of painting as social commentary. The enthusiasm which the younger Italians had for left-wing politics kept many of them tied to the subject, although the direction of their adopted styles could have easily led them to non-objective painting. The tension of subject and technique is seen in the painting of Guttuso, a young painter famous beyond his achievement, who uses a roughly simplified cubism, brash colors and images of workers and peasants. This is a fairly common synthesis. Others, like Birolli, Pizzinato and Cagli, have adopted the most obvious mannerisms of the middle-generation French painters: the swinging curve (a cubist shorthand) and broken color areas. But change is so rapid (Pizzinato, for example, is now extremely realistic) that we must regard much of this painting as experimentation with a wealth of new suggestions. It is this fluidity which makes it so difficult to write about the work—without photographs to illustrate my points and with few examples of the paintings available.

Recently there has been a turn on the part of some painters towards a more non-objective art. Afro, one of the most gifted, has moved to warmly colored, fluid canvases with only the slightest reference to the world; and other painters have taken up the suggestions of the latest French and American art (the 1950 Biennale showed de Kooning, Pollock and Gorky) to join an international style which is still being shaped.

I have spoken only of painting, and of that rather sketchily, in these few pages, although it is in sculpture that Italy has produced its most consistently successful artists. Marini is the most widely known among the sculptors, but others, Martini, Manzu, Greco have joined him to revive an art in which Italy was long pre-eminent.

Eric Bentley

THE ITALIAN THEATRE

In the first of a series of lectures organized by the University Fascist Youth in 1935, Pirandello called the Italian theatre "the first and most important theatre of the world." Yet in the previous year, at a world theatre conference in Rome (the Convegno Volta), the chief Italian spokesman, Silvio D'Amico, had, in effect, appealed to Mussolini to rescue this theatre from disaster. D'Amico quoted the American reporter Richard Watts as having said that the Duce had provided his country with great theatre by speaking from the balcony of Palazzo Venezia. If theatre could help the state in this way, D'Amico argued, couldn't the state help the theatre—with larger subsidies?

The contrast between the speeches of Pirandello and D'Amico dramatizes, I think, the contrast—baffling at first to the foreigner—in Italian theatre then or now: a contrast between what the brochures tell you and what you actually find, between what is professed by French students of *commedia dell'arte* and what you really see in Rome and Milan, between what the Italian theatre magazines blazon in print and what their editors confess in private. Here is a theatre which trumpets its own glories to the world and yet has been discussing for generations the question "Esiste un teatro italiano?" ("Does an Italian theatre exist?")

If the contrast I am talking about were merely that between a product as advertised and a product in itself as it really is, it would be of too simple a nature to require discussion. The fact is that the *splendeurs* are as real as the *misères,* Pirandello's claim as well-founded as D'Amico's demand. This is both the best and the worst theatre in the world.

THE WORST

Go to the average show by the average professional company, and you will find the standards of production lower than English repertory or American summer stock. The scenery is ragged, old-fashioned, and in poor taste. There seems to have been no director at all. The acting subsists on leftovers of Victorian style; no wonder the film directors prefer people off the street.

Sometimes a company of considerable pretensions is no better. No American college dare present so feeble a representation of *Murder in the Cathedral* as was offered in Rome and throughout Italy by the grand old man of the Italian stage, Ruggero Ruggeri (d. 1953). Seeing this chorus I was reminded of what an Italian conductor told me about singers. "All our singers are soloists," he said, "Italians can't sing together." Whatever degree of collaboration existed among the members of the Eliot chorus might have been established by a one-minute conference before the performance started. Again: no production at all. Just Ruggeri standing stage center where he could see and hear the prompter. Sitting in the front rows you got the whole thing twice: once in the prompter's loud whisper, once in Ruggeri's quiet falsetto.

I don't mean that there was no distinction in Ruggeri's acting—or, say, in that of Emma Gramatica when she appeared in equally shabby productions of Pirandello and D'Annunzio a couple of years ago. It is only that the undoubted distinction is beset by a mediocrity that would be tolerated in no other country. And that there is a conspiracy of silence about it in the press. The critics either don't see it or won't risk hurting anyone's feelings.

One should perhaps include theatre criticism as among the worst features of Italian theatre. I have no idea whether any of it is, in a strict and legal sense, corrupt, as it is in some parts of Europe. My impression is that, on the contrary, it is deprived of all intellectual interests by a misguided good will which makes of the critic an assistant to the press agent. He is so busy encouraging every bad performance of every bad play that he removes the incentive to serious effort. It may be that Silvio D'Amico—still a central figure in Rome—is a partial exception to the rule, as was his Milanese opposite number Renato Simoni (d. 1952). And the critic of *Unità* can be counted on for the communist brand of social criticism. (The keenest theatre criticism I know of in Italy was that of Antonio Gramsci and Piero Gobetti a generation ago; if there is nothing of the sort today, the rise of fascism and the degradation of Stalinism are responsible.) But the rule holds.

THE BEST

When Pirandello called the Italian theatre the best he was boasting in the familiar manner of his Duce, whose "sacred renewal" of Italian life his lecture invokes. But he was also referring to the archetypal character of earlier Italian achievements in the theatre, most notably the *commedia dell'arte*. The Mussolini regime was not disposed to acknowledge where that sort of tradition most conspicuously survives today—namely, in the dialect theatre. Yet, for all the government's opposition to dialect, some of the greatest names of the fascist era are those of dialect artists: Angelo Musco the Sicilian (Gio-

vanni Grasso belongs primarily in the previous era),
Petrolini the Roman comedian, and the three De Filippos. Only the De Filippos have survived into the present
Demo-Christian era—one of them was a DC candidate
at the recent election—but this is more than mere survival, for it was in the years following the fall of Mussolini that the greatest of them, Eduardo, came into his
own as a playwright. The latest edition of D'Amico's
history of drama is subtitled "From Aeschylus to Eduardo De Filippo." (D'Amico plays the same chronicler's
part in Italy that Allardyce Nicoll has played in England, John Gassner in America, Joseph Gregor in
Austria.)

Whatever his relation to Aeschylus, Eduardo is one
of the great artists of the contemporary theatre. Gordon
Craig finds him the greatest living actor. He is certainly
the leading Italian playwright. True, there are still
those who would grant such a title only to a writer of the
literary Italian language (*"lingua"*). Eduardo is nothing
if not Neapolitan, yet, at that, his plays are not purely
dialectal; he tends now to keep the pure dialect for the
lower-class characters. His plays are toured all over
Italy. One of them was the chief modern Italian exhibit
at a Venice festival. Another has been a hit—in translation—in Paris. This last is *Filumena Marturano,* the
tragi-comedy of a Neapolitan prostitute; if one has to
suggest an analogue in our tradition, it must be O'Casey.
It is not for the present writer to predict whether such
a play could ever succeed on our stage as he is already
at work on an American version.

The last play of Eduardo's that I saw was *Fear Number One* which is a comical treatment of our fear of the
third world war. That and its predecessor *The Big
Magic* showed Eduardo becoming increasingly reflective
and even intellectual and therefore (for an Italian)
Pirandellian. As played by himself, his sister Titina, and
his admirable troupe, these plays continued to fascinate

me, but whether the trend toward intellectuality is the right one for this author I would doubt. More probably, it is exactly analogous to Chaplin's later drift—a credit to an artist's earnestness but no boon to his art.

In the dynasty of the Neapolitan stage, De Filippo is the immediate heir of another Eduardo, the great Scarpetta, last of the Pulcinellas, favorite of Benedetto Croce. Gossip has it that De Filippo's best scenes are lifted from the Mss. in the older Eduardo's trunk. Which is a story that ought to be true if it isn't. The roots of Eduardo are in Neapolitan fun and fantasy. Any branching out into world culture, modern philosophy, or the Aeschylean empyrean is likely to be papier-mâché.

I add a warning to Americans: do not judge Eduardo by his films (*Napoli Milionaria, Filumena Marturano*), much less by other people's films in which he appears (*Assunta Spina, Seven Deadly Sins,* and a couple of dozen others). We have seen the talent of American actors somehow evaporate before the camera's eye, and just that happens to Eduardo's genius. Even on the stage, his style is elusive. He is the opposite of "Italianate." Nothing operatic here. The tone is low, the gesture—by Italian standards—understated. Then again, there is a great deal to learn before one can appreciate him. The Italian stage does not have an Oriental "gesturology," but various provinces, and Naples in particular, have what amounts to a system of gestures with accepted meanings.

The Teatro di Eduardo is perhaps all that is left of the greatness of dialect theatre. But since the war there have been notable achievements *in lingua*. Here, I believe, the outstanding personality is not a playwright (though some would nominate Ugo Betti [d. 1953]) but a director: Luchino Visconti. The closest American analogue is Elia Kazan. Both Visconti and Kazan are, in a loose and perhaps also in a strict sense, decadent. They transfer to the stage their own frenetic nervosity; Visconti even tends to a certain surrealistic deliquescence. Like

Kazan, he is saved from experimental mess by sheer showmanship. It may be that his great contribution has nothing to do with a particular style but consists in the fact that he is a craftsman and a perfectionist. Having a good deal of money has doubtless helped; he is one of *the* Viscontis and a duke. His production of *Death of a Salesman*—a play that has pursued me from country to country—was the only one anywhere to match Kazan's; for a man who had never touched American soil an amazing feat of sympathetic imagination. As for his range, it is wider than the American director's has as yet shown itself to be. He is as much at home with Shakespeare and Alfieri as with Williams.

NEITHER BEST NOR WORST

Though Italian theatre tends to be pushed to the extremes of good and bad, it would be folly to pretend it has no middling middle. Many of the famous *spettacoli all'aperto* belong there, though the grandeur of a Higher Impresario may seem to raise them higher. Then again, the rashness of trying to rival God—if every prospect pleases and only man is vile—can put a show in the lower category.

Highest in the middle category I would put the Piccolo Teatro di Milano and next underneath it the Piccolo Teatro di Roma. Here, no doubt, the real achievement was to create a repertory, as against a touring, theatre at all. I am told that I was not lucky in my choice of shows. Certainly I saw much that was competent or interesting without being first-rate. I also saw one show at each theatre which belongs in the highest category. *The Raven* in Milan and *Six Characters in Search of an Author* in Rome.

THE OUTLOOK

The Italian theatre is government-subsidized, and by now the cumbersome governmental apparatus, upset by the war, is working again. And there are three lavish magazines wholly devoted to theatre (as against the US's one): *Il Dramma, Teatro-Scenario,* and *Sipario.*

The question is whether it can be done this way, "it" being The Thing We All Want To Do in the theatre now; I hesitate to define it; like God, "it" has earned its vagueness. One's fear is that too much of the effort has been concentrated on the return to normalcy (i.e. 1939). On the other hand, there is *no* way of guaranteeing the appearance of young Salvinis and Duses, Pirandellos and Petrolinis. I am left with the classic conclusion of freshman theme and ladies' club lecture: Time Will Tell.

Two recent books are to be recommended: *Ritorno alla censura* by Vitaliano Brancati and *Spettacolo del secolo* by Vito Pandolfii. The Italian Society of Authors in New York would like to inform readers that the doings of the Italian theatre are annually recorded in an *Annuario del teatro italiano* and also, now, in an *Almanacco dello spettacolo italiano.* The Communist critic Luciano Lucignani is editing a review of theatre under the title *Arena.*

Parker Tyler

ITALIAN FILMS

The vitality of post-war Italian films takes up the great impulse of *Bicycle Thief,* which came in 1949, and amplifies it to the level of a permanent revival. In regard to merit among films, one should be careful before rushing into print. What is good can momentarily seem better than it is because of its automatic contrast with the disheartening omnipresent average. But the good peasant blood of *Two Cents Worth of Hope,* a distinguished *genre* comedy that appeared in 1953, has withstood the test of elapsed time. Now there are two items that define themselves as veritable peaks: *Strange Deception* and *Times Gone By;* also, an efflorescence of Anna Magnani: a revival in herself.

The metaphor of the life-blood is very worthy of the Italian revival, whose first impetus followed the war. "Life-blood" expresses the valual saturation of Curzio Malaparte's *Strange Deception,* which, without previous experience in the medium, the Italian novelist wrote and directed with amazing art, literally contributing his own music to what is a phenomenally "musical" treatment of motion pictures. Sound at the core and pure in flesh, the work in its full finesse can be appreciated only by lengthy analysis or actual experience of it. The hero, returning to his Tuscan village after ten years in a Russian prison camp, is in perfect health; as played by Raf

Vallone, he is indeed the image of peasant dignity and natural nobility: the pure thinking earth that Prometheus fashioned.

Yet, with peace restored, Bruno has come home to kill. The man he wishes to kill is the unknown-to-him betrayer of his younger brother, caught and shot by the Germans for being a Partisan. Thus, Bruno—and this is Malaparte's distinctive insight—returns not as the mortal avenger whom Electra took in her arms, nor as those prized murderers who stalked the Elizabethan and French neo-Classic stages, but as their opposite: a kind of Frankenstein's monster, a dreaded alien. Everybody knows the "Judas"; no one, not even Bruno's own parents, will identify him. The reasons are beautifully unfolded by Malaparte as Bruno wanders over his village. Hidden behind the very air now breathed by the townsfolk is the imminence of that violence which they are striving to believe has been exiled by God's will and the world's. Branded with the sign of the killer, Bruno's spectre sullies the Feast of the Virgin and taints the ritual wine-pressing. This atmosphere, created very remarkably, is all the more eloquent in the medium of photography which reveals the light of day and everything in it so literally and starkly.

All Bruno's human relations—of family, love, and friendship—have become involved in his fatal quest. The traditional Game of the Cross, in which the sexton, carrying a large cross, satirically dares someone to be crucified there, fulfills a symbolic function in the action. It is the dilemma and trap of Orestes, oriented to Christian sacrifice and forgiveness rather than to Classic nemesis and its Eumenidean balance. A saintly friend of Bruno, a kind of *deus ex machina*, arises to work out the climax of his vendetta. The irony is profoundly imagined and poetically executed. Possibly *Strange Deception* is to be considered a morally controversial work but its impact seems powerful enough to provide a catharsis for ideology as well as for pity and terror. Bruno is spared his last, worst crime by a curious dislocation of his avenging thrust. His final tremendous cry against the fate of the innocent, who bear the chief burden of guilt, pierces to the marrow and induces "classical" tears.

The six episodes of *Times Gone By*—with a framing story, a balletic introduction, and a revue-like song number—runs from strict folk comedy to post-Ibsen domestic tragedy. Perhaps the most happily contrived of all "omnibus" films, its grace consists mostly in a forthright grasp of costume-feeling and a perished sense of manners, portrayed, as a rule, with nostalgic satire and a refreshing elegance. Therefore the formula elements and the conventional sentiment are materially toned down. Clinching the high rank of this film in the Italian revival is the final episode, a broad comedy called *The Trial of Phryne*. It is a brilliant instance of revamping a literary legend to re-illustrate modern life and restore natural vigor to a hale "paganism." That the natural vigor here is both sexual and esthetic may be suggested to those who recall that Phryne is that criminal beauty whose conviction before the ancient Athenian court, the Areopagus, was avoided by the inspired wit of her lawyer, who simply tore off her robe before the judges. The sight of her naked physical perfections exonerated her without more ado. Dealing with the town where, a self-confessed poisoner of her mother-in-law but as beautiful as she is simple-minded, this short film is masterly in spirit and execution. The director of *Bicycle Thief*, Vittorio de Sica, is a *tour-de-force* as "Phryne's" lawyer, and Gina Lollobrigida brings as much intuitive rightness as visible loveliness to the role of "Phryne."

Anna Magnani is the only supreme actor-component of the Italian revival. Already seen here in *Open City*, *The Miracle*, and others, she has starred also in *Bellissima* and *Volcano*. She is curiously "right" for film pantomime, and for a screen actress, her range is to be

termed immense. She can *tower* and she can *subside,* and
with infallible timing. Always the true weight is there:
hers both individually and as a sex. Unfortunately, her
vehicles are of uneven merit, internally and by comparison with each other. Her role in *Volcano* oddly recalls
Sadie Thompson, to whose traditional image Miss Magnani's first get-up bears a chilling resemblance. A sort of
universal vulgarity spoils *Volcano,* the melodramatic
tale of a forcibly retired streetwalker's innate nobility.
But *Volcano,* like *Bellissima,* should be seen as a Magnani document. The latter gives the actress a superb
opportunity to do her stuff and as such is the classic "star
vehicle." C. Zavattini's story is ingeniously plausible as
a portrait of the common people while its narrow range
puts too much weight on the theme of a mother's obsession that her tiny daughter win a contest for a movie
contract. The amusing action becomes anticlimactically
tragic when the mother witnesses the impolite merri-
ment caused by her child's screen test, intended to be
serious; then, when the child wins the contest for being
a laugh-getter, the mother declines the realization of her
dream on the grounds that her daughter's success is inconsistent with human dignity. It is a provocative theme,
explored interestingly but superficially. However, considering the way Hollywood would have presented it,
one can do nothing but send up a prayer of thanks for
Italy and Magnani.

THE ARTS IN GERMANY

Joseph Frank

AN IMPENITENT PRUSSIAN

The name of Ernst Juenger is likely to be known to American readers, if it is known at all, as that of the author of *Die Marmorklippen* (On the Marble Cliffs)— a novel published inside Germany in 1939 that was unmistakably directed against the Hitler régime. Before that time, however, Juenger had been perhaps the most influential talent among those who paved the way for an acceptance of Nazism among the German intelligentsia. And, since the end of the war, Juenger has again emerged as the most authoritative voice among the writers of the "inner emigration," i.e., those who claimed to have spiritually emigrated from Hitler's Germany without having done so in fact.

In recent years, Juenger has published two major works which, German critics agree, are among the most important products of their post-war literature. One is a huge diary of Juenger's war experiences and reflections entitled *Strahlungen*. Juenger spent most of the war in Paris, attached to the staff of General Speidel; and his book gives an eerie glimpse into the fantastic, hothouse world of the anti-Nazi Prussian High Command in France—aristocratic, cultured, connoisseurs of French civilization, discussing Rimbaud and La Rochefoucauld in the Crillon and the Ritz while the Gestapo did its bloody work in the cellars off the Place de la Concorde.

Many of Juenger's friends from this period were later implicated in the unsuccessful bomb plot against Hitler; and Juenger's own opposition to Nazism, as *Die Marmorklippen* had already made clear, was rooted in this aristocratic conservatism.

Juenger's other book, *Heliopolis* (the title is the name of a fictitious state), is a massive allegorical novel of the future, his most ambitious creative work up to the present time. Set in the same imaginary Mediterranean landscape as *Die Marmorklippen,* it is written with all the kaleidoscopic brilliance of a writer who has nothing further to learn from the incantatory rhythms and fairy-tale suggestiveness of the German Romantics. The novel is, indeed, composed in the German Romantic tradition —loosely constructed, filled with philosophical disquisition and interpolated fragments, depending for its effects more on the relationship of certain key poetic symbols than on any dramatic narrative.

What there is of a narrative bears a striking resemblance to the secret struggle for power inside Germany after Hitler's accession. Two figures are engaged in this subterranean warfare: the Prokonsul and the Landvogt. The first, an hereditary aristocrat, controls the professional Army; the second, a demagogic upstart, whips up the mob with a gang of unscrupulous criminals. Caught in the center are the "Parsees," a highly civilized Oriental minority on whom the mob wreaks its fury with the Landvogt's instigation and approval.

The chief protagonist is a young officer on the Prokonsul's staff, Lucius de Geer; a scion of the *Burgenland,* the seat of the old nobility, where "everything was still in good order" and where there "was still room for honorable, yes, even for princely existence." Like Ernst Juenger, Lucius keeps a diary of philosophical annotations (all of Juenger's books before *Die Marmorklippen* were either diaries or highly personal essays); and he is an intimate of the small group of painters, poets and

philosophers whom the Prokonsul, like an Italian prince
of the Renaissance, entertains at his court. It is during
a Platonic symposium among this group that the theme
of *Heliopolis* first receives a clear enunciation.

"The Wise Men of all times and places" says Serner,
the philosopher, "are all agreed that Happiness cannot
be obtained through the Door of Desire or in the current of the world." And the writer, Ortner, reads a self-
contained short story—a variation on the Faust theme,
and one of the finest things in the book—about a man
who, after a mysterious eye operation, sees through the
surface of the world to its hidden mechanisms. He ob-
tains unlimited power; but this inhuman knowledge
makes joy impossible and life meaningless. And he
finally begs Dr. Fancy, the Mephistophelian eye special-
ist, to restore him to the degree of blindness befitting
the human condition.

This narrative is clearly intended to symbolize the
spiritual dilemma of man in *Heliopolis*, and to indicate
the direction in which it may be resolved. All parties
are engaged in a pitiless struggle for power, made even
more crucial because science has solved all its problems
(and *Heliopolis*, as a result, occasionally takes on a faint
air of science-fiction). "Mankind had become fully cal-
culable . . . But just as a new light casts new shadows,
so had the extremes of organization produced a new
consciousness of what was mysterious and inviolable."
At the conclusion of the novel, therefore, Lucius de Geer
quits the service of the Prokonsul and flies off on a rocket
ship to the "cosmic residences," convinced that all human concerns can no longer be sacrificed to the struggle
for power. Some day, he believes, mankind will realize
the nihilism of sheer power, and will then recall as its
ruler a quasi-divine figure (The Regent), "who unites
Power and Love."

This tenderness for what is "mysterious and inviolable" in man, and this antipathy to power, strike a new

note in Juenger's work; or rather, make explicit a note only faintly struck in *Die Marmorklippen*. For up to this latter book Juenger had glorified power in all its forms, and had ruthlessly insisted on the suppression of the individual to make way for the type—the interchangeable anyonymity whose life would be totally defined by his specific function in furthering the will-to-power. (The completest statement of this theme was given in a semi-sociological book, *Die Arbeiter,* published in 1932: a work taken, at the time, as the most powerful intellectual apologia for Nazism). Juenger still thinks *Die Arbeiter* contains a valid diagnosis of what is happening to modern man, and he has pictured the completion of the process in *Heliopolis;* but he is no longer able to regard it with the same approval as in the past. Man can no longer surrender to the will-to-power as an end in itself. But what principle does Juenger offer to replace it?

The answer given in *Heliopolis* is both theological and political, and the implications of the second cast a somewhat dubious light on the first. Pater Foelix, a Christian hermit, teaches Lucius a doctrine of suffering, sacrifice and love; and he is primarily responsible for Lucius' realization that power alone is not enough—"greatness cannot exist without goodness, without sympathy, without love." On the theological level, then, Juenger implies that power itself is evil. But Pater Foelix, who tends an apiary, also likes to dabble in political theory; and he holds up the inalterable caste system of the beehive as an image of the ideal state. "The power of love" he tells Lucius, "lives in the beehive completely undifferentiated"; each caste is happy to sacrifice itself for the whole; and this is an exemplar for the human state, "if we see the ideal of the State as the elevation of order to a pure relationship of love." On the political level, not power *per se* but power without "love" is the source of trouble.

Just what this means in practice may be seen from the description of the political situation in *Heliopolis*. The Prokonsul incarnates all the ruling-class virtues, and is quite willing to exercise power justly; but the irresponsible "Demos" refuses to recognize his lawful sovereignty and prefers to follow the siren-song of the Landvogt, who skillfully exploits its basest instincts. The catastrophic rise of the Landvogt, we are told, is directly attributable to the "theoreticians and Utopians . . . who busied themselves with the happiness and future of mankind"; they are the culprits who presumably destroyed the feudal equilibrium of "love." And the restoration of "love" can only come from the voluntary acceptance by the "Demos" of its old feudal bonds (metamorphosed, to be sure, into a transcendental principle of justice).

Juenger's ideal, in other words, is a feudal Paradise which, like the style and structure of his novel, is also in the German Romantic tradition. One thinks of Novalis and his very similar glorification of a poetically colored Middle Ages; and one remembers that this day-dream was invented by the German spirit to exorcise the trauma of the French Revolution. In truth, there is as little room for genuine individual freedom in Juenger's new feudalism as there was in the relentless mechanization of *Die Arbeiter*. Juenger has substituted a terminology of love for that of force; but in both instances the individual is lost in the function, i.e., his caste-status.

Juenger's aristocratic distaste for the "Demos" manifests itself all through the book, not only by specific animadversions but also by the unpleasantly self-conscious condescension with which he depicts all his lower-class characters. And except when he is rhapsodizing over the mythical feudal stability of the *Burgenland*, or celebrating the knightly virtues of the Prokonsul, *Heliopolis* lacks any note of personal passion, any echo of the torments and the sorrow of which we hear so much and feel so little. Juenger writes from a great distance, from the council-chambers of the mighty—from, as it were, the Crillon and the Ritz; not even the Landvogt arouses any indignation, only well-bred contempt. And one cannot help contrasting Juenger in this respect with Dostoevsky —a writer whose name he invokes himself, no doubt because the latter was also a political reactionary and a Christian. Dostoevsky's works, however, are totally penetrated with a humanity that wells up spontaneously from the brotherhood of man in Christ; and, whatever his political opinions, it is impossible not to respect the emotional depth of Dostoevsky's involvement with the insulted and the injured. There is a good deal of talk about Christianity in *Heliopolis,* and Pater Foelix's influence on Lucius is once described as the triumph of Christ over Socrates; but Juenger's Christianity, if such it can be called, has far more in common with the Teutonic Knights than with the New Testament.

In the next-to-last chapter of *Heliopolis,* a character supposedly possessed of supernatural wisdom remarks to Lucius: "We know your situation—it is that of the conservative spirit which tried to use revolutionary means, and failed." The irrelevance of this comment in the context of the book makes it all the more revealing; for Juenger, the impenitent admirer of the Prussian aristocracy, has indeed written their elegy—or at least the elegy of their attempt to use the destructive dynamism of Nazism for their own ends. *Heliopolis,* I think, springs far more from a feeling of political impotence and failure than from any profound emotional transformation on the part of its author. And the best proof, to my mind, is that the book lacks precisely those emotions which, in all the great religions, have always been considered the pre-requisite for any deep-seated spiritual conversion. I am referring, of course, to the emotions of humility and repentance.

Ray B. West, Jr.

THE GERMAN NOVEL AT MID-CENTURY

We were sitting in an apartment in the Russian sector of Vienna. In the rooms above dwelt a Russian general and a Communist official. Present were a poet, a novelist, a publisher, and our hostess and her husband. Our hostess' husband, an attorney, had just returned from six years' imprisonment in Russia. At one point in the conversation, talk turned to the days of German occupation and to the "official litterateurs" sent out by the Nazis to propagate the party line—young men who had recently published novels and verse celebrating the Aryan virtues.

"Where are these novelists and poets now?" I asked. My Austrian friends shrugged.

"Who can say," our host said. "They just disappeared."

"So many have disappeared," the novelist said. "In the 1930s it was the socialists, in the 1940s the Nazis. What can we say of ourselves? From what do we derive?"

"In a way, it's remarkable to have six people in one room who can talk about such things," the poet said. "In Vienna—in Germany—there are too many memories."

About the same time Alfred Andersch, a member of Werner Richter's *Gruppe 47*, was writing about German authors in the Frankfurter *Hefte*. "Maybe we have lost ten years," he said. "In that case it is just our destiny that we have lost them. In art one cannot make up for what has been missed." He continued, "It is impossible to express afterwards in a creative work the situation of foreign writers during the years 1933 to 1945. The poems Eliot wrote in those years," he said, "cannot be relived by us. In our art there will be expressed just this: that we read them too late."

In 1948 *Athena* of Berlin sent its readers a questionnaire, asking what authors best represented Germany. Hermann Hesse led with sixteen percent of the votes. Following were Thomas Mann, Melchior Vischer, and Ernst Wiechert with fourteen percent. Among the remainder, in approximately the order listed, were Jochem Thiem, Werner Bergengruen, Hans Carossa, Rudolf Alexander, Carl Zuckmeyer, Bertolt Brecht, Erich Kaestner, Alfred Doeblin, Ernst Juenger, Heinrich Mann, Frank Thiess, and Elizabeth Langgässer.

This list represents a generation that has almost passed from the contemporary scene. The best works of these authors antedate Hitler. At least two of them who might have served as a bridge between pre-Nazi Germany and the present have died: Ernst Wiechert and Elizabeth Langgässer.

It would be interesting to see the results of a similar questionnaire today, but it is doubtful that there would, even yet, be many young novelists on it. For a foreigner to say who the few might be would be presumptive and extremely risky. One must live longer than a year or two in a literary atmosphere before he can trust himself not to fall for fads or the promotion of cliques and literary reviews. It is not only that the proper emphasis will escape him; he is likely to confuse novelty with quality —and there is always novelty in a foreign literature. One must, however, risk certain generalizations, and mine would be as follows:

At first Franz Kafka's expression of the modern world

as chaotic and accidental seemed to appeal to a generation which had experienced the terror and destruction of war. The result was such novels as Hermann Kosack's *The City Beyond the River* and Ernst Kreuder's *Those Who Cannot Be Found*. But the Kafka vogue was waning elsewhere by the time the young Germans rediscovered him. Kafka represents the end of an era, not the beginning. Young novelists still felt the need for explanation, but not as an end in itself. Their chief problem, especially in Germany, was reconstruction; and so they sought desperately for solutions.

Naturally, a generation who had known nothing but war had but a single subject. Kurt Ihlenfeld's *Winter Thunder* which won a Berlin prize, portrayed the last days before the fall of Breslau. George Glaser's *Secret and Power* told the story of a young German Communist who fled to France before the Nazis and became a French soldier and citizen. Bruno Werner's *The Slaveship* recounted events from the burning of the Reichstag to the fall of Berlin. Albert Goes's *Unquiet Night* had as protagonist a chaplain experiencing the atrocities of war. Hans Richter's *The Vanquished* dealt with the defeat in Italy. Fritz Habeck's *The Boat Comes After Midnight* examined the disillusion of a German soldier in occupied France.

Novelists of a somewhat older, middle generation, such as Juenger, Thiess, Wiechert, and Langgässer, attempted to discover what had happened to their country. Novelists of this youngest generation, who had known less of the concentration camps than they did of the Hitler-Jugend and the army (even though most of them were classified as "politically unreliable"), examined themselves. When they looked beyond themselves, they did not so much return to the great figures of their own country, as they turned to France (and traditional Catholicism) or to America (and the primitive energy of

Hemingway, Dos Passos, and Steinbeck). The only fresh note—and for an American it can often become an exciting one—exists in a heightened sense of Europe's desperate need for moral and political reform.

After the first war the arts in Germany became experimental. When I first visited Germany in 1927 the younger literary generation was the *avant-garde*. Expressionism had become Bauhaus; Bauhaus had become surrealism. The tone since the second war has been very different. The first postwar period was one of rebellion against standards of the Hohenzollern-Hapsburg eras, anti-political (except for the Communists) and unconventional. In the second postwar period there has come a heightened respect for convention and a recognition of Europe's plight between America and Russia.

Take, for instance, two novels, Otto Rombach's *Gordean and the Riches of Life* and Fritz Habeck's *The Dance of the Seven Devils*. Both utilize historical settings to project problems of contemporary Europe, Rombach's work being concerned with the wars with the Huguenots, Habeck's with the Hundred Years War. Both novels consider the rights and obligations of the individual caught between powerful impersonal forces. As a reflection of the problems facing any European, Habeck's work is particularly effective. Technically, its picaresque and romantic surface may not represent a final solution to the problem of monotony in much of the pseudo-realistic war fiction, but it is a method which combines the traditional and the novel. It represents at least one means of expressing aesthetic and political awareness, qualities which must be central in any significant work dealing with contemporary Europe.

Much could be—and has been—written about the political attitudes of present-day Germany, but perhaps the most hopeful single thing to be noted, in respect to young German writers, is the absence of a strong, traditional nationalism. The young German novelist tends to think of himself as a European as much as a German; although, to be sure, it is often the attitude of the prodigal son who has returned only recently to the bosom of an upset family.

Joseph Frank

THE "DOUBLE LIFE" OF GOTTFRIED BENN

One of the most striking phenomena of German post-war literature is the sudden rise to prominence of Gottfried Benn. By no means a new or undiscovered writer, Benn published his first book—a volume of brutal, Expressionist poems called *Morgue*—in 1912, and he has been known ever since, to a small circle of readers, as a mordant satirist who can rise on occasion to heights of dissonant lyricism. At present, he is considered the greatest German poet since Rilke; but, curiously enough, it is not his poetry that has catapulted him into notoriety.

Since the end of the war, Benn has published a series of prose works of indistinct genre, somewhere between the dialogue, the novel and the personal essay. All are written in a raucous, highly individual style, filled with straight-from-the-shoulder slang and a cynical, hard-bitten eloquence. It is these works which have brought Benn to the attention of a wider audience, and evidently have struck an emotional chord that has a profound resonance in the German reading public. Among these works Benn has included a species of spiritual autobiography, published in 1950 under the title *Doppelleben* (*Double Life*). And this book reveals a good deal, not only about Benn himself, but about the state of mind that has found in Benn's recent publications an echo of its own obsessions.

The first part of the book, a series of fragments called *Lebensweg eines Intellektualisten* (*Autobiography of an Intellectual*), was written in 1934 under the impact of Hitler's accession to power. Despite the title, these fragments contain very little trace of any connected narrative structure; but they all focus on the spiritual dilemma of Benn and his literary generation. What was this dilemma? Quite simply, the fate of having come to maturity in a cultural climate created by Nietzsche—an atmosphere totally haunted by the opposition between Nature and Spirit (*Leben* and *Geist*). Nietzsche had undermined all principles of value, both religious and metaphysical, and no creation of Spirit remained viable to order the chaos of life. Or rather, only one such principle remained: Art. Art, Nietzsche had written, was "the final metaphysical activity within European nihilism"; and Benn's generation, the generation of Stefan George and Thomas Mann, had dedicated itself to this activity with selfless devotion.

Benn's fragments are a violent vindication of this metaphysical aestheticism—contemptuously called *Intellektualismus* by its opponents—as a valid and inevitable expression of the crisis of modern culture. He refers with savage scorn to the German bourgeois taste for the sentimental and the idyllic, for "forget-me-nots and apple-cookies"; and these thrusts may be taken as a riposte against the Nazi charge of *Kulturbolschevismus*. Regretfully, Benn records that "the new youth, who enter the scene under Hitler's star," will not understand the ideals of his generation; they are separated from their elders by the width of the abyss between Art and Might. But, in saying farewell to his past, Benn looks to the future with hope rather than despair.

For, it seems, another principle has been found to give Form and Order to the chaos of Life: the principle of Race. "There are two Laws that today, in Europe," Benn wrote in 1934, "have raised their heads in defiance of Life: Race and Art." Both are in the service of the same cause, "the maintenance of Order, the conquest of Form against the European degeneration." And though Benn, in a powerful concluding tirade, again identifies himself with "the formula of Art," it is clear that the Hitler-Jugend, in their own way, are sacrificing at the same exalted altar of the Spirit.

In 1950, Benn collected a second group of fragments published under the title that gives the book its name. These contain some extremely vivid descriptions of life in a German Army barracks while the Third Reich was crumbling into ruins. They also include a running torrent of invective against the "toy-soldier clowns and toilet heroes" who led to their doom "a mystical totality of fools, a pre-logical collectivity of the weak-minded— something very Germanic, no doubt, and only comprehensible from this ethnological point of view." Perhaps only the Nazis themselves have managed to equal the ingenious abuse that Benn heaps on their deluded followers; and he admits that his earlier complaisance for Nazism was a tragic error. Yet he continues to maintain (and this, too, is comprehensible only from an ethnological point of view) that his mistake, and presumably the mistake of the German people, was inevitable and even admirable.

In a fragment called "Shadows of the Past," Benn comments on his famous exchange of letters with Klaus Mann in 1933—an exchange published at the time as Benn's "Answer to the Literary Emigrés." The younger Mann, an ardent admirer of Benn's work, could not believe that the intransigent, *avant-garde* Expressionist would rally to the Nazi cause. Benn's slashing reply, however, filled with venomous insinuations, left no doubt that he upheld the will of the *Herrenvolk*. Certain passages of this reply, Benn admits, he would no longer write today, or at least not in so "romantic" a tone of "unpleasant exaltation"; but he reprints a long section whose reasoning he still supports.

Stripped of its bedazzling rhetoric, Benn's argument reduces itself to the contention that History, indeed social action of any kind, "proceeds not democratically but through Might"; and this places the intellectual in an insoluble quandary. "Killing animals is Might. Executing criminals is Might. Every traffic-cop is Might. Every Organization is Might." How is the poor intellectual to choose between conflicting Mights? Certainly not, Benn answers, by any process of ratiocination. "When things are mulled over too long, they fall into the void. Just so with this matter of Might and Spirit, Order and Chaos, State and Freedom. One must hang on to something, otherwise one also tumbles."

And so, presumably, one joins the "mystical totality of fools," one follows the "toy-soldier clowns and toilet-heroes" with a delicious shudder of abandonment only describable by that untranslatable German word *Schicksalsrausch* (intoxication with destiny). And one preens oneself, as Benn does, with the affirmation that "naturally, this conception of History is not that of the Enlightenment nor humanistic but metaphysical, and my conception of Man even more so."

Klaus Mann and the other literary emigrés, Benn now concedes, may have correctly diagnosed the diabolic evil of Nazism; they may have been more far-sighted than those who espoused the régime; but there are more important things than such superficial acumen. "Always to know everything, always to be right, that alone is not greatness. To err, and nonetheless to continue to believe in one's inner voice:—that is Man. And his glory begins beyond defeat or victory. The glory, namely, of having assumed his lot, whatever *moira*—one can, naturally, also say chance and occasion—have assigned him." Here, then, we have man's true glory; and every German who,

like Gottfried Benn, gladly accepted the dictates of Hit-
lerian *moira* has a rightful claim to his modicum.

Today, Gottfried Benn has become the apostle of
what he calls *Doppelleben*—"a conscious splitting up of
personality." In another of his recent works, a dialogue
called *Drei alte Maenner* (*Three Old Men*), he writes:
"We lived somewhat differently than what we were, we
wrote differently than we thought, we thought differently than we anticipated, and what remains is different from what we once had." This is the "situation—
1950" as Benn sees it, an absolute split between life and
spirit, between action and thought; and his only message
is to live this disruption to the hilt.

In the symbolic protagonist of his short novel, *Der
Ptolemaer*, Benn has pictured this schizophrenic salva-
tion. The *Ptolemaer* works in a beauty-parlor, but, while
occupied with the most mundane tasks, bemuses his
Spirit with intoxicatingly exotic hallucinations. "I work
over the ladies," Benn has his mouthpiece report, "but
inside me is a wine-harvest—and I feel extraordinarily
well as a result, in any case much better than in earlier
periods of my life when I did not possess this inner technique; when, as ordinarily occurs in Life, I suffered."

In the world of Benn's *Ptolemaer*, nobody is responsible for what occurs in the realm of praxis because Life
is a meaningless chaos. The self-induced hallucinations
of the spirit are, quite literally, the only reality; and to
cultivate these is the only morality. "Make no fuss about
going along with persuasions, world-viewers and syn-
theses to all points of the compass" Benn advises, "if jobs
and pocket-books require it; but keep your head free,
there must always be some empty space for the images
. . . this is his [the *Ptolemaer's*] morality." It is also the
morality of Benn's earlier metaphysical aestheticism,
monstrously adapted for the masses into the theory of
Doppelleben.

After this, it is of little use for Benn to assure us that

personally he has never acted out of opportunism. Benn himself, it is true, received nothing from the Nazis in exchange for his support except harassment both as a writer and as a practicing physician. He never belonged to the Nazi Party, and in 1935, to escape further difficulty, he joined the German Army and placed himself under the protection of powerful friends on the General Staff. It was at this time that he coined his famous phrase, which, as he reports, made the rounds of the High Command until 1945: "The Army is the aristocratic form of emigration."

But it is only the final inconsistency in this incredibly muddled book that a ferociously honest man should crown his life's work with an apologia for opportunism as a metaphysic. For what is *Doppelleben* if not a gigantic philosophy of opportunism? And one can well understand its appeal to a people desperately trying to convince themselves that, whatever the horrible consequences of their actions, the secret shrine of their Spirit had remained unsullied. No doubt the "inner technique" of *Doppelleben* has been of invaluable aid in this respect. Like the *Ptolemaer*, Benn's admirers no longer "suffer" from the complete disparity between their actions and their ideals.

German critics have praised these late works of Gottfried Benn as the most profound expression in German literature of the spiritual catastrophe of modern man. To a foreign reader, they suggest, far more plausibly, the spiritual catastrophe of the modern German.

William Becker

THE POSITION OF BERTOLT BRECHT

By far the most remarkable individual working today in the German theatre—one might well say, in the theatre anywhere—is Bertolt Brecht. He is the only living playwright whom one can justifiably rank among the master spirits of modern dramaturgy: Ibsen, Strindberg, Tchekov, Shaw, Pirandello, and Lorca. He is, in addition, a lyric poet of extraordinary gifts, and, as the French say, an *homme de théâtre* in the fullest sense. I suspect, in fact, that posterity will attach a much greater importance to the general theatrical aesthetic which he has formulated in his theoretical writings, and demonstrated in his stage work of the past few years, than to his plays as such. Today, a young playwright, seeking a way to repossess the great classical tradition of comedy—from Aristophanes to Ben Jonson on the one hand and the *Commedia dell'arte* on the other—could scarcely be better served than by submitting himself to the influence of Brecht's ideas. That few young playwrights have actually done so is one of the less urgent, but no less real, misfortunes of the Cold War. For Brecht has worked since returning to Germany from exile in America, under the Communist regime in East Berlin.

This has made the most ordinary information about him and his work very difficult to come by. In the ugly atmosphere of Berlin, where all standards except polit-

ical ones have largely disappeared, cultural affairs have
been absorbed into the general ebb and flow of political
hostility, and cultural reportage thereby reduced to a
minor division of the propaganda facilities. I was told
that neither Werner Krauss nor Berthold Viertel (who
has since died) would be well received in Berlin—Krauss
because of his former Nazi connections, Viertel because
of his left-wing background. Yet Krauss was the leading
actor under Viertel at the Burgtheater in Vienna—and
the Burgtheater is one of the best theatres in Europe. My
informant proudly spoke of Berlin's fine political awareness. The same sort of awareness makes it likely that
one will hear about Brecht either that he has been sup-
pressed by the Party, and is about to be purged, or else
that he has become a Party hack like the poet Johannes
R. Becher, and is now beneath consideration. Both views
were offered to me in Berlin; neither bore much relation
to the truth. Some of what one hears is, of course, wish-
ful thinking; more of it is malicious gossip concocted by
those caterpillar opportunists of cultural journalism
whom the general situation tends to attract. Almost
none of it tells us anything significant about how Brecht
has really fared under the East German regime.

One fact is frequently cited to exemplify Brecht's
supposed deterioration—that he has not written a new
play since his return. Actually the point—which is not
even true: Brecht has written a play about the 1871 Paris
insurrection called *The Days of the Commune* which,
reputedly, the Party thought too defeatist to be staged
—is quite irrelevant.

When Brecht left America, he had in hand at least half
a dozen plays, written in exile, which he had never been
able to stage. Among them were *Mother Courage, Pun-
tila, The Caucasian Chalk Circle, The Good Woman of
Sezuan,* and *Galileo.* By the time he arrived in Berlin
(there was an interim period in Switzerland), he also had
on paper the fundamental principles of his new anti-

Aristotelian theory of *theatrical alienation,* and they were largely untried in practice. What was needed was not more writing and thought, but some practical testing of these principles, and an opportunity to construct a permanent working theatre around them. These aims have been substantially fulfilled: Brecht's Berliner Ensemble is one of the three or four really formidable achievements of the post-war European theatre. (Anyone who wants to know how formidable has only to consult the huge volume of photographs and notes on all phases of theatrical art, published in Dresden, 1952, under the title *Theaterarbeit: 6 Aufführungen des Berliner Ensembles.*) It should also be mentioned that Brecht's literary talents have by no means been idle: almost every Berliner Ensemble production has involved textual revisions, or, not uncommonly, full Brechtian adaptation.

But what about Brecht and the regime? It is a complex and difficult question, and not one about which even the most scrupulous journalist can speak with much confidence. Yet some facts became apparent to me when I visited the Berliner Ensemble during a brief stay in Berlin immediately prior to the June riots of 1953, and it may be helpful to set them down for the record.

There can be no denying that, from an economic point of view, the authorities have treated Brecht superbly. There are now nearly sixty actors at his disposal in the Berliner Ensemble, all paid by the State at unusually handsome rates by current Berlin standards. Every actor has two months vacation a year with pay. Brecht himself lives in a fine suburban house on the Weissensee, and also keeps a country place within a few hours of Berlin. Furthermore, Brecht's frequent travels in Western Europe indicate that he has had liberal access to Western currencies: it has even been rumored that he received a substantial part of his State income in dollars.

The working facilities of the group are equally generous. Directly across a large plaza from the Deutsches Theater, a bombed-out ruin has been converted with State money into the artistic headquarters of the Ensemble. Here are housed a sizable library, several spacious work areas, and a main rehearsal studio which is actually a small auditorium, excellently equipped, under the supervision of Helene Weigel (the company's leading actress and Brecht's wife), with basic stage lighting, functional drapes, directors' and prompters' desks, and several hundred seats—all of the best modern design. I had never seen similar rehearsal facilities in any professional theatre; and I was reminded, more than anything else, of the lavish conditions in some American university drama departments. A few blocks away are the Ensemble's well-appointed and fully staffed business offices, looking much like the normal producer's offices in New York.

The chief difficulty up to the present time has been that the Berliner Ensemble has not had a theatre of its own. It has shared the Deutsches Theater with that theatre's resident company, and this has meant limited runs for not more than three or four productions a year. Consequently, I was told, the actors have at times grown lazy from enforced idleness, and few of them could be got to attend regularly the special classes in fencing and dancing which were offered to occupy them. The situation was presumably remedied, and Brecht's program made more ambitious, when the Ensemble took over in January of 1954 the Theater-am-Schiffbauerdamm, where Brecht started with *The Three Penny Opera* in the mid-twenties.

On the whole, I found a unique spirit in the Berliner Ensemble people. For one thing, they were young. For another, they inclined to be people of rather more general culture than one is accustomed to find in the theatre: many of them spoke several languages and most seemed to be intellectually involved in their work. They seemed to be largely without the usual affectations and crude vanities. Nor did I find any evident political fervor: I was told that politics plays little or no part in the normal course of the theatre work; and in general, I felt that Brecht's people spoke in a more honest and relaxed way about politics than most of the people I talked to in the West. About a quarter of the actors actually live in the West, and have continued to do so even while pressure was brought by the Eastern authorities to persuade them to move. It was said of Brecht himself that he keeps his politics to himself, insists that the focus of theatre work should be theatre, and is exceedingly deferential to those members of the company whom he knows not to share his own views.

Thus the advantages which Brecht derives from his commitment to the East are quite plain: the kind of operation most vital to this stage in his career has been made possible. But it would be foolish to pretend that he has not paid a price, even a heavy one. He has been under more or less constant attack by the Party critics recently, and two productions—*Urfaust* and his own opera, *The Trial of Lucullus,* with music by Paul Dessau—had to be withdrawn presumably not to be produced again. Perhaps even more important have been certain political quarrels at the top levels of the Berliner Ensemble which resulted in the loss of some of Brecht's best people to the West. Erich Engel, his chief director, has gone; Caspar Neher and Teo Otto, two Western designers of real genius who collaborated on some of the Ensemble's most outstanding productions, no longer work in the East; the principal actor in *Der Hofmeister* went back to Switzerland, and the production had to be withdrawn from the repertory for lack of a replacement; Therese Giehse and Leonard Steckel, both brilliant performers who had starring roles in the repertory, are at work solely in the West. This has left Brecht strapped for performers of star-quality, especially male ones—a limitation that operates with special severity against his own plays, inasmuch as one of Brecht's seldom-noted but most distinctive qualities as a playwright has been his faculty for creating great individual roles in the classical tradition. His *Galileo* (in which Charles Laughton starred here) remains unproduced in Germany for want of an actor of sufficient stature; in the West, Brecht might have had Fritz Kortner.

Nor can Brecht's work claim much of a following in the East. It has, on the whole, been too highbrow for the ordinary public, and too "formalistic" for the Party intellectuals. The Berliner Ensemble stands rather apart from the rest of East Berlin's theatre. I am told that Brecht is inclined to protest the blank artlessness of that "Socialist-Realist" *kitsch* which the Party critics promote (though he uses a similar vocabulary in talking about his own work), and it is perhaps significant that, while he ordinarily directs or oversees every Ensemble production, and notes the fact publicly in the program, he remained entirely aloof from the one play of this kind which the Ensemble has performed—a work about Soviet electrification projects called *The Chimes of the Kremlin* by an important Russian Stalin-Prize winner, N. F. Pogodin. Especially since the June riots, Brecht has reputedly stepped up his attacks on the *Kunstkommission* which controls artistic affairs in the East and establishes the Party line; but his larger point—that Brechtian Epic theatre is actually more appropriate to a Socialist society than is Soviet-type Socialist Realism—seems to have made little headway either with the authorities or with other playwrights and directors.

It seems likely, in fact, that Brecht might have commanded a larger following in the Western zones (which are pretty much without any vital forces in their postwar theatre) and perhaps wielded a greater influence; for his political position, as rendered through his plays and theory, has not fundamentally altered since the

days when *The Three Penny Opera* was the greatest
popular success in modern German theatre history. Probably Brecht had this in mind when after the war he
cagily chose to become, not an East German, but an
Austrian, citizen—a status which permitted him to travel
and produce his plays in the Western zones, and thus to
"ignore" (as he presumably intended) the division of
Germany. In the West he would unquestionably have
been intellectually freer, but he might also—in a country where most theatre is State supported and controlled
—have found it economically impossible to work. One
must remember that it was the American authorities
who put obstacles in the way of his settling in Munich
in 1948, and more or less forced his acceptance of the
original East German offer. But for us, the important
point which usually is missed in all the talk about
Brecht's "position," is that one cannot demonstrate any
necessary connection between Brecht's political position
and his aesthetic one, that Brecht is not, by any sensible
definition of the term, a "Communist playwright." That
one may deplore his political commitment, and still
profitably learn what he has to teach about theatre,
seems an obvious thing to say. Yet since no one apparently is learning, and so many are inclined to deplore, it
may also be necessary to say it.

Parker Tyler

THE GERMAN FILM

When Cocteau made his version of the story of Tristan
and Isolde, *The Eternal Return,* it did not occur to him
that the myth was other than literary; i.e., that the "return" could be more than something in the imagination
of an artist whose reconstitution of the Celtic myth was
intrinsically a way of flattering modern society. Hence,
The Eternal Return held all kinds of exotic and symbolic touches and fundamentally was parallel to *Hamlet*
in modern and *Love's Labour's Lost* in Edwardian dress.
This was because Cocteau was uninterested in the Wagnerian will-to-power that makes the contemporary German film, *Marriage in the Shadows,* a boomerang on the
aesthetics of Hitlerism.

Modern emphasis on psychology puts the love-death
tradition in the light of a kind of fantasy emanating
from virtually pathological states of love. It is a sort of
will-to-eroticism without objective necessity. However
authentic poetically and instinctively, this ignores the
importance of the circumstantial factor of external motivation and objective events. After all, the Oedipus-com-
plex is an abstraction from a plot of human actions.
Wagner derived a *music* of emotion from the plot of the
love-death, a music that in a sense is misleading because
it is the music of a power to *act* under whatever circumstances. The lover is a "great actor" for whom love remains the greatest action.

A German-made equivalent of *The Eternal Return,* but dealing with the Romeo-and-Juliet pattern, involved actors who play the Shakespearian tragedy. *Marriage in the Shadows* opens with two actors playing a love-death in a costume play in Berlin. The time is just before Hitler's triumph. The actress is a Jew and after the persecution begins, the actor marries her when she is forced apart from her fiancé because the latter becomes a Nazi official. The actor's proposal of marriage is technically precipitated by the sentiment of chivalry since a mixed marriage theoretically will protect the actress from persecution so long as she remains in retirement. Later, there are moments of stress when the husband accuses his wife of having submitted to a "marriage of convenience." But the time finally comes when, in optimistic mood, she at last appears in public with her husband, now a famous movie star, at one of his premières. The Secretary of State, introduced to her, learns she is a Jew, and personally affronted by the contact, starts deportation proceedings against her. The couple then, just as they seem to have out-weathered the long terror and to be truly in love, are compelled to commit suicide to preserve their union.

Not a memorable film artistically, *Marriage in the Shadows* handles its final sequence with an impressive finesse. Does part of this finesse come from consciousness of the large dramatic pattern? Eroticism, in any case, is not the factor emphasized. This film is far from being the free-floating, "psychological-aesthetic" fantasy that *The Eternal Return* is. It is securely within actual contemporary society and thus supplies a dramatic control and plausibility less mechanical than is apparent in the mythically isolated tradition of the love-death for which Wagner's opera, willy-nilly, is largely responsible and which preserves the personal ritual at the expense of the social context.

The vendetta animating *Marriage in the Shadows* is

the vendetta not of *Romeo and Juliet,* but of *The Merchant of Venice,* and raised to the political level, where in this case it is tragic. In Shakespeare's tragedy, the political force is apparently in favor of the lovers, enjoining peace between their houses. Such it is—also cumbrous and too late—in the *Orestes* trilogy. But as *Romeo and Juliet* is once removed from the internal family feud of *Orestes* to the clan feud, so *Marriage in the Shadows* is once removed from the clan feud of *Romeo and Juliet* to the "race" feud. But the basic economic motif remains a constant and here is thrust to the foreground. Thrones and palaces are as much "commodities" throughout the ages as are daughters, husbands, and lovers; so are professions, and at the climax of the film, the two actors have both been cast out of theirs. Incest is a strictly internal attack on the family, though it may of course be influenced by external factors such as Hitlerism, which was partly an external attack on all phases of family economy, spiritual and material.

The irony of the film is also constant and especially, paradoxically "poetic." For the mythical, sublimative blessing of the Wagnerian will-to-eroticism, which is the specific act of the love-death, was made available to Germans exactly by Hitler's persecution of German Jews— that is, available to such mixed marriages as that of the Jewish actress and the "Aryan" actor in *Marriage in the Shadows* (purported, by the way, to be founded on a factual case). The ancient Celtic sin of love at last became Jewishly motivated in its German transposition. Hitler thus was an unconscious director, rather than a conscious participant, of the actual counterpart of the love-death whose form he admired on the operatic stage. Which was inevitable, because he had no true appreciation of the erotic department of the will-to-power.

THE ARTS IN ENGLAND

Elizabeth Bowen

ENGLISH FICTION AT MID-CENTURY

In general, something is expected of, or at, the turn of a century. A term of time by being demarcated acquires character, which, as such, makes itself evident as it matures. So a century halfway along its course may be considered due to declare maturity, to have reached culmination-point, to make seen the fruition of its inherent ideas. The twentieth century's development, however, has been in some directions so violently forced, in others so notably arrested as to seem hardly to be a development at all, or at least to be difficult to recognize if it is one. In European countries, certainly, life and art are still seeking their footing in their actual time—both have the stigmata of an over-long drawn-out adolescence.

The mid-century call for an exhibition may therefore be said to have taken us by surprise, and found us unready, in disarray. As to art, it is *not* that there is nothing to show; the difficulty is rather in presentation—arrangement, classification and rating order. Individually, no potential exhibit is not expressive: now, however, is each so to be placed as to bring out its relationship with the others? For the warrant for and point of an exhibition must be its overall significance and expressiveness. In this case, one is tempted to ask, of what?

In England—if one may press the display analogy further—there would be particular difficulty in arranging the fiction stall. The novel, onward from 1914, has in different ways reflected the sense of flux. The cracking and splintering of the social mould during and after the first World War accounted for a shift, as to the subject, from outer to inner—from man as a public being, in public play, to man as a seat of isolated and in the main suffering private sensibility. For the greater part of the inter-war years, subjectivity hazed over the English novel; there was disposition to follow the stream of consciousness "from caverns measureless to man down to a sunless sea." With this went, it may now be felt, a misuse or perversion of some influences—the overheated for-or-against reaction to D. H. Lawrence, the attempted segregation of Henry James and Proust from their *beau monde*, of Tolstoi, Tchekov and Turgeniev from their thriving social-sensuous universe, of Thomas Hardy from his Wessex exuberance.

The intellectually respectable English novel for some time concentrated upon, insisted upon the victim-hero —whether at school, in love or at large in the jungle which by overgrowing the ruins of fixed society succeeded to what that used to be. There was almost a convention of disillusionment. The forte of the novelist was analysis. The alternative to the analytical was the caustic —the iconoclastic novel of ideas: for this, the still young Aldous Huxley gave the prototype.

The English inter-war novel, it seems now, was somewhat "out" in its concept of what makes tragedy. It did not finally diagnose the modern uneasiness—dislocation. Dorothy Richardson (still owed full recognition) and Virginia Woolf did best, in their stress on the interplay between consciousness and the exterior world; but these two delicate novelists of the senses cannot be called, in their last implication, tragic. The salutary value of the exterior, the comfortable sanity of the concrete came to be realised only when the approach of the second World

War forced one to envisage wholesale destruction. The obliteration of man's surroundings, streets and houses, tables and chairs sent up, for him, their psychological worth. Up to now, consciousness had been a sheltered product: its interest *as* consciousness diminished now that, at any moment, the physical shelter could be gone.

The second World War halted already-working novelists, and for obvious reasons produced few new ones. Few reputations, however, actually foundered (as had happened between 1914 and 1918). Graham Greene, for instance, and Evelyn Waugh, having begun to be prominent during the thirties, emerged from the war years to become still more so. It is they who have headed the novel's trend towards what might be called moral drama. Independent participants in this move have been Joyce Cary and, in his very different way, L. P. Hartley: both of these were writing before the war, but it would seem that the ensuing decade has given them special focus. Drama involves plot, action; on whatever plane, in whatever sphere—into the present picture, therefore, comes the intellectually-written adventure story, of which Hammond Innes is one exponent. P. H. Newby —like, again, Joyce Cary—is a dramatiser of character; both write about extroverts, domestic or social buccaneers. And one-man character-drama was epitomised in V. S. Pritchett's *Mr. Beluncle*—upon which followed the almost simultaneously written *Mr. Nicholas* of Thomas Hinde.

Those two novels, in each the father viewed by the son, link up with yet another development: family drama—as, indeed, does the L. P. Hartley *Eustace and Hilda* trilogy. This field, the English seldom desert for long. In the I. Compton Burnett masterpieces, the dialogue keeps shifting veil after veil from obsessions or passions bred by the blood-tie. But the main run of family novels now show a blend of pleasure in idiosyncrasy with a far more adverse regard for the institution

—the Rosamond Lehmann and Elizabeth Taylor novels exemplify this. Indeed, the attitude to institutions *as* institutions is more clement than it was, say, twenty-five years ago. A sort of aesthetic neo-conservatism may be found to have set in.

That, maybe, is helping to reinstate the social drama novel, which, having suffered eclipse in the twenties, began to make its way back, thanks to Evelyn Waugh, under the guise of burlesque or satire. A pre-1939 sequence of Anthony Powell novels made merry at the expense of coteries: this admirable writer's return, after twelve years' silence, has lately given us the more mellow, retrospective *A Question of Upbringing* and *A Buyer's Market*. Society, as it now provides material, might be described as the pattern formed by any frequentation of persons by one another through affinity or in pursuit of pleasure—dance, cocktail or week-end party, but equally the gathering in the pub or attendance at dog racing come under this. Henry Greene, outstanding social novelist and, like I. Compton Burnett, dialogue-expert, illustrates this necessary versatility: his *mise en scène* varies from the Mayfair drawing-room to the castle servants' hall, from the girls' school to the fire station. William Sansom has moved from firemen stories and Kafka allegory to the study of the upper or lower suburban rock pool. Nigel Balchin, master of hard-built plot, personalities the office and the laboratory.

Jocelyn Brooke is to be watched as a roving talent with, as yet, no special territory—he has, if anything, a semi-hostile addiction to type, as shown by his *Passing of a Hero*. Rex Warner continues to combine tautness with poetic distinction. Philip Toynbee is, of the younger group, probably the most interesting to his fellow-novelists: his *A Garden by the Sea* has been a controversial high point. Thomas Hinde and Emma Smith, who impacted with *The Far Cry*, seem so far to have no serious rivals among their young contemporaries.

At the moment, it is the political novel which is in eclipse. The ideological novel also is infrequent. As a general verdict, it might be fair to say that English fiction at present is at its most English: as an export, its value should rightly reside in that. A good deal may be felt to be germinating during this phase of apparent self-regard. What will have come of this, say, in ten years' time? Ideally, the exhibition should not open before then.

Kathleen Raine

ENGLISH POETRY AT MID-CENTURY

Perhaps in retrospect the early nineteen-fifties will be
seen to have an importance in the history of English
poetry that is at present not apparent. Writing as one
of the poets involved in this time I would say that never
has the sense of the overwhelming power of the forces
of evil flooding the world and sweeping away the good
(I mean in our own society, not at the other side of the
planet) been more heavy to bear and hard to overcome.
It is small wonder that many poets are silent—the wonder
is that any can write at all. Yet there are in all things
periods of growth and periods of decline, and a poetry
proper to the autumn of Magnus Annus as to its spring.
English poetry at present is passing through a period
comparable perhaps to the late seventeenth century,
when Vaughan, Herbert and Traherne withdrawn each
into his own rural solitude, sheltered a living quintes-
sence.

Whatever of value is being written at the present
time, it is not being written in London, where the
shadow falls most heavily. David Gascoyne, a visionary
poet highly sensitive to the spiritual atmosphere of the
world, is silent; as is Stephen Spender, who gave expression to the moral conscience of his generation in the
thirties. It is observable that poets who can tend to

move away from London. It is a centrifugal period: Herbert Read is living in Yorkshire, Edwin Muir in Scotland, Vernon Watkins and (as did Dylan Thomas) in Wales, Robert Graves in Spain, Roy Campbell in Portugal, George Barker in a country cottage. It is true that the young still come to London to seek their fortune: but poetry written "to be sold and sold quickly" to the BBC and elsewhere tends to degenerate into "features," nor is the competitive scramble calculated to ensure the survival of the wise, the sensitive, or the deeply feeling.

Two poets—Louis MacNeice and W. R. Rodgers—have made a serious attempt to make broadcasting a medium for their poetry. Someone had to make the attempt: and Louis MacNeice is certainly the best writer (with the possible exception of the late Dylan Thomas) of verse for broadcasting—*Nine Burnt Offerings* are longish poems, written to be spoken "on the air." Louis MacNeice is a classical scholar, an admirable translator, and is incapable of vulgarity in the use of words. His poems are pleasing to the ear, always humane and never silly: they are popular poetry of a certain kind at its best. Yet, to write public poetry that touches upon greatness demands something more than the throwing open of one's private world to forty million listeners.

With the best will in the world this kind of public-private relationship is tinged with unreality even when (as with MacNeice) it stops short of commercialism. A great sense of national glory gives a kind of validity to the poetry of Kipling or Mayakovsky, as to Churchill's speeches; or poets like Burns or Lorca, immersed in the life of a people, may be the mouthpiece of a race. In any case we should write for those we love and respect. Better for a poet to write for the eye of Ezra Pound alone than to make the public his critic. There is a lowering of standard in Louis MacNeice's latest work, as compared with his best poems, a verbal diffuseness, and a diffuseness of feeling also. The poems that sounded well "on the air" do not improve on rereading.

W. R. Rodgers' *Europa and the Bull,* a poem almost devoid of meaning, made a great impression when broadcast, because of the sound of the words, an effect almost purely auditory, and obtained by the free use of alliteration and anacrusis, in the manner of Thomas.

BBC poetry is only one manifestation of a great social change that has taken place in the last twenty-five years in England. There is no longer a dominant cultured minority that is the arbiter of literary taste and the custodian of the language. The Bloomsbury of Virginia Woolf was the last manifestation of a taste, language, and subtlety of feeling possible only among people reared in a tradition long perfected:

> A spot whereon the founders lived and died
> Seemed once more dear than life; ancestral trees
> Or gardens rich in memory glorified.

The poetry of Edith Sitwell is one last dry fine leaf upon that ancestral tree, "All that great glory spent"; we may think it just that an educated aristocracy (and the Universities already begin to reflect the change) should have given place to a half-educated democracy, but we cannot blind ourselves to the fact that the price paid for the many advantages of public education on a mass scale is the advent of a lower form of culture—at least for the time being. Above, the discipline of language and subtle thought of the educated minority is undermined: below, the deep roots of local tradition, folklore, and the richness of rustic speech, have gone. Memory atrophies as literacy takes its place: and the cultural heritage of the people, preserved for centuries in Wales, Ireland, the Highlands, and here and there in England—a tradition in which, as Yeats says, human events were "long steeped in the heart" has given place, within living memory, to the ephemeral newspaper and the wireless voices. Industrialism has produced a new kind of human being, and in a society so dedicated to the pursuit of the temporal, poetry, whose theme is the eternal, must find roothold in the stoniest ground, surely, that history has ever known. In America—perhaps in Russia and in China—there may be something humanly inspiring in the idea of Progress. But in England, we are aware of losing more than we gain by the transition —imaginatively, that is. Improved social conditions for the working class may not be too dearly bought at the price of culture and a language destroyed. Who can judge these things?

Poetry, at any rate, seems to flourish best where the past has not yet been completely obliterated, in Ireland, Wales, Scotland, and (among the young) in Oxford and Cambridge. A volume of poems by Ewart Milne, an Irishman, has just been published by Peter Russell that has the panache of eloquence and the myth-making gift of the tradition of Irish story telling. Patric Galvin, another Irish poet, has brought out the first number of a magazine *Chanticleer.* From Wales, besides Thomas and Vernon Watkins, comes good work by Lynette Roberts and Keidrich Rhys whose cadence and imagery bears the stamp of the language spoken by people, not emitted from machines. The late Dylan Thomas' *Collected Poems,* one of the two best volumes of verse published in the fifties is a poetry untouched by the machine. His rhetoric is a distillation of the speech of men in their houses and their fields, not the taught language of the schools or the inhuman language emitted by wireless sets and newspapers, now alas the language of an inhuman gabble.

The other notable volume comes from Scotland— Edwin Muir's *Collected Poems,* which, like the Thomas volume, contains new work as well as old. Like Yeats, Edwin Muir has reached a late maturity, and since the publication of the *Collected Poems* many fine new poems have appeared in *The Listener* and elsewhere. Muir writes in English, not in the fine vernacular made fashionable once more by Hugh Macdiarmid (who enjoys nation-wide fame in Scotland, a proof that there poetry is still a language understood by the people). Edwin Muir's imagery is drawn from a pastoral North, remote as memory and timeless as Eden. W. S. Graham, a younger poet, also writes in English, but, like Dylan Thomas, the vitality of his language and imagery derives from the life and speech of non-industrialized people. His long poem, *The Night Fishing*, first published in *Botteghe Oscure* has not yet appeared in book form. There are, I understand, other forthcoming poems by this poet. Sidney Goodsir Smith, another Scots poet, whose collection, *So Late into the Night,* was published early this year, writes in the Scots language (called "lallans" in the English papers) that lends its delicacy of feeling and fierceness of both scorn and passion to his fine lyrics. Tom Scott's translations of Villon into Scots are outstandingly good; similar translations of Baudelaire have not yet appeared in book form.

In England itself no poetry is being written as fine as that coming from Wales and Ireland. *The Laughing Hyaena* by D. J. Enwright, a poet who has spent much time in Cairo and was until recently teaching at Birmingham University, is an attempt to come to grips with the human landscape of the industrial city, and as a landscapist he is very fine at times, clear and incisive in his use of imagery, with an underlying intellectual toughness. C. Day Lewis has built for himself an Ivory Tower from the literary style and the sentiments of Thomas Hardy (a retreat into the pre-industrial past); and a younger poet, John Heath-Stubbs, writes out of a preoccupation with literature for its own sake rather than from the richness of long experience. At his best,

Heath-Stubbs is elegantly witty; at his worst, bookish.

There is some promise among the young both of Oxford and Cambridge. In Oxford, a group of young poets led by Martin Seymour Smith have sent themselves to school to learn from Robert Graves—nor could any better master of style be found (Graves' own latest book, *Poems and Satires,* slight as it is, is a model of English verse in the middle style). The Fantasy Poets, a series of pamphlets published in Oxford, represent the work of this group, and a volume by their best poet, Elizabeth Jennings, has just been awarded an Arts Council prize for the best first book of verse published in the last two and a half years. Miss Jennings greatly admires Edwin Muir: but, like Anne Ridler, she speaks with a personal voice of personal things—love, childhood, and delicate observations of scenes and people. In some ways it is easier for women not to lose their contact with permanent values, than for men, more implicated in the public and historic changes of the time. Anne Ridler's last book, *The Golden Bird,* contains a verse-play written for broadcasting, suffering from the diffuseness usual in such works, but besides this some lovely intimate poems in her more private, and truer, voice. At Cambridge, the leading poet is Thom Gunn, whose first book is also about to be published by the Fantasy Poets. He is probably a stronger poet, both in intellect and in passion, than Miss Jennings; but both are to be watched.

No one who has seen the available material will blame G. S. Fraser's anthology, *Springtime,* very much for being a very dull and uninspired collection. A few poets are better than the rest—besides the two poets just mentioned, John Hall and Thomas Blackburn stand out, (the former of the school of Muir, the latter a poetic disciple of the painter Francis Bacon). John Wain (also included in *Springtime*) is the leading spirit of a group of young poets who have chosen William Empson as their model. Wain's work, however derivative, shows, if not taste or imagination, energy and attack.

Innumerable little magazines come and go. The best of them is *Nine* in which Peter Russell attempts to maintain a standard of style and taste worthy of Ezra Pound; and *Poetry and Poverty,* edited by Dannie Abse, who is among those most troubled by the poverty of the poetry. John Lehmann's *New Soundings* on the BBC and the monthly poetry readings at the London Institute of Contemporary Arts have failed to discover hidden talent of a high order.

There is no sign of any flowering of young talent comparable with that of the thirties, or with the time of Geoffrey Grigson's *New Verse* that used to publish Dylan Thomas and David Gascoyne—or even Tambimuttu's wartime magazine *Poetry London.* Stephen Spender's new magazine *Encounter* seems in its first number to owe more to the past than to the present.

Nevertheless, with Dylan Thomas, Edwin Muir and Robert Graves writing their best work, the period could not be called sterile. George Barker is also at work on a long poem, not yet published. *A True Confession* is George Barker's last published poem; it contained some of his best flights of eloquence. Passages of his new unpublished poem promise no less.

Stephen Spender

ENGLISH PAINTING IN THE FIFTIES

The present state of English painting is comparable to that of contemporary English poetry. In both arts, the middle-aged practitioners continue to hold the advantage of doing work that is "new," according to the vocabulary of modernism. Graham Sutherland and Francis Bacon hold positions in painting, parallel to that of W. H. Auden in poetry. One looks to them for new developments in every stage of their art and their age seems only to have added power to their perpetual youth.

At the same time, there is a suspicion that perhaps we are misled through a confusion of vocabulary into expecting novelty of the young. Simply because, since about 1870, the young artist in Europe has always produced the new and the unexpected, we tend to identify innovations with youth, and feel that when they are lacking the young are without talent, or are prematurely aged and exhausted. But today the young start producing work which we expect from the old.

Recently, at the Royal College of Art in London, I inquired why the students give little support to an organization called the ICA (Institute of Contemporary Arts), which supports exhibitions and discussions about "advanced" art. The answer was that they were not interested in *avant-garde,* movements which they regarded as old-fashioned. And the puzzling truth is that the young regard as new just that kind of realism which an older generation regard as dated. To judge from recent exhibitions of student work several students who have been to Italy have come back with canvases of workers with thick wrists and fingers like carrots, sitting at the tables of grimy restaurants and eating vermicelli.

Yet despite a few examples of a rather crude realism to suggest that there is just a reaction towards the Zolaesque would be an over-simplification. The painter who above all dominates their imagination, is Francis Bacon. Painters are hypnotized by the vision of their more magnetic contemporaries to a degree which always rather amazes me. If Picasso paints leeks, the other painters don't paint carrots, but leeks and only leeks in exactly Picasso's way; and several young English painters now enclose their images in rectangles painted in white lines, suggesting a glass case or prison bars, in exactly the way that Bacon does.

So there is not, on the whole, a direct return to realism, but an attempt to relate a great many things which seem a far cry from realism back to observed facts. A recent exhibition labelled "realist painting" contained many abstract and fantastic works which seemed a far cry from any direct form of realism. Yet one can see the point of young artists, who have developed along the lines of modern painting, feeling that they are arriving at so many dead ends, and trying to find their way back to the realistic image. If they can do this without abandoning what they have discovered in impressionism, post-impressionism, surrealism, et cetera, their work is apt to be more interesting than that of the social realists.

The young painters, like the young poets, are in search of a touchstone which will at once relate them to the problems of their art and to the realities of their time. They respect their elders and to some extent follow them, but find that their work started off with a confident relation to another time: to the ideological passion of the 1930s, to the apocalyptic violence of the war, or to a religious revival which also had its aesthetic roots in the thirties and forties. No young poet or painter of the fifties has the same confident and contemporary relation to the fifties as Auden and Sutherland had to the thirties, Dylan Thomas and Francis Bacon to the forties.

Meanwhile the older artists are to some extent exploring the same problems as the younger ones. Their successes and failures at least show what appear to be fertile or infertile veins of development.

Shortly before the war, there was a very influential group of painters called the "Euston Road Group," led by William Coldstream, Graham Bell and Victor Pasmore. The name was derived from the road where was situated their joint studio and art school. All these painters used a French impressionistic technique to portray people, landscapes, objects. They reacted against surrealism, abstraction, fantastic and poetic painting.

Yet in spite of their return to reality which seems so parallel to what is going on now, the Euston Road school led to nothing. Coldstream, highly respected, has evolved into an academic figure. He is head of the Slade School of Art. Graham Bell, perhaps the most vital member of the group, was killed in the war. Lawrence Gowing, also a very talented painter, has taken to teaching and writing. Victor Pasmore has renounced impressionism and been through nearly all the modernist movements which the Euston Road Group renounced.

The poetic painters whose early work was perhaps a reaction from Coldstream and his group—Sutherland, Piper, John Craxton, Keith Vaughan and John Minton —have survived better, perhaps for two reasons. The first reason may well be that they are really poetic in the sense of being deeply interested in poetry. It is their strength and their weakness that they are "literary." Their weakness because I doubt whether the greatest achievements in imaginative painting can be made by painters who are largely concerned with trying to visualize and paint either what is a poetic image, or the kind of objects and scenes which are the subject matter of poetry (Piper's churchyards, mossy stones, remote mountains and lakes, et cetera). But it is also their strength because even if it does not lead to the greatest work, much good English painting has had connections with poetry: Blake, Palmer, the pre-Raphaelites in their earliest lyrical phase, for example.

The second reason why these poetic painters still have such a strong position is that, in spite of their being more "modern" and therefore seeming more obviously a "movement" committed to go in a certain direction, than the Euston Road Group, they have shown much more variety and flexibility. In the work of a painter like Sutherland, a pendulum seems always to be swinging between his dreamlike imagination and his researches into the real appearance of objects. When in doubt or in search of renewed inspiration, he turns back to objects. Most of his paintings are indeed variations on a theme, or stages of metamorphosis, in which a real object—a tree trunk, a country lane, a Welsh hillside, the crucifixion, Lord Beaverbrook or Mr. Maugham—are in process of turning from real objects into obsessive dream symbols.

The English appear to have great poetic imagination in literature, but easily exhausted poetic imagination in painting. Why this is so, cannot be discussed here, but it remains fairly true that it is fatal for the English artist to become over-attached to the visualized poetic pattern. Two examples of this danger are the work of Ben Nicholson, an excellent painter, who has not been able to get out of the rut of his simple yet poetic abstract forms (mostly squares and circles), and that of John Piper who, after having been stuck in abstractionism (before the war), was knocked off it by the fires and bombings and became one of the best war painters; after which he contrasted scenes of fire and bomb-damage, with the passionate quietness of his paintings of houses, churches, gravestones. But now Piper runs the danger of fixing his country scenes into rigid patterns which really conceal a return to his pre-war dry abstractions. Piper is a clear example of a painter who needs to drink at the fountain of real experience of nature, if he is not to lapse into a very parched abstractionism.

As with contemporary English poetry, it would be easy to generalize about painting by drawing attention to the dearth of outstanding major talents. Only Francis Bacon, with his vital, energetic and decisive depictions of faces which seem caught in the flash of an instantaneous exposure, and Graham Sutherland are today outstanding. Lucien Freud, an extraordinary painter and figure, belongs more to a German than an English tradition. But as with poetry, if one is dissatisfied with a facile generalization, one goes on to become deeply interested in contemporary English painting. Some of the painters who can least easily be classified, are among the most interesting. There is, for instance, Keith Vaughan, who has developed the least explored side of Cézanne—his manner of painting nudes—and whose landscapes are very satisfying. There are the very rare and intensely concentrated water colours of David Jones, a Catholic mystic who will, in his books and paintings, probably interest posterity far more than he attracts attention today.

During the present century, both in painting and poetry, a demand has been created for perpetual experiment and innovation. As was perhaps inevitable, the time has come when the most serious work can no longer satisfy this demand—with the inevitable result that there is a sense of disappointment. There is even a danger that this disappointment affects the artists themselves. They may know that to work seriously they cannot go on in directions already explored; they have to look around them at things, and go back to earlier stages of modern painting. But they may find it as disconcerting to do so, as we do to see them grouped as "realists" and the like. But the best response to the present situation is not to expect sensational results but to pay close attention to what is really a very interesting stage of development. Close attention will soon discover many painters whose work can be greatly appreciated.

Norman Demuth

MUSIC IN ENGLAND

The musical situation in England is dominated by the universally revered figure of Ralph Vaughan Williams, who continues in the flood of creative activity, each work in succession revealing some new facet of that fundamentally English idiom which he re-discovered and restored as a common language in his *Pastoral Symphony,* composed in 1922. From him stems a school of composers whose style is English as distinct from British and who have been influenced by no other culture. The other veterans, Joseph Holbrooke and Rutland Boughton (both born in 1878) and Cyril Scott and John Ireland (both born in 1879) rarely appear with new works. Holbrooke has announced that he will compose no more, having contributed an enormous number of works of all sizes to the repertoire, including three monumental operas; it was he who first championed the cause of the native composer in the early part of the century. Boughton nearly found an English expression in his Arthurian operas, but they came too soon and national operatic potentialities had not become realised. Scott in the first decade of the century was using harmonies hitherto unthought of in this country. By the twenties every composer was writing them. It is not generally realised that modern music owes a tremendous debt to this composer, and that it was he who set music rolling here towards a complete emancipation from traditional academicism.

Ireland, however, is a little different. His piano pieces, sonatas, songs, and his choral work *These Things Shall Be* are frequently performed and his influence exercises itself indirectly and quietly. His style has thinned out, but the old vigour, freshness, and poetry remain. He has always been an imaginative composer.

Imagination of another kind is the guiding factor in the work of Sir Arnold Bax. His symphonies and symphonic poems are impelled by picturesque Celtic folklore. Although at one time rated as exceedingly difficult, they now offer no insuperable difficulties to either performers or listeners. This charge of difficulty dies hard in England, and it is too often offered as an excuse for neglect. Bax has a following, but no followers; this is a pity, for English music could do with a leaven of his poetic imagination and picturesque writing.

The English School includes such names as Armstrong Gibbs, Gordon Jacob, and Herbert Howells among the older, and Gerald Finzi, Edmund Rubbra, and Michael Tippett among the younger. Armstrong Gibbs has composed innumerable songs of fine quality, and his Symphony for voices and orchestra, *Odysseus,* is a magnificent work. His chamber music is worthy to rank with all comers. Gibbs' technique adds strength to the dangerous tendency of the English idiom to be flaccid and vague. Gordon Jacob's music is intensely scholarly in the best sense. It is rather over-breezy, but is well-balanced. His powers to move his listeners are not as great as those of Herbert Howells, whose *Hymnus Paradisi* is one of the loveliest things of the century. His organ Psalm-Preludes and Rhapsodies are fine original works; they trace their technique from their composer's teacher, Stanford, but their language is strikingly individual. Howells' Rhapsodic Quintet is as fresh today as when it was written (1919) because, like all his other works, it lacks mannerisms.

Of the three younger composers, Edmund Rubbra is a natural symphonist with all the stuff of symphonic continuity and musical scholarship behind it. His works have a strength and stability which is absent from those of Michael Tippett, whose basic polyphony has no sinews and consequently lacks stamina. Tippett's *Concerto for Double String Orchestra* and *Symphony in A* have made an impression in certain quarters, but he is more likely to live with *Child of Our Time*, which is finely written, and is an outstanding landmark in the English choral tradition. The art of Gerald Finzi is altogether smaller and consequently has a more limited public; Finzi's settings of Shakespeare and Hardy add a great deal to English song. Of these composers, it is he who most nearly approaches the Vaughan Williams aesthetic.

The composers who do not subscribe to a self-consciously English idiom and are, therefore, "British" are headed by Sir Arthur Bliss, whose opera *The Olympians* was the first native work to be produced after the war at Covent Garden. Many unkind things were said about it by the quidnuncs, but the public liked its honesty and sincerity. These characterise all Bliss' music, and his personality.

Opinion varies as to whether the example of Sir William Walton or that of Benjamin Britten leads the younger generation. Walton is much the elder of the two, but his catalogue is infinitely smaller; he takes his time over each work and is not in a hurry for it to be performed. He constantly revises his scores, but this should not give the impression that he is uncertain in his touch; it simply means that he prefers other ways of saying things. It is significant that none of his works has

fallen into neglect, and each one makes regular and frequent appearances. Those who have heard what he has
completed of his opera are loud in their praises of it,
suggesting that it may prove to be the great opera of
the century in English.

Opinion on Benjamin Britten falls into three cate-
gories—those who think that everything he writes is a
masterpiece, those who see little merit in his music and
consider its value grossly exaggerated, and, more reasonably, those who take the middle course, regretting the
operas, except *Peter Grimes,* but admiring the composer's undoubted gifts in the smaller realms of choral
and chamber music. It is felt by some that Britten wrote
himself out operatically with *Peter Grimes* and that the
later operas strive after some kind of new expression but
fail to find it. Britten has extraordinary facility.

Arnold Cooke is one of the few English pupils of
Hindemith. His style is solid and workmanlike, clas-
sically impelled, and often inspiring. Similar strength
is found in Alan Rawsthorne who shows a curious
affinity with Roussel; of this he is probably quite unconscious.

Alan Bush, though once a tough nut to crack, has
simplified his style so that his music is now immediately
approachable. His *Nottingham Symphony* is most open-
handed and attractive, provided one forgets the early
works such as the Concert Piece for cello and piano and
the String Quartet, *Dialectic.*

Direct foreign influence has been felt by three composers of widely divergent points of view—Alec Rowley,
Lennox Berkeley, and Humphrey Searle. Rowley, the
oldest of the three, and Berkeley absorbed the Gallic
qualities of lightness and clarity. Of the two, Berkeley
is the more advanced and perhaps the more personal. In
his *Put Away the Flutes* and *Gold Coast Customs,* Searle
shows that he had found the secret of superimposing
emotional feeling upon an otherwise arid system of pure

mathematics. Few English composers practice such composition.

Most young composers today begin where others have left off, and it is almost the rule now that a newcomer should herald his arrival with a symphony; this usually leads post-haste to a second such work and this, impelled by a mind that has had no time to re-stock and re-fuel itself, is more often than not below the standard of the first. The symphonies of Peter Racine Fricker have substance, are extremely powerful, and are well thought out; but they are uniformly gloomy and pessimistic. There is nothing wrong in this outlook if the composer really believes it, but it sometimes happens that depression is mistaken for profundity. Similar works by John Gardner, Richard Arnel, Daniel Jones, William Wordsworth, and William Alwyn (an expert film composer and considerably older than the others) adopt a different attitude and if they do not say anything particularly new (one particularly over-emotionalised work puts the clock back considerably, but is none the less popular for that) they are well-varied. Gardner and Jones are the most advanced—there are few signs that the young English composers have any wish to ruffle the placid waters of English music-making, although the music of Malcolm Arnold suggests that here is a slightly turbulent spirit.

Operas are composed by the score, but few are chosen. Arthur Benjamin's *A Tale of Two Cities* contained all the stuff of opera and was dramatically well-pointed. Benjamin allows the singers to *sing*. Alan Bush had to go to Germany for the production of his *Wat Tyler*. In spite of competitions and the commissioning of operas from composers, nothing permanent has appeared so far, and the question arises as to the value of these prizes and commissions when no arrangements are made for production. It is to be feared that realization of and admiration for British Opera are paper- and lip-service only.

Of the foreigners who have become British subjects, Roberto Gerhard has a pretty knack in opera and Egon Wellesz is a real scholar as well as being a composer of the highest integrity.

The Composers' Guild of Great Britain works strenuously to promote the cause of native composers in a perfectly and necessarily objective manner, receiving sympathetic co-operation from orchestras and performers. The situation is intensely active and music is pouring out in quantities as never before. The race for fame and survival promises to continue indefinitely. However, it is time that England produced the really great *universal* work that will rank in importance with *Le Sacre du Printemps, Wozzeck* and Oliver Messiaen's *Turangalila Symphony*.

William Becker

ENGLISH THEATRE: A BUDDING TRADITIONALISM

The single outstanding development of the post-war period in British theatre has been the tentative emergence of what may yet prove to be a fully operative traditionalism. Such an observation is likely to surprise some Americans. For one often hears in this country, both from Anglophiles and from apologists for Broadway, that the supposed superiority of the British theatre to our own is entirely due to British "traditions." But the fact is that England's theatrical culture is still much less "traditional" (in a functional sense) than, say, France's or Germany's: it operates, on the whole, much like ours, with precious few opportunities for workers in the theatre to feel themselves part of an enabling theatrical continuum. Nothing in England, until Stratford, could even have borne comparison to a really traditional theatre like the Comédie Française. And it is important to remember that Stratford had only a token existence before its post-war reformation suddenly brought it into international prominence, and that even the Old Vic before the war had a purely national reputation and was only intermittently successful.

Today the achievements of the post-war period look considerable, though the situation remains tentative and unstable—especially at the Old Vic, whose history over the past few years has reaffirmed the evident fact that institutions, at least until they become the agencies of a traditional discipline, are no better than the people who run them. Two years ago in a fantastic tangle of malice, stupidity, and opportunism—all woven into complex intrigues of truly Machiavellian proportions—the Old Vic was nearly destroyed. An interfering Board of Governors, animated by the genteel Philistianism of its Chairman, Viscount Esher—according to reports circulated at the time—was ultimately at fault; but the showdown was precipitated by a bureaucrat named Llewellyn Rees, with the result that everybody of purpose and talent resigned, and the Vic was left in the hands of a young director named Hugh Hunt. In the process, a long-term plan, devised by the triumvirate of brilliant and dedicated men who were forced out—George Devine, Glen Byam Shaw, and Michel St. Denis—and involving a national theatre, a school, an experimental theatre, and a traveling company, was abandoned. With it temporarily went all hope of an organic development which could ultimately have assured a traditional existence to the Old Vic's operations. Meanwhile recent seasons, under the directionless guidance of Hunt, have been disastrous. The *Henry VII*, for example, was a rundown recast version of a production originally done by Tyrone Guthrie for Stratford. Its general atmosphere of orphaned poverty seemed to depict the Old Vic's present condition with perfect accuracy. It had the incidental effect of reducing the grandiose groupings and hammy timing of the Guthrie style to an absurd shambles: since the Vic stage is a good deal smaller than Stratford's, the actors found themselves stumbling over the set and each other at all the most characteristic Guthrie moments, and one realized, as one seldom can when the Guthrie spectacle works, what a hollow and precariously superficial thing it actually is.

The Old Vic has undergone a reorganization: Hugh Hunt has been replaced by Michael Benthall, a director of taste and ability, though occasionally given in the past to heavy-handedness and over-decoration; and it has been announced that, during the next five years, the company will perform all of Shakespeare's plays in turn, on a single stationary set. That, at least, sounds like the kind of groundwork on which a traditional theatre might be erected; and one only regrets that so completely a fresh start became necessary at all. The function of an institution is to turn history into tradition; Mr. Hunt's administration presided over the reversal of that process.

Stratford is an entirely different story. Privately supported and unhampered by professional committee-sitters, it has developed steadily into an institution of the very first rank. It owes this development largely to the administrative genius of its Director, Anthony Quayle, who, after John Gielgud, is probably the most valuable single individual now at work in the British theatre. Quayle's combination of talents is rare, but it is also an imperative one for the sort of post he holds. For Quayle is fundamentally art-, not bureau-, directed (to paraphrase a fashionable sociological distinction): he is a gifted and extraordinarily versatile actor as well as a perceptive stage-director, and he owes his administrative success largely to his special faculty for knowing just how and when to use everyone of superior theatrical talent in England. Stratford, unlike the Comédie Française, is broadly eclectic: the individual productions have varied greatly in quality and tone, and one cannot speak of a "Stratford style." Yet the recent ones, even at their least inspired, have all seemed to share a clarity of statement and a sensible respect for the text—and these, of course, may be the first indications of that inherent discipline which is the hall-mark of genuine tradition.

What I saw of a recent season at Stratford (Marius Goring in *Richard III*, Michael Redgrave in *The Mer-*

chant of Venice, and Redgrave and Peggy Ashcroft in
Anthony and Cleopatra) did not impress me in anything like the degree that the season of 1951 did. The
1951 productions of the historical tetralogy (*Richard II*
through *Henry V*), directed by Quayle, with their con-
summate attention to the meaning of the action in its
total political context, were unquestionably the best
Shakespeare productions I have ever seen. Nonetheless,
there were deep satisfactions to be had on this occasion,
too. For me, the greatest were Harry Andrews' performances—as *The Merchant,* as Enobarbus in *Anthony,*
as Buckingham in *Richard III.* Andrews is one of the
few actors who can truthfully be called a product of
Stratford: over the past several seasons, he has developed
from a quite ordinary talent into one of the most useful
Shakespearean actors in England. Such a development
is obviously the chief thing that a functioning tradition
can promote; and Harry Andrews' career may be a more
generally hopeful sign than anyone yet realizes. So
powerful a stage personality has he become that Marius
Goring's competent but uninspired performance as
Richard II was thrown quite out of perspective, so that
the play often seemed to be more about a king-maker
than a king. And the superiority of Andrews' Stratford
Enobarbus to the performance he gave in that role for
the Oliviers two years ago was surely no accident. So
long as Stratford cannot or will not maintain a single
permanent company like the Comédie Française, a
career like Harry Andrews' is likely to remain exceptional, and the fullest traditionalism not likely to be
achieved. Meanwhile, however, it would be ungrateful
to carp: Stratford is far and away the best English-
speaking theatre that exists.

Parker Tyler

BRITISH FILM: PHONETICS, *FUMED OAK,* AND FUN

England made *Breaking Through the Sound Barrier*, as good a scientific thriller as modern filmic times have produced. Is it a coincidence that it has to do with the dynamics of sound? Perhaps not. The fusion of effective diction with an optimistic version of reality seems the peculiar documentary-fictitious realm in which Great Britain excels all other nations. During the thirties, it was Britain which gave most imagination, technical skill and seriousness of purpose to the Documentary Film, and the impetus of that period of full activity is still felt. *Cavalcade, In Which We Serve,* and *This Happy Breed,* were epic-sized films from England, stating—with an obvious desire not to overstate—the historic patriotism of a people. The element of an imaginative or fictitious art there emerged as of lesser importance in favor of what might be termed The Record. A full-fledged fiction is more or less "off the record" in England; that is, not to be taken too seriously. For example, *The Importance of Being Earnest,* a film received with much gratitude from the epicures of high comedy, has the elegance, airiness, and hieratic assurance of a court masque.

There are, however, two ways to take the highly stylized humors of *The Importance:* hermetically and not so hermetically. If the life of joy and fancy can be expressed completely by Gilbert and Sullivan, Wilde's great bagatelle should seem but a rather esoteric nuance of that very tuneful philosophy. Like *Patience,* it proves specifically that the English have a faculty for heavenly fun with a perfect talent for self-portraiture. But in the modern world (and what can remind us better that we are in the modern world than the three films mentioned above?), *The Importance* becomes a socially delimited conceit. Noel Coward's trio, *Tonight at 8:30,* came along to prove that an equal linguistic and phonetic competence, several rungs down on the social ladder, reveals the other side of the comic coin; which is to say that the faculty cited above is equally utile for *horrible* fun.

It is the second part of Coward's film, *Fumed Oak,* that exhibits this repellent triumph. Could any other nation, indeed, find a truth so horrible productive of so much amusement and so permissive of an objective craft to render it? Coward has been as tireless among lower middle-class clichés, unconverted by wit and imagination, as Wilde among upper-class clichés, converted by wit and imagination. The imaginative element in *Fumed Oak* is the moral revolt of a middle-aged floor-walker who takes unholy joy, before chucking everything and leaving for the South Seas, in telling off brutally his family of three—wife, mother-in-law, and daughter—because for seventeen years he has been persecuted by their phonetic powers. His unforeseen forensics effectually quells them, making the better part of the piece one long curtain-line and producing in the hearer a sort of goose-flesh of mirth. *Fumed Oak* might be called a paradigm of what may suddenly happen to the vulgar and the vulgate if nothing has happened to them for seventeen years. Of course, a war may "happen" and serve the same purpose as the middle-aged floorwalker's long-nourished vision of freedom in Noa-Noa Land. (At any rate, the "sound barrier" is broken!)

A Queen Is Crowned, aside from cheering, marching music, and the documentary convention of oral commentary, is notable for its phonetic austerity and verbal sparseness. Its main event is the most solemn public spectacle of our time and properly prodigious in a nation which produced such a court satire as *The Mikado* and such a vision of the Peers as that in *Iolanthe*. The Coronation, however, is The Record. The modern English temper has followed its documentary bent by also producing on film a court romance about the first Elizabeth of England, featuring her speculative ("off the record") romance with Admiral Thomas Seymour. This is *Young Bess,* an officially lavish and perfectly mediocre item, whose high distinction remains, alone, a full-fledged diction.

Do Americans tend to overstress the aesthetic, not to say also the social, importance of British speech? It would be natural in a nation whose parent stem is chiefly England, from which its social standards, its manners of all kinds, largely derive. The beauty of that speech achieves a dominant, however "insular," place in Shakespearean films as though it were one of Prospero's magics. British film productions of Shakespeare have seemed to this witness to leave much to be desired. British accent and British diction almost, but not quite, saved the American-made *Julius Caesar* from artistic mediocrity. The case is that, in international films, the only prime excellence of England, artistically speaking, is the craft of speech. This is true despite such superlative and steady film performers as Laurence Olivier, Margaret Rutherford, and Alec Guinness. As I mean "performers" rather than actors, I mean "personalities" rather than artists.

Phonetics all to one side, the meat of an art is the whole conception. The retreat of a set of stage-film actors in America, led by Charles Laughton, to "drama quartets" may be interpreted as a revolt against the boredom imposed by inferior material on actors with British speech standards. Quite natural, of course; and quite natural that the voice should be the instrument on which predominant reliance is placed: vocality in a *decent* setting. There is no vocal institution to retreat to in America, such as Racine and Corneille in France, for Shakespeare is not an *institution* on our own stage. I have heard a great deal of Olivier's voice, both in American and English films. Capable of humorous as well as pathetic inflections, that voice has often been a pleasure to listen to; it has even made me inattentive to what was being said. Sir Laurence's speaking of the narration for *A Queen Is Crowned* was in every way satisfactory. It was more than satisfactory when he gave vent to his final "God Save the Queen!" These words were said with the fervor of a living knight. They were not shouted or choked-up; they were not "emotional." They were dramatically articulated speech and clearly above the commonplace level to which the camera was rigorously limited here as a representative agent. People found moving images in *A Queen Is Crowned* but I think that these must have been entirely connotative and not due to any cunning of the plastic imagination, either in the ceremony itself or the way it was photographed. The Coronation was an occasion when actions, as words, were strictly prescribed, their force not being subject to modes of representation and hence not being "aesthetic."

THE ARTS IN THE UNITED STATES

Malcolm Cowley

AMERICAN NOVELS SINCE THE WAR

An essay as short as this, dealing with a subject as broad as postwar American fiction, has to be a sort of aerial survey, not critical but topographical. Looking down as if from a slow observation plane, we examine the jumbled landscape to learn what it reveals. We can scarcely see the people, let alone hearing them talk, but at least we can see their fields, their roads, and where these converge in groups of houses, each different from any other group.

The largest of the groups is composed of novels about the armed services in World War II. There are now so many of the novels, by such a varied company of authors, that one can find, if not a published book, then at least a manuscript about every arm and rank of all the services in every theatre of operations and in every major battle from Pearl Harbor to Okinawa—not to mention other novels about occupation troops, prisoners of war, soldiers and sailors on leave, and patients in psychiatric hospitals. It is as if a commission in Washington had summoned a meeting of all the novelists and had given each of them the task of writing one volume about a single phase of the conflict. And it is as if the chairman of the commission had said, "Some of you can be original, to lend variety to the undertaking, but we expect the rest of you to use the same methods and approxi-

mately the same style, so that the volumes will fit together into a vast collective history of the war."

Many of the novels are so much alike that dialogues
and episodes could be transposed from one to another
without a change except in names. There are indeed a
few individualists among the authors: notably there is
James Jones, who is the only one to write about the
Army as an institution and a permanent way of life;
there is Norman Mailer, who has a political sense that is
rare among writers of his generation; and there is the
late John Horne Burns, with the strained but persuasive
lyricism that he achieved in *The Gallery,* and never
achieved again; but these and a few others are exceptions. Most of the authors write like contributors to a
symposium. Although the sameness of their novels is
their great defect as separate works, it is also a virtue of
the undertaking as a whole. Together the novels form a
production of lasting value, one that may well be richer
and more complete than the contemporary account we
possess of any nation's part in any other war.

Even in a topographical survey I should make two
other remarks about the second-war novels. The first is
that, on the average, they are better written than all but
a few of the war novels produced in the 1920s. Fictional
methods, and especially the technique of presenting
"what really happened in action"—to borrow a phrase
from Hemingway—have been refined during the last
quarter-century, and young writers have been quicker
to learn the methods. A second remark is that in general
the sense of historical perspective has to be supplied by
readers of the novels as a group, since it is singularly
lacking in most of the individual novelists.

Most of them write as if they were immersed in the
war and as if, instead of being an exterior event to describe, it had become an inner condition of their lives.
Their state of mind is expressed by one of the two principal characters in *Point of Honor,* by M. L. Kadish, a

thoughtful and neglected novel about the fighting in Italy. The character is Sergeant Holloway, who goes into action with a battery of howitzers. As the guns fire, "Holloway eases into a kind of peace. Now he lives compact within the space of action. He can eye the present the way he saw a small snake eye a bird's nest once before the war."

Many of the novels give us just such a narrow-focused, intent and snake's-eye picture of the fighting. Even when the novelist, in imagination, soars over the battlefront, his picture is lacking in perspective. Lieutenant Evans, the other hero of *Point of Honor,* is an artillery observer in a Piper Cub who muses as the battle unrolls beneath him. "Had he thought once that the war had an issue? Anti-fascism, perhaps? Under aerial observation, war sheds issues. War was Fact, Thing-in-Itself, Existence sheer beyond argument; it spoke from the Rapido and beyond. 'I AM THAT I AM,' it declared to you. 'I AM MY OWN JUSTIFICATION.'" In general the novelists do not presume to judge the war. They do not think much about its causes or consequences and, unlike the novelists of the other war, they do not rebel against it. Their heroes accept the war as they would an earthquake and try to do their best in the circumstances.

A second group of postwar novelists includes the authors of what might be called the "new" fiction, to correspond with the new criticism. Like almost all the influential critics, many of the novelists are employed by universities, usually in the department of English. They listen to the critics, perhaps too intently, and try to win their grudging approval. Both critics and novelists are more interested in problems of structure and texture than they are in subject matter or ideas. If there are ideas in the novels they are seldom directly expressed and the social subject matter is nearly non-existent.

The new fiction represents the extreme point of a reaction from "social realism" as practised in the 1930s.

The new fictionists—I am thinking of young men and women like Frederick Buechner, Jean Stafford, Truman Capote, Robie Macauley and Paul Bowles, to mention a few of the more talented—are determined not to deal with public issues or social environments. Instead they try to give their stories a permanent human value by writing about the moral dilemmas of individuals, usually in isolated situations where the dilemmas can be studied like specimens in a laboratory.

Favorite settings are plantation houses on the point of collapse, abandoned summer hotels, decaying villages in Georgia or East Texas, lonely ranches in Colorado and the international colony in Rome or Tangier. Favorite themes are the initiation of a pre-adolescent boy or girl into the knowledge of sex or evil (as in *Other Voices, Other Rooms* and *The Mountain Lion*), an adulterous love affair as seen through the eyes of a child (as in how many novels), a wise old woman's death and its effect on her family, and a young woman's flight from reality into the womblike comfort of drugs, nymphomania or catatonic dementia (as in *The Sheltering Sky*). Women are likely to play the more active roles in the stories; the heroes are dummies or victims. There are scores of novels, published or in manuscript, that describe the ruin of a sensitive and truly artistic young man by his possessive mother.

It would not be accurate to say that the new fiction never presents a political idea. One that has been dramatically suggested in many novels, including some but not all of those with a Southern background, is the foolishness of racial prejudice. Another common idea is the weakness and cowardice of liberals and still another, expressed in terms of character, is the selfishness of reformers. Some of the novelists like to hint that their sentiments are conservative and often they depict very old men and women admiringly, as if to demonstrate that the past, with its simple codes of conduct, is better than the present.

The fact remains that most of the ideas to be deduced from the new fiction are moral rather than political or social. Usually they can be translated into statements of a highly generalized type: for example, "Evil is in the human heart"—which is the hidden thesis of many "new" novels—"Ripeness is all," "Little children, love one another!"—for the novelists like to use the words "love," "good" and "compassion"—and very simply, "Mother was to blame."

Another large group of postwar fiction is composed of naturalists—if we give a broad meaning to the term and apply it to any novelist who is primarily interested in his subject matter. The naturalists like to write about a community or a social environment. Some of their postwar subjects are a small city with its interwoven lives (*Sironia, Texas*), a Midwestern county over the years (*Raintree County*), the Chicago slums (*Knock at Any Door*), the motion-picture business (*What Makes Sammy Run*), a boys' military school (*End as a Man*) and the younger generation on the Pacific Coast (*Corpus of Joe Bailey*).

The central themes of such novels are usually quite simple. In some the protagonist—we can't often call him a hero—is warped by his environment, tempted into crime, and ends in the electric chair. In others he succeeds in business because of faults that keep him from being truly human. In still others he fights false social standards and achieves a sort of emotional maturity. Since the novelist is interested in the mechanism of social success or failure, and since he deals at length with many other characters who cross the path of the hero-victim-villain, he ends by writing a very long book. If a manuscript comes to a publisher's office in a single neat folder, it is likely to be new-fictional. If it arrives in

The Arts in the United States

a suitcase or a wooden packing box, it is either historical or naturalistic.

As a group the naturalists are more interested in the exterior drama of events than they are in achieving psychological depth. They pay comparatively little attention to the inner structure and texture of their novels. In their huge manuscripts a few of the episodes will be grotesquely swollen, and the editorial reader will blue-pencil them, while other episodes will be lacking in detail. The style is likely to be conventional or pedestrian. Frank Norris—not Dreiser—was the grandfather of most of the present-day naturalists and he often expressed his contempt for careful writing. "What pleased me most in your review of *McTeague*," he said in a letter to Isaac Marcosson, "was 'disdaining all pretensions to style.' It is precisely what I try most to avoid. I detest 'fine writing,' 'rhetoric,' 'elegant English'—tommyrot. Who cares for fine style! Tell your yarn and let your style go to the devil. We don't want literature, we want life." Yet Norris' novels are full of "fine writing" in the bad sense and usually end with a deep-purple passage.

Most of the present-day naturalists have followed Norris, both in his contempt for elegant English and in his failure to see that he sometimes wrote with bogus elegance. There are others, however, who show a sense of respect for the sound, the color and the infinite possibilities of the English language. While retaining the naturalistic interest in subject matter, they have tried to get beneath the surface of events and to present their characters as felt persons, not as observed specimens. Sometimes they transform the naturalistic story into a tone poem of anger or longing or mystery or degradation.

At this point I am describing what is really another group of postwar novels, smaller in number and harder to define than the three preceding groups, but perhaps no less important. Indeed it seems to me that novels like

The Man with the Golden Arm, by Nelson Algren, *The Invisible Man,* by Ralph Ellison, *Lie Down in Darkness,* by William Styron—for its last two chapters—and recently *The Adventures of Augie March,* by Saul Bellow, represent the most hopeful tendency now to be found in American fiction. The work of such novelists has faults, easy to discern, but these are the price they pay for taking chances that the new fictionists have refused to take. They deal with human characters, involved in human dilemmas, but don't make the mistake of presenting them as if they were divorced from society.

There are other good novels in all the classifications I have been trying to map as if from a distance. That is the weakness of a topographical or taxonomic survey: it indicates the sort of qualities, usually weaknesses, that are common to a group, but not the more important qualities that make a novel survive as a separate work of art.

Take for example *The Member of the Wedding,* by Carson McCullers. From the standpoint of our survey it belongs to the genus New Fiction, species Southern, variety Coming to Knowledge of Pre-adolescent Girl (or *rite de passage*) and thus can be filed away with half a dozen books by other writers. What the survey does not reveal is that it is written with an intensity of feeling and a rightness of language that the others fail to achieve; it has the power over the reader of a perfectly spoken incantation. Or take a rather neglected novel by Harriette Arnow, *Hunter's Horn.* This time the genus is Naturalism (with symbolic overtones), the species Hillbilly, the variety Obsessive Pursuit of a Wild Animal. Once again the survey does not reveal the special quality of the novel, which is partly the poetry of earth, partly the sense of a community and partly a sort of in-feeling for the characters that makes it better than any other novel about the Kentucky hill people since Elizabeth Madox Roberts' *The Time of Man.*

The postwar period in American fiction has not produced any novels that the future is likely to call great—only the future is entitled to speak of greatness—but it has produced many works, famous or neglected, that are unique in their species and deserve to be read for years to come. The faults of the period are easy to indicate, even at the end of this very brief survey. Most of the authors—not only war novelists but new fictionists and naturalists as well—have shown a peculiar lack of the historical sense; they can write "time passed," but they rarely give us the feeling of experienced time. They have been generally timid in their choice of subjects and characters and wanting in deep convictions.

As justification for timidity they can plead the dangers of this age, which has not been friendly to experiments in living or thinking. Yet the age has produced fundamental changes in the American character without producing equal changes in the novels, most of which are traditional in their form, as in their sense of life. The novelists are serious, skillful and perceptive, but one feels that most of them are without a definite direction —not stumbling, or not enough, but walking briskly, heads erect, eyes forward, within fences that mark the limit of their explorations. If they learn that the fences can be climbed, as I believe they will, we may enter a new period in American writing.

Arthur Mizener

AMERICAN POETRY IN THE TWENTIETH CENTURY

The poetry of any age is distinguishable—if it is—by the constellation of attitudes and ideas which constitutes its particular sensibility and by the rhetoric with which it defines this sensibility. It is always dangerous to discuss the poetry of an age. Poems, if not always written by fools like the gentlemen who said they were, are written by men whose art it is to be particular.

The most remarkable characteristic of American poetry in the twentieth century is a wry, depreciatory honesty. Ezra Pound described its style in a sentence which illustrates the style well. "Poetry," he said, "ought to be at least as well written as prose." Perhaps only in the poetry of Hart Crane, with its romantic rhetoric ("The sea's green crying towers a-sway, Beyond/And Kingdoms/naked in the/trembling heart—"), and of Wallace Stevens, with its rhetoric of elegance ("Soon with a noise like tambourines./Came her attendant Byzantines"), is this attitude a minor element.

The shift to it begins with Robert Frost. Professional New Englander though Frost is, however, he was first recognized in England. T. S. Eliot, though much influenced by The Big River and Cape Ann, is as much a British as an American poet. Contrariwise, Auden, who is Yorkshire enough, is also the bard of Forty-Second Street. These examples are not meant to suggest that

American and British poetry cannot be distinguished; there are clearly American qualities in all American poetry, from Pound's mock yawp to Eliot's English accent. But though many of these distinguishing characteristics are far from superficial, the profound qualities of our poetry are common to American and British poetry and, except for convenience, it would be foolish to treat them separately.

The characteristic depreciatory honesty of the age is very striking in Frost. He makes his most serious assertions in a homely, conversational manner, as if he felt he could authenticate his insights only by making the minimum claims for them, and none for himself. The laconic, country-bred New Englander who speaks in almost all his poems provides the anticlimaxes which are characteristic of his best poems, such as "The Most of It," where the speaker cried out that life wanted "not its own love back in copy speech/But counter-love, original response"; and then a great buck swam across the lake,

> Pushing the crumpled water up ahead,
> And landed like a waterfall,
> And stumbled through the rocks with horny tread,
> And forced the underbrush—and that was all.

This same attitude comes out in the very American poetry of William Carlos Williams and Pound, showing itself in the homeliness of their subjects and in the slight touch of comic exaggeration in their manner, as in Williams' directions for a funeral:

> For heaven's sake though see to the driver! . . .
> up there unceremoniously
> dragging our friend out to his own dignity!
> Bring him down—bring him down!
> Low and inconspicuous! I'd not have him ride
> on the wagon at all—damn him—
> the undertaker's understrapper!

In a quite different way it is the unwobbling pivot which steadies Pound's most serious passages, in which

> we have heard the fauns chiding Proteus
>   in the smell of hay under the olive-trees,
> And the frogs singing against the fauns in the half-
> light.

In such passages Pound's verse is as lovely as any in the twentieth century, but its grave and responsible eloquence comes from a cool precision rather than an extravagance of rhetoric.

But much the most influential of the early poets of the age has been T. S. Eliot, despite his rather forbidding intellectual-puritan temper. ("How unpleasant," he once wrote himself, "to meet Mr. Eliot:/With his features of clerical cut,/And his brow so grim/and his mouth so prim. . . .") The source of Mr. Eliot's influence is his awareness of our profound sense of inadequacy and his ironic self-possession in the face of this knowledge. If, after such knowledge, there is no forgiveness, still, nothing is to be gained by ignoring it or giving way to hysteria. From Prufrock, obsessed by the absurdity of his heart, anxious not to forget that he is Osric rather than Hamlet, sure that he has no right to make a tragedy of his inability to hear mermaids singing, to the graver, less youthfully self-conscious voice of the age's greatest poem, *Four Quartets,* Mr. Eliot has known how to speak to that part of our nature we do not even know we have which underlies our opinions and even our beliefs. That special power is evident in the simplest phrases of the *Quartets:*

> I do not know much about gods; but I think that
>   the river
> Is a strong brown god. . . .
> Home is where one starts from. As we grow older
> The world becomes stranger. . . .

Each in his own way, the poets who succeeded this first group have shown a similar attitude. The profoundly strange and original poetry of Allen Tate, for example, is full of it:

> This is the day His hour of life draws near,
> Let me get ready from head to foot for it
> Most handily with eyes to pick this year
> For small feed to reward a feathered wit.

It is in the nicely shaded control of feeling in John Ransom's poetry:

> There was such speed in her little body,
> And such lightness in her footfall,
> It is no wonder her brown study
> Astonishes us all.

It is in the deeply serious, wry primness of Marianne Moore, with whom New England is not a dramatic pose but a passion of the mind:

> 'No water so still as the
>   dead fountains of Versailles.' No swan
> with swart blind look askance
> and gondeliering legs, so fine
>   as the chintz-china one with fawn-
> brown eyes and toothed gold
> collar on to show whose bird it was.

The middle generation of twentieth century poets was not so fortunate as the first. Whatever may have been the ultimate causes of its difficulties, it suffered from the widespread attempt to imitate Yeats' *Persona,* which ill fits the boy from Providence or Kansas City; and, as Randall Jarrell has remarked, the influence of the late Dylan Thomas came close to corrupting a whole generation (it is still at work in so good a poet as James Merrill). In any event, only a few poets stand out in this generation: Mr. Jarrell himself, Robert Lowell, Delmore Schwartz.

Of these the most gifted and the most troubled is Mr. Lowell, who has recently been struggling to escape from the excessive metaphysical complication of his own thought into some kind of direct, narrative poetry, perhaps like Frost's, as if, after the range of metaphor in *Lord Weary's Castle,* he found this the best way to his meaning. Occasionally his gift comes clear, as in the beautiful "Falling Asleep over the Aeneid," and then he is the best poet of his age in America. A similar development, this time in a modification of Auden's influence, is at work in Mr. Jarrell's latest work, for example, in "Money." "Money" is ironic about the rich man who speaks it, but it is also ironic about the easy way we are all ironic about such people. "*I*'d talk down money if *I* hadn't any," the old man says.

But in a way the most interesting of these poets is Delmore Schwartz, in whose work the period style was first firmly established. Its harmonious blending of effects from such different poets as Pound, Eliot, Yeats and Auden—to name only the predominant influences— is a very considerable achievement. It allows Mr. Schwartz to create his own voice within the range of a familiar voice, as did the best of the Elizabethan sonneteers and of the eighteenth-century couplet writers:

Let these romantic critics go elsewhere,
Elsewhere pretend that happiness is not like this.
Do we not have, in fine, depression and war
Certain each generation? Who would want more?
O what unsated heart would ask for more?

This style, at once conventional and personal, is widely possessed in the latest generation of poets. It is elegantly practiced by Richard Wilbur, whose Tom Swift

> worked at none but wit's expense
> Putting dirigibles together
> Out in the yard in quiet weather,
> Whistling beyond Tom Sawyer's fence.

It is funny and a little frightening in Reed Whittemore's Paul Revere:

> Is it one if by land, two if by sea?
> Or two if by land? Or what?

The great virtue of an established, period style of this kind is that it makes for a very high level of general performance. If the latest generation of twentieth century American poets has produced no poets-as-heroes, as did the first generation, it has produced a surprisingly large number of good poems by a surprisingly large number of writers, as any reader can see who will look through the excellent volume of *New Poems* by American Poets recently edited by Rolfe Humphries.

Delmore Schwartz

RECENT LITERARY CRITICISM

Since the war, literary criticism in America has become an active and flourishing industry to so great extent that it has provoked an antagonism which I think ought to be examined and illustrated.

I remember a famous American poet, and a truly great one, beginning a reading of his poetry by speaking of the present state of criticism, poetry, and the criticism of poetry. Some poets, he said, write for other poets, some poets write for the critics, some critics write poetry because they are critics of poetry, some critics write poetry for other critics, and finally some critics write criticism for other critics. His audience was overjoyed. As they laughed, a flashlight photographer lightened the scene near the platform, directing his camera at the poet, who looked more guilty than startled. One cannot be sure but he seemed to look as if he had been caught in the act of saying what he did say.

A literary critic expressed the same antagonism when he was asked about a piece of abstract sculpture in his living room by the electrician who had come to repair the wiring in his apartment. "What does it mean?" the electrician wanted to know. "Do you like girls?" the critic replied. The electrician admitted that he did. "Do you ask what a pretty girl means?" the critic said then.

The electrician made his departure. The important point is that he remained dissatisfied.

Then there is the antipathy which Randall Jarrell has expressed with characteristic eloquence in his recent book, *Poetry and the Age*: this is, he says, an age of criticism: "there has never been an age when so much good criticism was written—or so *much* bad." And when you examine the leading literary reviews, "each of these contains several poems, and a piece of fiction—sometimes two pieces; the rest is criticism . . . I am talking as a reader of the criticism of the last few years and am assuming its merits and services, which are great. . . . The magazines which enjoy attacking them are almost ludicrously inferior to them. But, I think, they print far too much criticism and far too much that is attractive to critics and lovers of criticism than it is to poets and fiction-writers. . . . Some of this criticism is as good as anyone could wish: several of the best critics alive print most of their work in such magazines as these. Some more of this criticism is intelligent and useful—it sounds as if it had been written by a reader for readers, by a human being. But a great deal of this criticism might just as well have been written by a syndicate of encyclopedias for an International Business Machine. It is not only bad or mediocre, it is dull; it is, often, an astonishingly graceless, joyless, humorless, long-winded, niggling, blinkered, methodical, self-important, cliche-ridden, prestige-obsessed, almost autonomous criticism."

Mr. Jarrell's description is precise, or at any rate, my own feelings are so much akin to his that it seems precise to me. But perhaps our own feelings are not important when measured against the state of literacy in America and the endless necessity for the training of an educated class. The state of affairs which Mr. Jarrell describes has come into being through the new union between literary criticism and the teaching of English. Some of the criticism to which Mr. Jarrell objects is produced by overworked instructors who must earn academic promotion by publication: in the past, most of them would have published scholarly papers in the scholarly journals; but now, although academic standards of scholarship remain unaltered, the teacher's worth is increased, from the point of view of a university, if he functions as both a critic and a scholar. Consequently there has been a *rapprochement* between scholarship and criticism instead of the senseless separation which existed for far too long. The teacher has been drawn toward criticism and the critic toward scholarship in a way which cannot but be good for both criticism and scholarship.

But more important by far, the practice of criticism has increased because of a definite social and cultural need. Much of the criticism which distresses Mr. Jarrell is given over almost entirely to an analysis and interpretation of the meanings of the literary object, which is certainly a one-sided and limited kind of criticism at best. But at worst it has helped to create and to keep alive a consciousness of literature at a higher and more serious level than at any time since the Civil War. The proof of this is that if it is an age of criticism, it is also an age of the reprint. For the ascendancy of the New Criticism has been accompanied by an important related phenomenon, the literary revival, which has restored the living as well as the dead. There have been valuable books and collections of essays about Faulkner, Fitzgerald, Hemingway, Eliot, Joyce, and Yeats, among others, a fact which must be connected with the state of affairs twenty years back when it was extremely difficult for a critic to get a book of criticism published at all. The literary revival has resurrected James, given the novels of Faulkner and Fitzgerald the attention of which they were deprived by the concerns of criticism during the depression; and classic American literature has established itself clearly and fully. We have only to think of

Melville, Emily Dickinson, and Mark Twain to see there has been a real advance: the gulf between the present and the past which existed in virtually every other period has been greatly diminished, and this has come about chiefly because so many critics are teachers. Faulkner is perhaps the best example of how genuine the progress has been: in any other literary period, he might have suffered the fate of Melville after the writing of *Moby Dick.*

Nevertheless Mr. Jarrell's judgment is just in itself. It would certainly be very nice if all the critics in question wrote well, in a lucid style, free of cant, jargon, and preciosity; if their analysis of the meaning of poetry were balanced by a sense of the being of poetry, and a historical sense of literature; if they were more often able to recognize that a method which developed out of the analysis of lyric poetry cannot be directly translated to the criticism of fiction and the drama; and if more of them shared the social and moral values of Van Wyck Brooks and Edmund Wilson, instead of those of T. S. Eliot. It is easier to criticize the New Criticism than to shoot fish in a barrel; and it ought to be criticized; at the same time, in criticizing it, one ought to remember a fact which Mr. Jarrell cites elsewhere in his book, in his essay on the obscurity of the poet and the indifference to poetry in America: "One of our universities recently made a survey of the reading habits of the American public; it decided that forty-eight percent of all Americans read, during a year, no book at all." It is within this context, from the point of view of the sociology of literature, that the recent growth of criticism must be estimated. It is true enough that the most one can say, adopting this point of view, is: *better than nothing.*

It is better than nothing in this sense: if on the one hand it is now often necessary, because of the New Criticism, to insist that *Moby Dick* is about a white whale and whaling, whatever its more elevated and profound meanings may be, on the other hand *Moby Dick* was not mentioned at all during the first seventy years after it was published. In a like way, as the poems of Emily Dickinson were not published during her lifetime, so Edwin Arlington Robinson and Robert Frost suffered for twenty years from the lack of understanding and recognition which Emily Dickinson would have experienced if she had been published. For the time being at least, the New Criticism has diminished the kind of deafness and darkness with which these poets were confronted.

The consolations of a historical perspective can be overestimated. Yet, going back twenty-five years, one has only to read the pronouncements of H. L. Mencken on the art of poetry as a pack of lies, the *avant-garde* as a pack of poseurs and pretenders, the puerility of Thorstein Veblen and John Dewey and the nobility of war to see that the supposed glory of the first postwar period is mostly a nostalgia for exuberance. And if one goes back fifty years to the time of Howells, George Woodberry, Hamilton W. Mabie, Henry Van Dyke, and Barret Wendell, one comes upon a literary scene which was an appalling gentleman's club inhabited by a host of genteel mediocrities most of whom were devoted to impersonating that familiar ghost who has haunted American literature since the time of Washington Irving, the imaginary Englishman.

Although in the ancient past, Sisyphus was condemned by the gods to roll a rock to the top of a mountain, today Sisyphus is a literary critic. Every time he finishes a book review, he has to begin a new one: his task, being the task of criticism is endless and without termination. But now as the imaginary Englishman returns dressed in the tunic of the new conservatism and as the howling Comanches of mass culture whoop it up on the TV screen, Sisyphus cannot help but see the new critic's love of literature in a redeeming light.

Kenneth Rexroth

THE YOUNGER GENERATION AND ITS BOOKS

Right now we're in one of those cyclic crescendos of fret about the younger generation, several decibles above the fret about Clara Bow. Much of this is just the eternal worry of the old as the young discover the secrets of life. There is a brief transition period of human life— a penumbra, alas all too narrow—between the discovery of the Truth and the acceptance of the Social Lie. Those humans who are living in it always frighten those who have outgrown it.

It is in music that those who have entered the brief span of comparative wisdom known as youth have spoken most clearly. The music of Gillespie, Parker, Young, and Tristano, Brubeck, Mulligan is the specific idiom which speaks of, for, to, and by the young. This is the clear unmistakable, insistent voice of rejection. You cannot begin to understand what is going on until you realize that all over the world "Fouilles-tu l'Oiseau?" has taken the place of "Soviets partout."

The descent from music to literature for them is a drop of several qualitative levels. Ask your younger brothers, nephews, sons, "Does Norman Mailer speak for you?" The answer will be, "No, I don't recognize anybody I know in that book." It is necessary to remember that there are three distinct age groups of writers: the one that began to publish during the war—even I belong to this one, so does Kenneth Patchen, so does Nelson Algren, and so does Henry Miller, old enough to be everybody's grandfather; the group that began to write during the war and published immediately afterwards, of whom Mailer is a good example; beginning to breathe down all our necks is a group that has had to take the wars, not twice in a lifetime, but twice in childhood and youth. These are the boys nobody wants to face.

There are several spurious youth running around whom it would be well to challenge. The literature of the International Set, the denizens of Tangiers and the suburbs of Florence—Paul Bowles and Truman Capote —is thriller-diller stuff on the lowest level, comic books for the vulgar. I don't know anyone under thirty who reads them. Like Michael Arlen in another epoch, their audience is shop girls and housemaids who save their nickels to subscribe to the more expensive flapper fashion magazines.

Secondly, there's plain money-writing—some of it on a fairly high level and, because of the rough house demand of the pocket book audience, able to get away with a degree of social criticism unknown in earlier popular literature. Jones is the type, and the science fiction writers—although some of the latter are beginning to move over into the pseudo-sophisticated slick magazines, for example, Ray Bradbury.

I think that the nature of popular fiction, the never-ceasing demand for dames overthrown by force and violence, makes it the most socially significant writing, aesthetics to the contrary, taking place. The genealogy runs Hemingway-Hammett-Cain-Chandler-Horace Mc-Coy, with Henry Miller in left field, a mixed metaphor which will cover the blood on the scanties school and the Brooklyn boy approach direct. Possibly Farrell, Algren, and other Chicago realists had a hand in it too; but they are altogether too elegiac in pace for the prose which now rules the roost in front of the local drug store. The secret of this kind of writing is that it isn't buying anything and it isn't selling anything; and it hasn't since it first began to appear in the pages of *Black Mask* where the style was deliberately and consciously developed before the war.

Two recent books are outstanding examples of this style and they interest me more than any of the others in this article—Manchester's *City of Anger* and Mandel's *Flee The Angry Strangers*. There are all sorts of things wrong with them, Manchester's cast is an enormous collection of Harry Stack Sullivan case histories, rather than people or even archetypal caricatures of the Dickens order. I should imagine that it was Dickens he was aiming at. In spite of thinness of characterization, his huge web of "interpersonal relations," to use the fashionable term, does catch up and hold something of the living or living-dead reality of the city of anger, the city Bunyan's Pilgrim fled from, the city waiting for the Bomb, the city where we all live.

Mandel's relationship to the metier is certainly rather remote. I imagine the cats in the village bars get up when he sits down. The book, especially in the opening chapters, sounds like a collaboration of Little Joe Gould, Maxwell Bodenheim, and a collegiate imitator of Damon Runyon. But he learns by doing, and the latter half of the book is probably as true a picture of the totally alienated as you're likely to get.

Chester Himes is another writer on the pocket book level. He is possibly more vulgar than Ralph Ellison, but he is more convincing, and both of them present the same picture of Negro total rejection. I would say that Himes is more popular with Negroes because of his confident and simple identification with his material. Most Negroes I know find too much extraneous worry in Ellison and are suspicious of his ambition.

There is an intermediate group which includes Bour-jaily, Burns, Merle Miller; still young, they are not quite money writers, super slicks, or *avant-garde*. It may well be that one of these people—and there are several more than those I've named—will crawl up to the head of the track in the next ten years.

I'm not sure where to put Salinger. His *Catcher In the Rye,* a re-take of F. Scott Fitzgerald's *This Side of Paradise,* concerns the adolescent problems of a prep school youth. I don't know any prep school youth, and I don't know anybody who does. But in spite of this specialization, Salinger does get across the same indict-ment: for youth, even some rich youth, this is a world of strangers, going about their lethal, clandestine, and wrathful business, all of them enemies.

With young Roman Catholic writers, rejection is absolute and it is very assured. J. F. Powers is, in my opinion, the best short story writer to come up in many years. His work is a cunning blend of Farrell, Bernanos, and the most savage whimsy of the *New Yorker,* ortho-dox but self-critical and eminently humane. Merton I find a trifle over-decorative, but he is certainly a con-siderable poet. My own taste runs more to the rougher, more direct poetry of Brother Antoninus, OP, for-merly William Everson.

Last, there is the world of the quarterlies, for better or worse. The young people I know condemn all of it as "school teacher literature." Art with a capital "A" has become polite, or at the best "social worker art" in the eyes of the disaffiliated. I'm inclined to agree, but I'm also inclined to make a few exceptions. Writers like Saul Bellow, Jean Stafford, Elizabeth Hardwicke, Mary McCarthy, Eleanor Clark are such. Pre-war versions of the forgotten—the highbrow writers—are Harold Frederick, David Graham Phillips, Robert Herrick, or Edith Wharton, none as good as Mrs. E. L. Voynich.

This is the world of *haut cuisine* presided over by E. M. Forster and Virginia Woolf. It can safely be left to the classrooms—nobody among these young strangers cares anything about it.

Of course these writers are not very young. They were all formed by the transition of the American academic intellectual from the 4½ International to the European Defense Community. You can hardly expect a youth who sat out the Korean war to read these authors even if the GI bill pays him to sit in a classroom and listen to it.

There has, of course, been a continuous production of books by the younger generation of Southern writers, but it is easier to name bad ones than good ones. The only good ones that occur to me are *The Heart Is A Lonely Hunter, Reflections In A Golden Eye,* and *Lie Down In Darkness.* These are essentially reworkings of Faulkner. The great danger, and a danger to which Carson Mc-Cullers may already have succumbed, is that she and William Styron will have graduated to swimming pools and yachts before they have learned how to write.

This is the great danger all around. I cannot agree with Aldridge's *After The Lost Generation* that novels by and large perform the social function of a constant symbolic criticism of values. With few exceptions in the history of literature, novels have been written for the immature. Aristotle was right—tragedy must deal with the problems of adults. A real mastery of fictional dramaturgy comes late, and if Hollywood is there with a checkbook before you reach the age of 25, your goose is cooked. Where would Joseph Conrad have been, pray tell, if someone had handed him a check for $100,000 for *Almayer's Folly?*

I suppose I should write something about poetry. Since I write poetry myself, I guess I'm less tolerant. It seems to me something terrible has gone wrong with poetry. After the generation of Hollywood, the Communist Party, the WPA, and *Time* magazine, poetry was never able to raise its head again. The poet the young read is Kenneth Patchen, not themselves, except as a sort of duty.

There are a few poets in the quarterlies who have come up since the war. Probably the best are Richard Wilbur, Jean Garrigue, Ruth Herschberger, Paul Goodman, Theodore Roethke, Robert Duncan. The only young poet who shares the total rejection of the novelists and musicians is Philip Lamantia. James Laughlin puts him in what he still calls *New Directions* whenever he can get something, and Lamantia turns up periodically in such magazines as *Horizon, Tiger's Eye, Portfolio, Botteghe Oscure.* He is the one young American poet included in all European collections of American verse.

Theoretically there should be a large popular poetic literature taking off from Fearing, Patchen, Sandburg, and the better, if there were any, proletarian poets, and saying the same things that the pocket book writers say. Alas, there are only academic exercises, wearily tapped out on the typewriter to add grace to the final accolade of a teaching fellowship in English in a small college.

There is a sort of poetic underworld in the mimeographed little magazines. Curiously enough the editors of these publications seem to write better than most of their contributors, unless they are other editors. I have the feeling that in each case the editor starts a poetry magazine in hopes that out of the mail will drop something really good, the kind of poem he himself has always wanted to write. One of the curious things about post war poetry is that a hero of the young is the author of the longest hymn of hate in literature, Ezra Pound.

Older than most of the contributors to these mimeographed publications is Charles Olson, and, I suspect for this reason alone, he is probably the best known. Robert Creelcy, Richard Emerson, Fred Eckman, Gil

Orlovitz are the best of the younger people. Eckman and Emerson edit the magazine—printed, not mimeographed—called the *Golden Goose*. I know them well, and I know they try to find and print the poetry the young are waiting to see.

Robert Richman

AMERICAN PAINTING AND SCULPTURE

If it can be said that American letters and American architecture are no longer those of a Colonial culture and have had a major influence on the literature and architecture of Europe, it must also be said that the influence in painting and sculpture has been that of Europe upon America. And on many levels: we are at the stage in these visual arts when a Colony seeks its cultural independence and having broken from the mother culture can walk along with the significant artists of Europe that influenced the Americans many of whom like Cézanne, Matisse, Picasso, Braque and Moore remained in Europe, and those who among others emigrated to America—Gabo, Mondrian, Duchamp, Tanguy, Chagall and Steinberg.

The decade of the 1950s in American painting will surely be landmarked by the influence of three native painters whose work has been revalued at the event of their deaths: of John Marin in October of 1953, who stands in the highest order of our artists; of Arthur Dove in 1946; of Marsden Hartley in 1943, more rugged, less lyric than Marin and less mystic than Dove, more somber in color and less aerial; all of whom have had a profound and generative influence on the young painters and still loom large as America's three Internationalists, who are gathered together in our memory as being that generation of artists who broke from the naive imitation of European styles with the eloquent encouragement of Ryder before them pointing the way. As Melville, Henry James and Edward Arlington Robinson were to American letters, Marin, Dove and Hartley seem to be to our painting, along with one other—Lyonel Feininger—whose painting in a very special way is the unique combination of the European version of geometric abstract painting which he helped to form, while he taught at the Bauhaus, and of the indigenous art of America from which he springs.

These are the senior native painters and it would seem that theirs has been the most formative modern tradition rising up from the American continent to shape its contemporary painting. The middle generation of the native born—Stuart Davis, Georgia O'Keefe, Mark Tobey and Karl Knaths and the next generation of I. Rice Periera, Loren MacIver and Willem de Kooning have each made original variations upon this modern tradition shaped by the senior painters and born out of the abstract art of modern Europe. There are other formative influences also: that of the pre-Colombian art of the Toltecs, the Aztecs and the Mayas; of the pottery of the Arizona Indians and the Navajo sand paintings; of American folk art as it was rediscovered by the WPA artists who illustrated it for the Index of American Design; and of the International style in our architecture, parkways, contour-plowed fields, industrial arts and graphic design. In naming these climates of influence on contemporary American painting and sculpture, I imply in the best artists only those relationships of the winds in erosion to the rocks. The conditions of painting in our milieu are not simple: no Titian works in the studio of Giorgione.

The condition of sculpture has not been as complicated. The senior sculptors are the American-born Alexander Calder; the Russian-Americans—Naum Gabo, the Constructivist and Archipenko, the Cubist; and the younger Isamu Noguchi—American-born of Japanese parents. These artists all seem to be in the prime of their creative lives; and especially Gabo, who for me symbolizes the really modern artist at work in America because he is both explorer and first resident citizen of constructivism—a land of art he helped to discover, like Henry James, T. S. Eliot, Cézanne, Braque, or Paul Hindemith, each one of whom has not only been an explorer, each has been a first settler as well, even to the point of financing his own Massachusetts Bay Company, without the protection of the British Fleet.

There is one artist unique in the 1950s whose works resemble the position of the works of Paul Klee held in their relationship to the tradition of painting and drawing. Moreover like Klee's work, his cannot be copied or used. I refer of course to the Rumanian-American, Saul Steinberg, whose work is as matchless for the humor and ease of his drawing as for the penetration of his vision into man.

This argument does not seek to run aground on the issue of national roots—those of Europe, Asia, South or North America—and surely not for reasons of chauvinism. All the same, this is the age in which, for the first time, American artists did not have to go to a Rome or Paris of Art. The European painters were instead coming to America to live; and they brought their works, their easels and their influences with them. The Transatlantic passage of influences in the visual arts began with the International Exhibition of Modern Art in 1913 at the Armory in New York City; it became a two-way exchange, as indeed the travel of the artists themselves was to become two-way. Here in the visual arts, then, in America, there is a new international—or it could be a post-national—spirit in painting, sculpture and architecture quite like the spirit of Europe in the Age of Erasmus, which was pre-national, with the Latin language for intellectual and cultural intercourse, except that the geography and population of the new internationalism has no boundaries and there are no language boundaries in this Paris-Rome-Berlin-New York-Chicago axis of art. In the presence of this spirit, the early Marin, Dove and Hartley with good reason called themselves "The Internationalists."

Since there have been fewer sculptors at work than painters, it is easier to see the finest work and the more direct trends in this decade. The work of Naum Gabo is becoming more and more well-known in America. In the eight years he has been living and working in New England—four miles on one arm of a triangle from Alexander Calder and four miles on the other from Yves Tanguy, the Surrealist painter—Gabo's work has taken its place rightfully in the major private and museum collections of the world. His sculpture stands, in my opinion, as the finest of its genre—a formal geometric abstract art—as pure as a theorem, as graceful as a generalization in philosophy, and in its reach one of the highest flights of the creative spirit, as the best fugues and poems are.

Spontaneity is Calder's major achievement and contribution to another genre—that of organic abstract sculpture. That is not to say casualness, for his sculptures have the order, the pattern and the passion of a leaf's right to move on its twig, the twig on its branch, the branch on its trunk, down to the very roots. Calder reminds one of Brancusi and Moore—in that he too "shared credit with his materials"; and in his mechanical organization alone he resembles the Russian Constructivists. The best of Calder's work intertwines botany with engineering, behaving as a plant behaves in the wind, with a choreography among the leaves that one usually associates with a school of very small fish. These are joyous procedures and high achievement.

To Gabo and to Calder, the work of Isamu Noguchi

must be compared as that of a peer with his peers. With those sculptures we call the Constructivist or geometric abstract work, and the Realist (in Cézanne's sense) or organic abstract work, it is essential to compare the third type, or the Symbolic in the work of Noguchi. All three are types of abstract art: Calder's art progresses by abstracting from the visible forms in Nature, and proceeds by synthesis; Gabo's art progresses by abstracting from the conceptual laws upon which Nature operates invisibly, and proceeds by analysis; Noguchi's art progresses, as rites and rituals do, by abstracting from the elemental emotional experiences of man—what Freud called the "primitive" or racial experiences. And Noguchi's procedure is mimesis, that of a Western man (he apprenticed to Brancusi) and of the Oriental craftsman —the Sung caligrapher or potter—who lets the form autogenetically evolve out of the materials. This is at the opposite pole from the Constructivists who as a mirror to their concept create their images and construct them with materials. Their concepts of space and motion differ not in kind among these three types of abstract sculpture, but in degree and emphasis. Each derives from the new physics.

Of the younger generation, the work of Richard Lippold looms best, certainly most considered and sound in its use of the tradition of Gabo, Calder and Noguchi whose work he has assimilated in the best sense and from which he has made original departures to achieve his own style and idiom. His sense of form stems from the Constructivists and from music, which gives his work one aspect of lyricism, the other aspect of which seems to be like Calder's use of Nature, particularly of snowflakes. From Noguchi he employs a variation of symbolism; Lippold has taken one facet—the surface instead of the core of the ritual, not unlike the manner in which a poetic image works. Other younger sculptors have made an even less satisfactory use of symbolism than has

Noguchi. And their use of materials differs from the Brancusi, Moore and Noguchi techniques in which the artist "shared credit with his materials." In the works of David Hare, Mary Callery, Herbert Ferber, Theodore Roszak and David Smith are reflected these and the influence of Giacometti, Moore, Arp, Lipschitz, Zorach, or the Surrealists. The influences of Rodin and Matisse and of Malliol's idealizations of the nude body in either the underweight variations of Lehmbruck or the overweight variations of Lachaise are on the wane.

It seems important that Gabo, Noguchi and Calder have turned back the concerted campaign in the twenties, thirties and forties, of the International stylists in architecture—especially by those trained in the Bauhaus in Germany and in the New Bauhaus in Chicago—and the designers of industrial art to capture painting and sculpture, to colonize and to exploit them into decoration, the subdivision, of what was then reverently called Design. What actually happened was more in accord with historic precedent: these sculptors influenced the architects and they in turn influenced the former in a reciprocal manner. Many of Gabo's works, particularly his models, were monuments that were married to architecture and engineering, and as such they exerted influence upon the International style in architecture and in industrial art. Noguchi has actually influenced the design of furniture not only indirectly by his sculpture in which he has been the vehicle for transmuting the methods of Brancusi's use of materials but directly by the tables and lamps, and by the stage sets for the dance theatre of Martha Graham and of Erick Hawkins, which he has designed and executed. These sets are high peaks in scenic art and have had salutary effect on the work of the Abstract-Expressionists. Calder's influence has quietly and happily been absorbed by such designers as Charles Eames, who in designing his well known chairs learned from the "leaves and branches" of Calder.

The painters have had far greater difficulty in withstanding the stylistic invasions of the Bauhaus designers and the architects of the International Style and the Abstract-Imitators (the naive copists of Mondrian and Malevich). Even though the best of the painters—as did the best of the sculptors—repelled them, the infiltration devastated much professional painting and nearly all amateur painting in the forties and fifties. "Abstract Art for Abstract Art's sake" is now a popular movement. It is the mode for not only the Sunday painters but for most of the lesser weekday painters—the tenth to the third-rate ones. Even the second order of painters seems to be united with them in their fallacy. And it is the historic fallacy of the right to revolt in art for the wrong reason. Amid the many strands of influence from the turn of the century to date and among the many trends in style, the second and third generation painters are now poised at their crucial phase of history—at what, as it were, is the phase of their articles of confederation.

The contestants have literally though loosely drawn camps—not as the French did in Dadaism complete with a group, a manifesto, and an agreed aim. And the factions in American painting have been many. The principals are embittered partisans and they paint for a small though partisan set of critics and audience. The factions which come the closest to a working majority in this Chamber of Painterly Deputies are two: the reactionary Right is the Geometric Abstract painting of the Post-Cubist and Constructivist movement (this movement is the one which is imitated by that group of naive copists who comprise nearly a popular front of the Sunday and the Lesser Weekday painters); and the radical Left is called the Abstract-Expressionist movement—epitomized by Jackson Pollock—which demands a freedom of form and of symbol and in this condition has an affinity with, and prompts a revival of, romantic painting. Arranged between these two opponent movements in contemporary painting in America is the snarled multitude of vestigal and chthonic though minority movements.

The roots of the snarl reach to 1908 when a group of American painters formed "The Eight" of which John Sloane is its memorable artist; but another of "The Eight" was to be the cause of a greater influence: it was Arthur Davies who was the guiding force in organizing the famous 1913 Armory Show comprised of 1600 pieces of the new art mostly from Europe. Surely never has so concentrated a revolutionary influence from a foreign culture been dropped so abruptly in the midst of a native culture with so profound a cataclysm—all nearly within a week-end. Evolving out of that exhibition was a group of American artists—Marin, Joseph Stella, Hartley, Feininger and Dove, who, though heavily under the influence of the new art of Europe, were near enough in age to the advent of the Fauves and of the Cubists so that they grew and flourished simultaneously with Matisse, Picasso, Braque, Klee and Kandinsky.

Marin, Dove, Alfred Maurer and Hartley, and other Americans also called "The Internationalists," worked predominantly in either geometric abstraction or organic abstraction. These artists and their descendants were to encounter the second unique influence nearly thirty years later, when Mondrian, Duchamp, Gabo, and Gropius, Albers and Moholy-Nagy—teachers from the Bauhaus—and the Surrealists, Yves Tanguy, Max Ernst and William Hayter among others moved from Europe to America and made their homes. An exhibition in 1913 and an European emigration in the thirties—in which, for the first time in American history, artists came West from Europe—were to intensify the normal change in styles of art, all with sudden speed.

The impulse and regeneration of the second wave from Europe helped bring to a close the movements of Regionalism and Social Realism which had their birth largely in reaction to the first wave of twentieth century

European Art. A violent reaction to the 1913 Armory Show, which gave courage and affirmation to the Internationalist painters in America was to be expected: it came seventeen years later after the World War, the Russian Revolution and the Great Depression. But the delay merely built up the pressure of the reaction; and for the first time, before or since—roughly the years between the Depression and the Appeasement at Munich —American painters grouped together on one agreed theme: to destroy the Abstract Art of the Internationalists in America, and, in general, that type of influence from European art. There were actually two of these reactionary groups: one was Regionalism—Edward Hopper, Charles Burchfield, Grant Wood among others who were anti-abstract and pro-romantic in their preferences of art; the other was Social Realism—Ben Shahn, William Gropper, Jack Levine among others who espoused the Marxian theory of art in which the subject matter differed from that of abstract art *ex officio*.

Both the Regionalists and the Social Realists were doubly effective for in many instances they worked for a single patron, the WPA, and painted the "American Scene" or the "American Suffering" prolifically and profitably. What is now obvious, but was then befogged, is that Regionalist and Social Realist painters, either of the first order or the second, were reacting against the whole of the European tradition in the modern movement begun by Cézanne, though they assumed that they were revolting only against an ill-advised group of Americans, the Internationalist painters whom the 1913 Armory Show had degraded. Although Hopper and Burchfield outgrew the confines of Regionalism, as Charles Sheeler and Niles Spencer did, the second order in this movement perpetuated the mistake and ignoring the real tradition of painting in the West became fanatic or monastic disciples of realism like John Curry, Thomas Benton and, later, Grant Wood.

Near the end of the thirties Marin, Hartley, Dove and Georgia O'Keefe; Feininger, May Ray, Stuart Davis and Karl Knaths—the list is incomplete—had established an important belief: it was that the tradition of painting in America was one of a continuous evolution out of and with the art of Europe; and that the adjectives *American* or *European* could not properly be used to restrict painting that was essentially *Western*. This new idea also attracted the generation of Willem de Kooning, Loren MacIver, I. Rice Periera, Morris Graves and Robert Motherwell, in whom with variations on their senior generation in American painting, abstract art—the organic and the geometric—was to move into its second phase in America; because whereas the energetic output of the Regionalists and the Social Realists waned, so too did their influence on the younger first rank painters who were attracted to the symbolic and the abstract in art.

Before the imminent outbreak of World War II, the artists and intellectuals of Europe came in exodus to America; the event paralleled the Armory Show of 1913 which was held in the shadow of an earlier war. In the forties, this influence of the artists themselves though slower, was to become as profoundly deep as that of the Armory Show. Most of these artists who came were individually at work within the strict confines of doctrinaire schools either of geometric abstract art or of the Surrealistic or of the fantastic, et cetera. The important ones were Mondrian (the de Stijls), Gabo (the Constructivists), Archipenko (the Cubists) and Léger, and a group of artist-teachers—Ozenfant (the French Purists) and Gropius, Moholy-Nagy and Albers (from the Bauhaus). Then there was Duchamp (Futurist), Tanguy (Surrealist) and Chagall (Imagist). There were other emigrant artists who were ministers of similar schools of European painting; but the influences coming from Europe in the work of Klee, of Braque, of Picasso, of

Henry Moore and of Miro were more vital and formative than those of the lesser emigrant artists. Cézanne, too, was now being discovered directly by the younger Americans, and no longer by way of the Cubists and the Constructivists.

Throughout the thirties and the forties other strands of influence were being formed, like the important one by Mark Tobey, O'Keefe and, later, Morris Graves who among others made of their American and European sources a direct fusion with calligraphy from Oriental art. And other influences on the painters were those indirectly of pre-Colombian artifacts, of prehistoric Arizona Indian pottery decorated in amazingly modern conventionalized design, or of Navajo sand paintings. These pre-Colombian influences and the Oriental, the younger generation of American painters have interwoven with the works of Klee and Miro. Such as William Baziotes, Robert Motherwell and Theodore Stamos—in a manner similar to the Expressionists for they use a less contrived idea—have revitalized organic abstract art in the fifties with their special use of mythic and primordial symbols. They paint freer, more biomorphic forms than the geometric abstract group—Davis, Knaths, Periera and Bradley Tomlin; but all these abstract painters, the organic and the geometric, have made a proper and salutary use of the native twentieth century tradition of Marin, Dove, Hartley and Feininger; of the American-European tradition of Gabo, Mondrian and Duchamp; and of the European tradition of Cézanne, Braque, Moore and Klee, who though leaders were also individually greater than the movements they led.

It is nearly commonplace to say that since 1940 the tendency to abstract has had major emphasis among the best artists in America; that, as movements, Social Realism and Regionalism have become decadent; that Surrealism, as a movement, has blended into the genre called the Symbolic Abstract; and that with this genre, the Geometric Abstract and the Organic Abstract are each moving from their experimental into their classic phases, which is to say in another way that these three variations of abstract art have merged with the dominant tradition of Western painting in America. Here innovations and gains are consolidated as they were in all classic periods of art—in Byzantium, in the Middle Ages, in Sung China, or in Greece.

There is yet a fourth development in America—that called Abstract-Expressionism—which is marked mainly by the work of Jackson Pollock, Frederick Kiesler, Mark Rothko, Edward Corbett and Clyfford Still. It is a variant breaking from the Symbolic Abstract—a far left revolutionary movement which marks the beginning, roughly at 1950, of the third wave of our abstract art. Paralleling this, though by no means related to it nor deriving from it, is the formation of a Popular Academy of "abstract" art by miraculous conversions of that multitude of amateur painters who ten years ago were transfixing upon their canvases instead "The Connecticut Hills at Dusk," or "A Nude of Academe," or "A Still Life with Digitalis."

All the same the Abstract-Expressionists may share a common aesthetic error with the Popular Academy: they too seem to have lost sight of the reasons for the revolt that began modern painting. These Expressionists though high professional talents do not demand of themselves what Cézanne demanded—preciseness of vision and integrity of form. Upon these two postulates, and upon a new philosophic theory of reality, modern art was founded and must for its growth depend, with each artist engaging the three—vision, form, reality—at first hand and intimately. Pollock cannot use extrusion and dripulation merely because Cézanne adapted Poussin's realizations of Nature and varied Seurat's use of pointillism—color architecture. For his methods Pollock must have the reasons for use that Cézanne had for his: any work of visual art must come from the direct encounter with precise vision and with the search for an integrity of form by which to create that new reality, the work of art. Cézanne differs from Poussin not because he took up where Poussin left off: rather, Cézanne looked more deeply into the same problems of vision, of form, and of reality, where his forebears began.

The Abstract-Expressionists must look deeply into these and not just at the problems solved by Cézanne, Braque, or Miro, if they are to enrich the traditions of Western painting by giving it their shape and direction in the next half-century. They cannot proceed by abstracting from abstraction—that is, from the body of twentieth century abstract painting and sculpture. To do this bodes deterioration of the movement into anarchy. Indeed the loss of precise vision is revealed by their lack of an integral or evolved form, for, as it were, paintings of Pollock (*Number 7, 1950* and *Number 30, 1950*) or Frederick Kiesler's (*Galaxy*) "endless painting" (the term is his) or the work of Still, reminiscent of relief maps in black and white, very nearly could have been formed without material damage by extending or cutting the length or the width a few inches. Corbett and Rothko have more formal sense. Of the movement as a whole it must be said that experimental though it is, the Abstract-Expressionists are trying to cope with the ever-present struggle to weave the figurative with the abstract. Indeed Pollock's work in 1953, *Ocean Greyness* and *Greyed Rainbow* show this change.

Juan Gris wrote in his notebooks in 1924: "painting for me is like a fabric, all of a piece and uniform, with one set of threads as the representational, aesthetic element, and the cross-threads as the technical, architectural or abstract element; and if one set is lacking the fabric does not exist." In the past forty years there have been in America many attempts to separate the threads, either to keep the two apart or to let them reunite in new combinations. The novelty of the union in Abstract-Expression is not enough; but in the very latest works in each of the other three types of abstract painting and sculpture, the best artists have made some and announce other such tapestries.

Robert Evett

Until the early part of the twentieth century, the fine art music of the United States was imitation European music, always behind the European fashion, and usually intrinsically poor as well because of the academic spirit which motivated it. Composers born just after 1870—Arthur Farwell, Carl Ruggles and especially Charles Ives—are generally thought to have broken the silver cord with the parent culture, and it is true that Ives wrote an experimental music which in many ways anticipated certain European radical innovations. Farwell's music has already been forgotten, and Ives and Ruggles are easier to admire in the abstract than they are to listen to. None of these composers founded a school; Ives, in particular, owes his fame to the work of younger men in his behalf. In retrospect, the Ives *chic* of the thirties and early forties seems to have been little more than a gracious gesture from a younger generation toward an older man who had, in some ways, anticipated the rhythmic and tonal developments of the twentieth century.

Perhaps the golden decade of American composition was that of the thirties. At that time, a group of young composers appeared whose work compared favorably with the best of their European contemporaries. Of these, Roy Harris and Aaron Copland were by far the most fortunate in their relations with the public. In their early days they were unified by an identity of purpose with Walter Piston, Quincy Porter, Roger Sessions, Virgil Thomson, and the Mexican, Carlos Chavez. They were flanked on the left by experimenters—Edgard Varèse, Ruth Crawford, and Henry Cowell. On the right, there were Randall Thompson, Ernst Bacon, Otto Luening and Douglas Moore. Howard Hanson, though not motivated toward a modern style, was generous in his assistance of many of the others. Wallingford Riegger, whose stature has not yet been fully revealed to the public, was evolving his style slowly.

These composers worked under optimum conditions. Their music was sufficiently novel to shock at least part of the public out of its apathy: they had the support of at least one superb critic, Paul Rosenfeld, and the sympathetic interest of several less erudite reviewers; they were among the first to enjoy the financial support of the Guggenheim foundation, of Yaddo and the Mac-Dowell colony; many of them were championed by a superb European virtuoso, Serge Koussevitsky, whose authority was sufficient to provoke the emulation of other conductors. Yaddo, the League of Composers, and the International Society for Contemporary Music encouraged their production of chamber music; Copland and Sessions organized their own concert series. In California, Henry Cowell and others published new scores on a subscription basis. The *Modern Music* magazine, which expired in 1946, served as an invaluable forum for the exchange of ideas. Commercial recording companies and publishers, dance groups and motion picture companies began to commission works. Academic institutions began to show preference for the younger composers, with the result that, as the 1929 depression began, there were few unemployed modern composers in the United States. The world was being very, very kind.

As these young composers matured, their individual developments pointed up serious discrepancies in their basic aims. Piston became the champion of post-classical tradition while Sessions developed a rather abstruse radical style. Copland began to specialize in light, cheerful music while Harris aimed at monumentality of design and concept.

The growing breach, based as it was on style, developed into a really serious rivalry for the few performances that mattered. Koussevitsky and Mrs. Elizabeth Sprague Coolidge offered not only performances but really handsome fees which everybody wanted. Every performance by the Boston Symphony, the New York Philharmonic, or by Mrs. Coolidge's chamber groups at the Library of Congress meant an enormous increase in prestige.

A certain equilibrium was maintained as long as most of these composers lived in or near the city of New York. At first, "near" meant that Princeton and Boston were not too remote, but gradually, Piston, who took a chair at Harvard, proved to be too far away, and Sessions and Harris, at Princeton, began to lose out. The desire for a better living took Harris farther away from New York, and Sessions to the University of California, where he virtually disappeared. Chavez went back to Mexico City and he, too was talked about less and less in the United States. Quincy Porter, at Yale, lost out even more. This left, in New York, only Aaron Copland and Virgil Thomson of the first-generation moderns who had started out so auspiciously. Varèse, who was also there, stopped writing for a long time. Cowell, Riegger, Moore, Luening and Randall Thompson moved to that city, though Thompson's involvement with it has been casual, but none of them has been able to really get all of his chestnuts out of the fire.

While the careers of these first-generation moderns were expanding and contracting, a second generation was growing up, largely under the tutelage of the older men. Most of the younger composers took teaching positions outside New York, and a strange kind of parochialism began to develop. Gifted young men, like Halsey Stevens and John Edmunds of San Francisco, Cecil Effinger of Colorado, Robert Palmer and Hunter Johnson began to lose access to the performances in New York from which they could be expected to get some prestige —not only the orchestral performances, which have always been a luxury, but the chamber music performances which were once thought to be their right. The most celebrated of these composers are William Schuman and David Diamond, who stayed in New York.

When Roy Harris left New York, he had grand visions of the future of music in the United States, in which the virtuoso tradition would become a thing of the past, and in which every town with a good composer or two in it would become a little Athens. The plain fact is that provincial cities were and are over-aware of their subservience to New York; Hollywood and Washington, both world capitals in other fields, are not cordial to their resident composers. The late Ruth Crawford had to live in Washington for almost a generation before her work was honored by a performance by the symphony orchestra of that city. There are at least three other fine composers there: Esther Williamson, Robert Parris and the Reverend Russell Woollen, who have never been performed by the National Symphony, or by any other large orchestra.

This situation is paralleled all over the country. Most of Vincent Persichetti's enormous orchestral output has never been heard in his native Philadelphia, nor any place else. Even the Boston composers, Lukas Foss, Harold Shapero, and Irving Fine, are relatively neglected, but they are well-off when compared with Howard Boatwright and David Krehenbuell in New Haven.

Because of the sorry state of affairs in the provinces,

most of the youngest American generation look on leaving New York with horror, and will do so only if the big foundations guarantee them a temporary living. Actually, most of them have no place to go, as the teaching jobs which lured their seniors away are full; there are virtually no vacancies to be had for which their training would qualify them. New York is glutted with composers who are afraid to leave, unemployed, or barely employed. They operate addressograph machines, they work at Brentano's and Howard Johnson's, and a few lucky ones, like Alan Hovhaness and Ben Weber either teach an instrument or act as copyists and autographers. In less than thirty years time, the American musical scene has been turned from a desert into a slum. Like all slums, this one has its gangs, its group wars and private murders; such order as it has is maintained by the moral equivalent of a corrupt police force.

This situation is the result of an overproduction of composers, and the overproduction is the result of a generous intention. In a nation where most intellectuals live by wages, intellectual education takes on the coloration of vocational training. As a consequence, any advanced training has a professional intention, and in music, where even amateur standing can be reached only with deadly intensity, all training is for a professional end. Academic standards for training in composition are so loose that it is virtually impossible to establish and maintain high standards. The result is that a young person with neither talent nor fortitude can be graduated from schools as a bona-fide composer; he can, in fact, pay several thousand dollars in return for certification as a composer. It shouldn't take a ouija-board to show that talent in musical composition cannot be bought and sold. In a period when style is undergoing considerable change, however, it can take more than that to recognize talent.

After the supply and the demand have been regulated

by proper training, the first half-century of real American composition will provide a field for study rather like that of the baroque era. Some composers will be lost altogether, others will have proven to be the Bachs and Vivaldis of their time.

At present, so much is being written and so many manuscripts are inaccessible that a proper evaluation of what has been done is impossible. As candidates for a later, probably posthumous, evaluation, one may list Roy Harris, Walter Piston, Roger Sessions, William Schuman, Robert Palmer and Lou Harrison; some of these will surely have to yield to persons less known.

The ugliest single phenomenon of American composition is the system of decades by which it is measured. One says, for instance, that the twenties was the decade of dissonant counterpoint, the thirties the decade of fugue writing, the forties the decade of Mozartian lightness, the fifties the decade of post-expressionism, and so on. Nobody but the music historian wants this, primarily because no composer is confined to ten years of creative effort.

Since 1940, the only composers who have made names for themselves in the United States have been the ultra-conservatives, like Gian-Carlo Menotti and Samuel Barber, and those radicals who are to the left of Schoenberg, notably John Cage and Morton Feldman. These composers represent neither the direction of music in general, nor that of its phase in the United States.

The problem of American composers is not to surpass the Europeans, either in radicalism or in reaction, but to remain part of Western culture, arriving simultaneously with Europe at superficial qualities of technique and style while allowing individual personalities to develop. The only composers who don't know this are those enjoying a vogue at the present.

Eric Bentley

GIVE MY REGARDS TO BROADWAY

The profoundest analyst of American culture, Tocqueville, suggested that democracy was not conducive to democratic art. And the twentieth century, without removing any of the obstacles to theatre which the French critic listed, has added a few more, notably the movies in its second decade, radio in its third, and TV in its fifth. This being so, the surprising fact is not that the theatre is harassed but that it exists at all. Nowhere have the substitutes for theatre been so developed and accepted as in America. Yet there is still an American theatre. Why?

One thing we have learned is that in the present phase of history one medium's gain is not always the other's loss: the phonograph record has enlarged, not depleted, the audience at symphony concerts. The theatre affords, perhaps, no precise analogy to this famous triumph in the musical field. The old "road" theatre *was* largely wiped out by the movies; the Broadway public *is* very small compared with the movie and TV public. Nonetheless, the spread of community and university theatres goes some way toward replacing the road companies. And, in New York there is a wide response to almost any good play when it has a good—or even just a glossy —production. In short, the idea that the theatre is dying

—like certain churches—because the public has lost interest and is busy elsewhere is simply not true.

Professionally, the theatre retains the primacy which many of us believe to be its natural right; it is by virtue of no empty traditionalism that the theatre page (or column) precedes movies, radio and TV in the papers or takes precedence over them in a magazine like the *New Republic.* The three newer arts remain to a remarkable extent parasites: they draw talent from the theatre, not vice versa. When we hear of a movie actor appearing on the stage, we find either that he was stage-trained or that he is no good. There is of course the third possibility: that he has had stage training *and* is no good; he *had* to go to Hollywood.

We are reminded that, in the early days of film, an actor had to come from the stage, there being nowhere else for him to come from. Isn't it possible, we are asked, for some other medium to become the main source of supply? It is possible, we have to reply, but there is no sign of its happening. On the contrary, one has only to attend a few TV rehearsals to see how utterly TV producers depend upon a technique of acting that could never have been acquired—nor even, perhaps, maintained—under the conditions they impose. Some of these conditions could be changed, though they probably won't be. Others seem to be inherent. The stage alone offers the actor full play—allows him to give a performance in an unbroken curve and places him in direct emotional contact with his audience. That is why real actors are dissatisfied with the substitutes.

The theatre exists. The snag is that it does not exist spaciously and variously enough to satisfy any of those who have its interests at heart. The producer's point of view has been that entertainment the public doesn't pay for, the country can do without. There is common sense in this; and, even in art, the businessman is far less of a fool than other people. A show doesn't get to be a hit without meeting standards of showmanship. There is more fun, more craftsmanship, even more art in the average commercial show than in the average serious play. The serious play as currently known to Broadway is a bore and an imposition. The cry of pain that goes up when reviewers pan these plays is emitted either by interested parties or disinterested muddleheads. Why should a businessman invest in anything other than, say, *South Pacific,* when *South Pacific* has the artistic as well as the economic edge? The nest of serious theatre has been fouled by a foolish subintelligentsia.

Yet—we must convince our prospective investor—there *is* a need for a non-commercial, or less commercial, theatre. In part that need derives precisely from the theatre's primacy among the arts of entertainment: in order to make money in radio, movies and TV, invest it in actors, invest it in theatre. Then again, the commercial theatre itself needs a non-commercial division. I believe I am uncovering no secret when I say that the impetus toward the creation of a professional experimental theatre at Columbia University is coming, not from "serious playwrights," but from the author and the composer of *South Pacific,* Rodgers and Hammerstein. They know that workers in the theatre need a training ground, and that there is a public—if not always a large and wealthy one—for other shows besides *South Pacific.* I do not mean that the audience for a non-commercial show must always be small and poverty-stricken. The box-office of a small art theatre often has occasion to rob the rich. And perhaps the strongest of all arguments in favor of a subsidy for theatre is that it opens the doors to millions who would otherwise never pass through them; by subsidy, we can lower the prices and admit the people who otherwise take their dollar to the movies. Hence, the subsidized theatre, far from being an attempt to force something down "the public's throat, is a democratic institution, signalizing a refusal to limit the audience to the well-to-do. Yet it is not a threat to the commercial theatre. In Paris, commercial and subsidized houses live side by side in reasonable amity. And one notes that, artistically, they do each other a lot of good.

It may be thought that in invoking the European idea of subsidy I have wandered too far from the situation in America. Here we have yet to repeal the entertainment tax; and even when that step has been taken, we shall perhaps have to forego the word Subsidy (like the word Socialism) so as not to antagonize such cultural isolationists as might otherwise be our best friends. But the economics of theatre in America already includes much besides business enterprise. Help for the non-commercial effort is coming from at least three very rich sources: individual philanthropists, local communities (which may mean philanthropists in a group), and the state legislatures. By philanthropists I mean men who are investing money with very little hope of getting it back (let alone with interest) in productions which they happen to like. The community theatre, though not yet as successful, perhaps, as English repertory, has its recognized triumphs in Dallas, Cleveland, Pasadena and not a few other cities. The state legislatures, whatever they may think of Socialism in general or Subsidy in particular, pour money into the theatres of the state universities which—in Wisconsin, say, or Indiana—are among the chief theatres of the region.

In short, the fact that money does not come to our non-commercial theatre in the European way, should not delude us into believing that it cannot come at all. Under the Eisenhower Administration, it may be vain to talk of a federal theatre in the sense of a *Comédie Américaine* but it is not vain to recall that our actual Federal Theatre of the thirties was no such thing but rather a brilliant improvisation of a characteristically American sort—a triumphant piece of private enterprise in the public domain. The American way, I take it, is to seize your chances as they come up, for America is a country where you believe—most of the time—that they *will* come up.

Parker Tyler

THE AMERICAN FILM: TRENDS IN THE FIFTIES

There are certainly two aspects of human spectacle in
which American movies are incomparable: the floor-
show and the gun-battle. It is to be noted, in any summation of trends in American films, that these two spec-
tacles have an historic and related status, a status origi-
nating with the growth of show-business in America. An
alternative to the gun-battle—one just as much relished
and just as elegantly done in American movies—is the
fist-fight, both amateur and professional. A famous film
of the teens, later remade, was *The Spoilers,* which set
the standard for that sort of thing in movies over the
world. During the forties, a Technicolor Western appeared in which it was flatly indicated that the grudge
fight between hero and villain in the Old West was far
from being the edifying moral event many have supposed, and instead was a kind of gambling show, pro-
moted by bettors who regarded the two warriors much
as they would two bears drawing blood, perhaps life,
from each other. In other words, the fist fight was the
masculine contribution to the floor show, then as now,
on platform or off, consisting of girls.

After mid-century, the knightly ethics of the lethal
gun-battle have given way before the pressure of com-
mon-sense and humanitarian criticism, and if now the
gun-battle survives in the higher film brackets, it does

so as the form of competition that certain sports are today: a benign superstructure of the brute impulse to kill. Jennifer Jones as a female gun-battler was an anticlimax a few years ago when even the habitués deemed her role excessively bloodthirsty. After all, she was a girl. It was no coincidence that in *High Noon* a formal sense dominated the visual style to a degree conspicuous in a Western. The fact is that glamor was removed from the two-man gun-battle which is the film's crisis, so that the event becomes the mere routine of the sheriff doing a single-handed job on the notorious outlaw: uppermost in feeling is the stark formalism of it all. In *High Noon*, a social element is emphasized by the defection of the law-abiding group, which is cowardly. The catch is that the townspeople, in terms of moral prejudice, prefer (for whatever reasons) to be the spectators of the event. It was too bad that they couldn't get it by Television. But the usual show is at least what the customers in the movie house get. The man in the audience and the townspeople of the film represent two forms of "innocent bystanding" that are curiously akin in the light of total morality.

Humanely, our century—which has already killed more than any other century—assumes that killing is morally hideous; even the execution of the criminal can bring little moral edification. Yet the spectacle of killing (which the 3-D's make "thrice" real) continues to have its floor-show appeal as well as its automatic documentary or "newsy" calibre. *Cease Fire* is a three dimensional perspective on the Korean fighting, while *Red Garters* focusses on the traditional two-man gun-battle as a floor-show burlesque of any illusion that the Westerns keep ancient chivalry alive. Why the term, "floor-show"?—it signifies the intimate element, the aesthetic relationship most easily fusing spectator, in our time, with spectacle. "Ringside seats" indicates exactly what I mean.

Deep thinkers in these subjects are faced with a paradox: every other little boy in the street has Gene Autry or Roy Rogers or Bill Boyd for his gun-toting hero, and yet the heroism of saving a lovely woman from being scalped or raped and pegging the dirty villain for a fareyouwell is presumably as morally dead as historically outdated. Lately, the movies have not been behindhand in focussing on the little boy of indeterminate age as the reservoir of chivalric myth. The chief popular knight-errant in the American second quarter of the century has been the Lone Ranger. In the documentarily and humanely slanted *Little Fugitive*, there is a mock killing played as a trick on a little boy to make him believe he is his big brother's murderer. In lone flight, the little "killer" unintentionally lands in Coney Island, which to him is the most available land of real adventure. But his ideal of the cowboy has been explicitly derived from Television movies. Ostensibly it is all perfectly harmless, everything ending happily, but the image of Coney Island as an outdoor floor-show involving let's-pretend Wild West stuff is the impression that survives of this miniature odyssey.

The mock death of the big brother is emblematic of the mock death rendered in theatrical make-believe itself. On the pure level of fantasy, there is bound to be a fusing ambiguity. Is art, even as in the plebian movies, primarily a land of wish-fulfilment behavior where honorable murder is the old-wives' tale of a dead-and-gone culture? *Shane*, the runner-up to *High Noon* in terms of scrupulous production, tells the story of a good-bad hero through the eyes of a little boy who worships him. A less distinguished Western recently allowed a little boy to believe, for quite a spell, that his own dad was no hero but a low-down, murdering horse-thief. Indeed, the eyes of the young must judge these matters; must judge, in short, what constitutes the "heroism" of killing. Not long ago, Audie Murphy, of all people, played the role of a professional killer with "virtue"; that is, one who follows a code of fair fighting (and who reforms, of course, at the picture's close). Movies do not hesitate to play up such moral ambiguities. The audience, no less than the film-makers, cannot be blind to the indirect commentary on war that is involved in these mid-century entertainments. "Is the modern soldier a hero?" is the blunt if obfuscated proposition. Peculiarly enough, this is much like the question asked by Hamlet of the tragedy of blood. Does honor consist, that is to say, exactly and entirely of demanding blood for blood, life for life?—and who, precisely, is the corpse? Perhaps *his* virtue is in doubt.

In *Red Garters,* filmed entirely with backgrounds equivalent to stage-sets of the musical-comedy genre, the cowboy hero arrives on the frankly artificial scene to avenge the death of his brother. Every element of the standard Western is deliberately present with a special spoof-it-out-of-countenance accent embodied in frequent songs and dances. So one may ask whether *Red Garters,* having absolutely everything that *Oklahoma* has, isn't making a euphemistic joke of the contemporary reality behind the cowboy charade. It is interesting that a great effort is made in the film to reveal the absurdity of the chivalric duelling tradition. Both participants here, worked on by the humanitarianly inspired heroine, deliberately fire to miss. Meanwhile a self-confessed coward shoots from ambush to kill one of them, but fortunately the heroine has had the foresight to place blanks in the skunk's guns (etc.). If one conforms with the apparent wish of this and other movies to consider all the world a floor-show, questions are not in order. But if any relation to reality is meant, one may ask all the questions admissible to a courtroom concerning motives in this "illegal" duel.

Re the soldier as knight errant, *The Knights of the Round Table* and *King of the Khyber Rifles,* two of the more or less classic Romantic vintage, have gained a new transfusion of charm from the ambitious dimensions of CinemaScope and they announce that the spectacle is Definitely Revived by the 3-D's. The diagnostician of trends inevitably must remark that nothing recent or current hints of any diminution of confidence in film-makers that some refabrication of a mouldy old stereo won't do very nicely for the time being, especially if it has the con-man's Dietrich, Marilyn Monroe. Envy of Television might seem enough to make Hollywood producers take supreme risks but a look at Television itself explains why envy is not enough. There is nothing in Television that hasn't been in the movies—by which I mean *all* kinds of floor-shows.

Glancing to one side at the artistically serious efforts of film-makers to present classics or near-classics, there springs to view Orson Welles' example of simonizing Shakespeare for the mobile camera, *Othello:* a brilliantly skillful and inevitably and aridly impertinent piece of work. 1953's *Julius Caesar* was an emulation of the British productions of *Henry V* and *Hamlet,* but cannot be said to have solved the problem of transferring Shakespeare to the screen any better than did its models, and in some respects it falls below its models. A pretentious kind of art-film has reached the fiction genre. Huston's *Moulin Rouge* had some superlatively successful atmosphere but the treatment of its hero, Toulouse-Lautrec, while apparently it heralds similar exploitations, leaves out almost everything to be desired of a film about a great artist.

Othello, in English, was produced as a sort of international enterprise. Economic factors, indeed, have made American enterprises on foreign soil attractive to both actor and producer. Bing Crosby surprised by coming forward with *Little Boy Lost.* Made in France and released by Paramount, it is a remarkable example of disciplining the glamor ego down to sensible size. Bing is nothing if not sincerely modest in it and plays a beautiful foil for a mesmeric child actor, Christian Fourcade. There have been many child heroes in the latest decade of film, and if any promising or aesthetically hopeful trend exists in American movies, it is the humane dignity and care and chaste sentiment which a child's presence has the faculty of conferring on—or at least awakening in—his handlers. As obvious as *Little Boy Lost* is, it profits by its contact with France and French actors and never overflows into vulgar sentiment. If the Western hero is about to be revaluated in America (though one scarcely dare hope for anything so epoch-making) perhaps it *is* sound to start with a small boy's hero-worshipping (as in *Shane*) subjected to the laws of a child's direct observation. If little Christian Fourcade can render Crosby sober and serious, perhaps some other little boy can laugh Roy Rogers and colleagues off the wide-open Western screens. Which suggests that the broad tongue-in-cheek fantasy of *Red Garters* is not altogether without interest, especially as it has a conscious grasp of the underlying ritualism of the chivalric duel and its negative component in modern life.

One must account for two impulses in human temperament regarding the taking of life by man: that of the young soldier, Zossima, in *The Brothers Karamazov*, who repudiates the ritual duel as wanton killing, and that of Ilusha, the little boy in the same novel, who so passionately wants to avenge his father's humiliating chastisement by Dmitri Karamazov that he throws a stone at Dmitri's saintly brother, Alyosha (a "Karamazov"), and bites his hand. Personal and family honor is the sole content of the ritual duel. Only blood can wash away a moral stain. As Zossima understood, every instance of the ritual duel is a direct challenge to the adequacy of Christ's sacrifice. Modern wars, however, make all Christian scruples into metaphysical and individualistic issues. It is to the mortal verve of Ilusha, the "natural boy," to which we must look for predictions about the ethical status of human killing. Many might agree that Jesus is no competitor of Roy Rogers as a mythical hero without relinquishing the faith of socialist thinkers in the power of reason. But the history of reason as collaborator with human and aesthetic emotion, beginning with the French revolution and its revision of neo-Classic tragedy, does not inspire confidence in its controlling power, unless as a mere discipline of the static ideal of patriotism. But in the latter case, it must be remarked that there is no dividend in tragedy, which is the prime interest of the aesthetic motive.

The cynicism of *High Noon*, if this film be considered in the light of Corneille's *Horatii*, is that brother betrays brother in the family of just society. One seems to read a vague parable of propaganda for the United Nations, with the United States as a possible "lone sheriff" pitted against a certain deadly "menace" while the rest of the world neutrally looks on. But this interpretation, however formally plausible, makes *High Noon* a fantasy difficult for reason to justify. The United States in the international field can hardly justify the small boy's faith in the Lone Ranger simply because it will probably not be necessary for it to do so. Nevertheless, the longevity of the Lone Ranger as a fantasy-hero seems unlimited. One is constrained to wait without much hope for the unique child who, parallel with the one who perceived that the emperor really wasn't wearing any clothes, perceives that the Lone Ranger is something hanging in a dressing-room.

NOTES ON THE CONTRIBUTORS

WILLIAM BECKER is the drama critic for the *Hudson Review* and a contributor to the *New Republic* and other periodicals. His experience in European theatre as actor and critic stems from his travels in Europe while he was a Rhodes Scholar at Oxford University.

ERIC BENTLEY is the drama critic of the *New Republic*. He has directed in leading theatres of Europe and America. He is the author of four books—the latest is *In Search of Theatre*—and the editor of six. He lectures on Elizabethan drama at Columbia University.

FRANCIS BIDDLE is the author of several books: on law, on civil liberties, a novel, a biography, and essays. He is at present writing his memoirs, which will cover among others his years as Attorney General of the United States and as president of the Americans for Democratic Action.

ELIZABETH BOWEN, the Anglo-Irish lady of letters, is well-known on both sides of the Atlantic for her novels— among others *The Last September* and *The Heat of the Day;* for her short stories; for her essays and her astute criticism. At present she is writing a new novel.

NICOLA CHIAROMONTE has lived in the United States, France, and Italy, where he is now drama critic of *Il Mondo,* the Italian weekly. He contributes to the *Partisan Review* and the *New Republic,* among others, writing on European and American letters and politics.

MALCOLM COWLEY was literary editor of the *New Republic* in the thirties and is equally well-known for his book, *Exile's Return,* which is a literary odyssey of the twenties. He is an editor of The Viking Press.

NORMAN DEMUTH is professor of composition at the Royal Academy of Music in London. He is a prolific composer and the author of books on music theory and of music criticism, primarily concerned with contemporary work.

ROBERT EVETT is the music critic of the *New Republic.* He is the composer of considerable chamber music and a recently published choral cycle, *The Mask of Cain.*

WALLACE FOWLIE is an authority on modern French literature, and the author of books on Rimbaud and Mallarmé, among others. He is a member of the faculty of Bennington College.

JOSEPH FRANK has contributed criticism to leading American and European periodicals, both from Paris, where he held a Fulbright Fellowship, and from the University of Chicago, where he holds a Rockefeller Fellowship.

KERMIT LANSNER, formerly on the staff of *The Kenyon Review,* a member of the faculty of Kenyon College, then a Fulbright Fellow in France, is on the editorial staff of *Art News.*

ARCHIBALD MACLEISH is Boylston Professor of Literature at Harvard University. His collected poems have received the Bollingen Award, the Pulitzer Prize, and the National Book Award. Under Roosevelt's administration, he was Assistant Secretary of State, then Librarian of Congress.

PAOLO MILANO has been living and teaching in the United States since 1939. He has published critical works on European and American literature and is a member of the faculty of Queens College.

ARTHUR MIZENER is the author of *Far Side of Paradise*—a critical study of F. Scott Fitzgerald—contributes regularly to the literary quarterlies and to the *New Republic.* He is professor of English literature at Cornell University.

HENRI PEYRE is a professor of French literature at Yale. He has published numerous books of criticism, both in the United States and France. His latest book is *The French Novel* (Oxford University Press, 1954).

KATHLEEN RAINE is a poet, her most recent collections of verse being *The Pythoness* and *The Year One*. She is writing a book on Blake. Her criticism appears regularly in the *New Republic*, and the *New Statesman and Nation* in England.

JOHN CROWE RANSOM is the editor of *The Kenyon Review*. In addition to his many books of poems, which received the Bollingen Award, and of criticism, he is the author of a perennially controversial volume, *The New Criticism*, and of *The World's Body*.

HERBERT READ, author of over two dozen books—poetry, fiction, autobiography, aesthetics, and criticism of literature and the visual arts—was knighted in 1953. He is president of the Institute of Contemporary Arts in London. In 1953-54 he gave the Norton lectures at Harvard and the Mellon lectures at the National Gallery of Art in Washington.

KENNETH REXROTH, poet, playwright and critic, is the author of many books, among them: *The Art of Worldly Wisdom* and *The Phoenix and The Tortoise*. He is an editor of *Perspectives USA*.

ROBERT RICHMAN, literary editor of the *New Republic* (1952-54), is director of the Institute of Contemporary Arts in Washington. The editor of *The Arts at Mid-Century*, he is writing a book of criticism of the several arts and is preparing a volume of his poetry, which has appeared in the literary magazines.

MARK SCHORER is a novelist and a critic of modern literature. He has edited several anthologies and published novels and a collection of his own stories, *The State of Mind*. His latest novel is *The Wars of Love*.

DELMORE SCHWARTZ is equally prolific as a poet and a critic, especially of poetry. He is an editor of the *Partisan*

Review. Among his books are: *Vaudeville for a Princess* and *The World Is a Wedding.*

STEPHEN SPENDER is the author of several books of poetry, fiction and literary criticism. He has also written extensively on social problems; his recent book, *Learning Laughter,* is about Israel. He is the editor of *Encounter.*

ALLEN TATE is the author of many volumes—fiction, biography, poetry and criticism. His recent book, *The Forlorn Demon,* is a set of critical essays. He is professor of literature at the University of Minnesota.

PARKER TYLER has lectured and written extensively on motion pictures since he published *The Hollywood Hallucination.* He is a poet and a playwright as well.

RAY B. WEST, JR. is an editor of the *Western Review* and a member of the faculty of the University of Iowa. His criticism appears regularly in American periodicals.